AF600710

BREWING LEGAL TIMES

Things, Form, and the Enactment of Law

Brewing Legal Times

Things, Form, and the Enactment of Law

EMILY GRABHAM

UNIVERSITY OF TORONTO PRESS
Toronto Buffalo London

Toronto Buffalo London
www.utppublishing.com

ISBN 978-1-4426-4605-6

Library and Archives Canada Cataloguing in Publication

Grabham, Emily, 1977–, author
Brewing legal times : things, form, and the enactment of law / Emily Grabham.

Includes bibliographical references and index.
ISBN 978-1-4426-4605-6 (cloth)

1. Time (Law) – Philosophy. I. Title.

K579.T5G73 2016 340'.11 C2016-901648-X

This book has been published with the help of a grant from the Federation for the Humanities and Social Sciences, through the Awards to Scholarly Publications Program, using funds provided by the Social Sciences and Humanities Research Council of Canada.

University of Toronto Press acknowledges the financial assistance to its publishing program of the Canada Council for the Arts and the Ontario Arts Council, an agency of the Government of Ontario.

Canada Council for the Arts
Conseil des Arts du Canada

Funded by the Government of Canada
Financé par le gouvernement du Canada

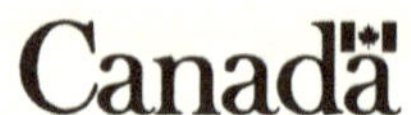

For Martina

Contents

Acknowledgments

Thank you to the great number of people who have supported this book.

Many people read chapters, and made them much better. My sincere thanks go to the wonderful Donatella Alessandrini, Kate Bedford, Emilie Cloatre, Davina Cooper, Judy Fudge, Hyo Yoon Kang, Andreas Mihalopoulos-Philippopoulos, Martyn Pickersgill, Nick Piska, Flora Renz, and three anonymous reviewers for the University of Toronto Press for their careful and generous comments.

I have been carried along in the writing of this book by the warmth of friends, colleagues, and kin: Donatella Alessandrini, Mehmet Altunatmaz, Diamond Ashiagbor, Nicola Barker, Olivia Barker, Siân Beynon-Jones, Susan Boyd, Doris Buss, Emilie Cloatre, Vicky Conway, Joanne Conaghan, Davina Cooper, Carys Craig, Emma Cunliffe, Marieke de Goede, Anisa de Jong, Stacy Douglas, Laurie Duggan, Nadine El-Enany, Máiréad Enright, Luis Eslava, Ruth Fletcher, Judy Fudge, Mary Gabrimichael, Sarah Gibbons, Finn Gibbons-Ford and his dad David, Emily Haslam, Lois Harder, Zoe Harper, Lydia Hayes, Didi Herman, Rosemary Hunter, Suhraiya Jivraj, Vinita Joseph, Sarah Keenan, Sarah Lamble, Sonia Lawrence, Julie McCandless, Jeremy Marshall, Renisa Mawani, Brigid Morris, Claire Mummé, Rose Parfitt, Nick Piska, Lucas Platero, Barbara Prainsack, Erika Rackley, Sinéad Ring, Yvette Russell, Sally Sheldon, Anastasia Tataryn, Mariana Valverde, Claire Young, Matthew Weait, Toni Williams, and Ania Zbyszewska.

Thank you and big hugs to my siblings Jessica and Matthew, my niece Charlotte, and my parents Sarah, Chris, and Diana. A warm hello to the Bedfords and Holdsworths. Thank you to Olive, for bringing a sense of perspective, and to Martina, Borka, and Celie for having been there. Thank you so much to Kate Bedford for morning cups of coffee and for sharing with me your Crunchies and your newly discovered interest in beer. I look forward to many more adventures together.

Many academic communities have sustained the currents of thought and debate to which this book hopefully contributes. Thanks to the journals *Feminist Legal Studies* and *feminists@law*, the AHRC *Technoscience and Law* network, the AHRC *Regulating Time* network, the *Social Critiques of Law* research cluster, and Kent Centre for Law, Gender, and Sexuality, among others.

Warm thanks to the Institute of Feminist Legal Studies at Osgoode Hall Law School in Toronto for providing a home for repeated research visits to Ontario. I have treasured the many long conversations I've had with the inspirational Sonia Lawrence over the past few years and hope these continue. Remaining in touch with Carys Craig for nearly twenty years now has been a joy. Thank you to Emma Cunliffe for long walks in B.C. Thank you very much to Ruth Buchanan for directing my last visit to IFLS. I hope that I can repay this hospitality in coming years.

I am grateful to the Canadian Federation for the Humanities and Social Sciences Awards to Scholarly Publishing Program for financially supporting the publication of this book. Research contributing to the book has also been funded by the Economic and Social Research Council under grant reference ES/K001108/1, the United Kingdom Socio-Legal Studies Association, the University of Kent Social Sciences Faculty Fund, and Kent Law School Research Support Fund. Kent Law School has provided consistently excellent research support and generously accommodated sabbaticals in 2012 and 2015. Sarah Slowe, Cathy Norman, and Sarah Gilkes have given wise advice and gotten me out of scrapes.

The book could not take the form it has done without the generous involvement of many interview participants in Canada and the United Kingdom. I am indebted to these people for stepping out of their busy lives and providing thoughts, reflections, and in-depth analysis of issues that have structured their own lives. Many of these people also read and commented on sections of the book, for which I am particularly thankful.

I am very lucky to have had Daniel Quinlan as an editor. Daniel's incisive feedback and his consistently engaging and calm manner have been wonderful to experience. As the book neared publication, Barry Norris contributed delightfully accurate copy-editing, and Wayne Herrington and Luciano Nicassio were cheerful, patient, and efficient. Karen Howatson's indexing saved the day.

Parts of this book have been published previously. Thank you to the following publishers for allowing partial reprinting of material in the following sources: Taylor and Francis for "A Likely Story: HIV and the Definition of Disability in UK Employment Equality Law, 1996–2005," in Emilie Cloatre and Martyn Pickersgill, eds., *Knowledge, Technology and Law* (Routledge, 2015), pp. 206–22, and for "Legal Form and Temporal Rationalities in UK Work-Life Balance Law" (2014) *Australian Feminist Studies* 29 (79): 67–84 (see further http://www.tandfonline.com/toc/cafs20/current); Cambridge University Press for "Doing Things with Time: Flexibility, Adaptability, and Elasticity in UK Equality Cases" (2011) *Canadian Journal of Law and Society* 26 (3): 485–508; and Sage for "Governing Permanence: Trans Subjects, Time and the Gender Recognition Act" (2010) *Social and Legal Studies* 19 (1): 107–26 (DOI 10.1177/0964663909346200).

Many thanks to the Frank O'Hara estate, to Carcanet Press, and to Penguin Random House LLC for granting their permission to reproduce part of Frank O'Hara's poem "Interior (with Jane)" from *Frank O'Hara: Selected Poems*, edited by Donald Allen, 2005. "Interior (with Jane)" from *The Collected Poems of Frank O'Hara*, by Frank O'Hara, copyright © 1971 by Maureen Granville-Smith, Administratrix of the Estate of Frank O'Hara, copyright renewed 1999 by Maureen O'Hara Granville-Smith and Donald Allen. Used by permission of Alfred A. Knopf, an imprint of the Knopf Doubleday Publishing Group, a division of Penguin Random House LLC. All rights reserved. Any third party use of this material, outside of this publication, is prohibited. Interested parties must apply directly to Penguin Random House LLC for permission.

BREWING LEGAL TIMES

Things, Form, and the Enactment of Law

Introduction

The "Eagerness of Objects"

The eagerness of objects to
be what we are afraid to do

cannot help but move us Is
this willingness to be a motive

in us what we reject? The
really stupid things, I mean

a can of coffee, a 35¢ ear
ring, a handful of hair, what

do these things do to us?

– Frank O'Hara, *Interior (with Jane)*

The bureaucrat with the hourglass did not just keep the time; he *started* it and *stopped* it. He literally created time and ended it with each intervention of the advocate.

– Carol Greenhouse, *A Moment's Notice*

In the early 2000s I worked for a legal collective in London, England, providing advice and representation to queers on employment issues. My position title, "lesbian caseworker," dated from an earlier era, but I kept it because it neatly, if ambiguously, juxtaposed identity and function. Bikes and stacks of papers littered our open plan office. Alongside a large bank of filing cabinets stood our "homophobic" photocopier, so named because it would jam during marathon copying sessions on the evenings before important tribunal dates. Our pink headed notepaper, alternately a source of embarrassment and pride when corresponding with City law firms, became progressively more out of date; we kept it because we couldn't afford to replace it. We didn't have time, either, to clear out the ten years' worth of voluntary sector leaflets homed in our meeting room.

Working there, I felt like I was living in the 1980s. This wasn't altogether unpleasant, as it conjured idealized notions of collective organizing, flat working structures, and genuinely free-of-charge legal advice. Yet there were difficulties. Our local government funding was cut in a wave of reductions that pre-empted later austerity measures by a decade. On the horizon was a set of legal measures against sexual orientation discrimination, required by European Union law and soon to be implemented in the United Kingdom by means of regulations.[1] But we were not there yet, and every week we told people that, without bringing a speculative human rights challenge, they had few formal legal options to challenge workplace problems relating to their sexuality. Ostensibly the organization that could have led on providing advice under the new legal regime, we were heading for closure just at the point when the new regulations would be coming into effect.

I look back at that period as a strange combination of treading water, degeneration, and what Elizabeth Freeman has so eloquently termed "temporal drag" (Freeman 2011). Treading water, because we knew the new rights were coming soon, but we could not use them yet. Degeneration, because the building, as well as our operating budget, was falling apart. And drag, because of the sheer kitsch of our continued existence.

Freeman writes that it "may be crucial ... to complicate the idea of horizontal political generations or waves succeeding each other in progressive time with a notion of 'temporal drag' thought less in the psychic time of the individual than in the movement time of collective political fantasy" (Freeman 2011, 65). Our collective political fantasy valorized an organizational and funding structure from an era of relatively left-wing local government in London, and maintained revolutionary visions of sexual politics that nevertheless sometimes would struggle with "queer" identities and practices. Yet we were on top of the latest legal developments, we attended the policy forums, and we provided up-to-date responses to government consultations. We were no less technically minded than we were idealistic; we were as interested in the finer points of discrimination legislation as we recognized

1 These were the Employment Equality (Sexual Orientation) Regulations 2003, implementing Directive 2000/78/EC establishing a general framework for equal treatment in employment and occupation.

law's exclusionary effects. Davina Cooper terms "everyday utopias" those groups that "work by creating the change they wish to encounter, building and forging new ways of experiencing social and political life" (Cooper 2014, 2). We were somewhere in the hinterlands, living a peculiarly draggy legal utopia.

In the midst of all of this, the piles of paper on the desk of the "gay men's caseworker" were steadily outgrowing the usual bounds of polite messiness. Not an untidy man by nature, he often found himself inundated with medical reports, disease manuals, and correspondence with clinicians. As a result of advising numerous people living with HIV, my colleague had developed a practice expertise in disability discrimination law. He spent hours writing instructions to medical experts, drafting and arguing over medical reports, and attending tribunal hearings, all so that his clients could make the preliminary legal point that their HIV met the definition of "disability" for the purposes of the discrimination laws in force at the time. This was before these people had even arrived at the real substance of their work problems: the fudged "risk assessments" that excluded them from jobs, the shunning, employers' mistaken assumptions around HIV transmission and life expectancy, all with real and apparent material effects. The relevant legal test, which we will meet again in Chapter Three, was whether their condition was "more likely than not" to be an impairment in the future. In this context the irony of having to provide evidence of a poor prognosis to an employment tribunal just at the point at which antiretrovirals were transforming many people's experiences of HIV was not lost on any of us.

Some time later, having left legal practice for an academic job, I tried to make sense of these experiences. Engaged in research on law and time, it became apparent that what my colleague was doing in the early 2000s was no less significant to the creation of a specifically *legal* temporality – "likelihood" – than anything else would be. This is not to say that he was some kind of magician, conjuring time from nowhere, but rather that, in the process of his everyday work, he contributed to the emergence and stability of "likelihood" in mundane ways, even as he was critical of it. Far from being abstract and metaphysical, likelihood was constituted in tangible ways, through interactions between people, technologies, things, and laws. In this case likelihood was dependent for its survival on medical reports, the retrovirus itself, and the means through which clinicians were able to measure its existence, prevalence, and effects (for example, through viral load tests and T cell counts).

In this book, I argue that our relationship with "things" creates legal time. These things include objects in the legal field such as case reports, medical reports, medical tests, drugs, files, and classification systems, for example, as well as ways of doing law with these things: adjudicating, litigating, documenting, and certifying. The following chapters engage with generative and object-friendly concepts of time, raising the question of how cells, tests, forms, reports, railway signalling boxes, legal technicalities, and legal documents contribute, alongside people, to the materialization of time in legal networks. I focus on three broad areas of legal regulation: HIV-related discrimination, gender recognition, and work-life balance. I propose that the temporalities that have emerged in relation to these areas – progression, likelihood, transition, and balance, as well as their many accomplices – are constituted through diverse relationships between people, things, and laws. In this theorization, human action does not exist *within* time, but instead generates temporalities, including legal temporalities, in specific assemblages of other human and nonhuman actors. In following this enquiry, I ask what our understanding of law and time might look like if we followed things as well as people, if we allowed objects to open access to new worlds, and if we paid attention to the agentic potential of, for example, matter, metals, and particles, and not merely conscious human behaviour.

There is a growing contemporary scholarship on time (see, for example, Bastian 2014). Within studies of labour, research has focused on qualities of time and temporal orientations found in the so-called "new economy" (Adkins 2008; Amoore 2004; Waldby and Cooper 2010). Feminist and queer scholarship has critiqued the heteronormative underpinnings of familial and reproductive time, its cultural formations and political effects (Dinshaw et al. 2007; Freeman 2005, 2011; Halberstam 2005), as well as its implications for queer intergenerationality, utopia, and hope (Edelman 2004; Muñoz 2009). Critical rereadings of postcolonial temporalities, furthermore, provide new perspectives the politics of revolution, memory, and mourning (Scott 2014).

More specifically for the purposes of this book, social and political theory has already developed rich accounts of the close interconnections between inventions, institutions, and new understandings of time, which can inform our understanding of time's relationship with objects and matter. A wide range of work has accounted for the significance of objects and material artefacts in culture (Candlin and Guins 2009; Henare, Holbraad, and Wastell 2007; Pottage and Mundy 2004).

Actor-network theory and object-related anthropology have helped to uncover the many ways in which things exert effects (or can be understood to "speak") in networks or assemblages of human and nonhuman actors (see, for example, Holbraad 2011; Latour 2005). Importantly for the purposes of this book, research in political theory increasingly focuses on the participation of nonhumans in political events and the significance of the temporal paradigm of the "anthropocene" for thinking about human action (Bennett 2010). Technologies such as clocks, schedules, calendars, railroads, and "standard time" have helped to create particular temporal paradigms, which are culturally specific (O'Malley 1996; Zerubavel 1985). As the anthropologist Kevin Birth puts it, "[t]he artifactual determination of time does not represent a coherent, consistent cultural system ... but represents instead the sedimentation of generations of solutions to different problems" (2012, 2).

Similarly, however, recent theorizations of time in social and political theory help us to understand how changing temporal orientations – apparently uncertain worlds and futures, new configurations of labour time, horizons of speculation – authorize multiple shades and tactics of intervention (Adkins 2012; Amoore 2013; Amoore and de Goede 2008; de Goede 2012). Time is something that is both technically achieved through objects and norms and brought about through "horizontal resonances" between fields previously imagined as distinct: commercial consultancy and state security, for example (Amoore 2013, 11), clinical and medical concepts of prognosis (Chapter Three), or drug trials for AZT and military personnel classification systems (Chapter Two). Hence the theoretical perspectives and methodological tools already exist across a range of disciplines for a more thorough investigation of time's relationship with things.

The problem that has emerged in my research, however, has been how to understand the relationship between time and things in a *legal* context. Although a vibrant body of work already exists on law and time (for example, Cooper 2013; Douglas 2011; Engel 1987; Mawani 2014; Richland 2013), it has not yet considered to any great degree the specific role of objects and legal artefacts in creating legal temporalities. Furthermore, growing scholarship theorizing the material in law (Lynch and McNally 2003; Pickersgill 2011; Pottage 2012), while friendly to this kind of approach, has not yet taken it up in relation to the study of time. The analysis in this book, therefore, has required drawing together a range of hitherto disparate literatures to formulate new conceptual perspectives on law, time, and materiality. My argument departs from existing scholarship on law and time by emphasizing the specificities of law's material forms. It extends existing literatures on time by confronting the multiple, mundane ways in which time is enacted through legal assemblages. And it challenges scholarship on the *materialities* of time to consider what emerges when we consider specifically *legal* modes, raising issues that are not present elsewhere (such as dilemmas over the status of legal form).

Law and Time: From Mechanisms to Things

Focusing on "things" was not my intention at the outset. My research on law and time initially conceptualized time-related legal provisions or principles, such as the concept of likelihood we have just seen, as temporal "mechanisms," shaping behaviours, subjectivities, and institutional action. But this approach in itself did not help me to understand the shades of agency exerted by the HIV retrovirus and its associated tests and treatments in Canadian law in the 1980s and 1990s (Chapter Two), or the performative function of the statutory declaration forms required by the United Kingdom's Gender Recognition Act (Chapter Four), or even the insistent reappearance of vehicles and transport systems in work-life balance disputes (Chapter Five). Here, I provide a short account of these conundrums in order to clarify my focus on time, things, and matter.

Through projects on transgender recognition laws, the four-day work week (Grabham 2010a), and work-life balance, I initially focused on tracing time-related legal provisions and constructs as specific examples of productive or biopolitical power – shaping legal subjects and experiences by shaping their temporal horizons, histories, and possibilities (see also Craven, Fitzmaurice, and Vogiatzi 2006; Melissaris 2005). Different types of legal time could have different effects. For example, a provision in the United Kingdom's Gender Recognition Act requiring transgender people to promise to remain in their "acquired" gender "until death" could be understood to impose a type of permanence in the service of legal rights (Grabham 2010b). The concept and legal machinery of work-life balance, with its promise of equilibrium, could be seen to have significant effects in shaping women's work practices and expectations around the unpaid care burden (Grabham 2011).

Drawing on the work of Pierre Bourdieu and Elizabeth Freeman and on governmentality studies (Dean 1999), this analysis adopted for legal analysis some well-known debates about temporalization and agency. Temporalization refers to the process of making time through actions and relationships. Bourdieu's scholarship, for example, challenges metaphysical notions of time with an account of agency based on power, chances, and embodied action that continues to hold contemporary resonances. Bourdieu wrote about how unpredictability, forcing others to wait, and taking people by surprise all constitute the exercise of power through manipulating time (2000, 228). He used the notion of temporalization to describe how practice makes human time, in contradistinction to a metaphysical account through which actors exist within, and act upon, empty time (206). Describing the ways that agents produce social relations by acting in and on the world, Bourdieu proposed a timely account of what he terms "habitus" (dispositions and systems of perception) by focusing on its relationship with the "forthcoming": "Habitus constructs the world by a certain way of orienting itself towards it, of bringing to bear on it an attention which, like that of a jumper preparing to jump, is an active, constructive bodily tension towards the imminent forthcoming (*allodoxia*, the mistake we sometimes make when, waiting for someone, we seem to see that person in everyone who comes along, gives an accurate idea of this tension)" (144).

The "jumper preparing to jump" – or embodied sense of the forthcoming – is thereby a nonconscious orientation to future action (207). Agents create a sense of forward motion in time when they have the capacity to invest in their surroundings and the social spaces around them (what Bourdieu calls "field") and when their actions align with the norms attaching to those spaces. As Bourdieu puts it: "So it is in and by practice, through the practical implication that it implies, that social agents temporalize themselves. But they can 'make' time only in so far as they are endowed with habitus adjusted to the field, that is, to the sense of the game (or of investment), understood as a capacity to anticipate, in the practical mode, forthcomings [*des à venir*] that present themselves in the very structure of the game" (213).

Time, in these accounts, is thus intimately linked with power and social relations. Elizabeth Freeman has expanded on Bourdieu's work on temporalization in writing about what she calls "temporal mechanisms": social and political techniques that reproduce biopolitical status relations – that is, relations that reproduce norms of the family, citizenship, health, and work – through the exercise of time (2005, 57). Freeman describes as "chrono-normativity" the ways in which "genealogies of descent and mundane workings of domestic life interlock through temporal schemes" (2011, xxii). This shift away from an account based wholly on Bourdieusian concepts of field and habitus allows for an analysis of dominant temporalities as tactics within particular fields of intervention, including, for example, transgender recognition projects or, as we will see, the legal regulation of HIV as a disability.

Influenced by these perspectives, it is possible to understand time-related concepts as having distinct legal functions and consequences, forming the conceptual backdrop that shapes practical legal solutions to social problems, for example, or putting limits on how people can use law and what people need to do to access rights (through commencement dates, for example, or qualifying periods). Running through this broad approach to law and time was (and still is) the proposition that legal temporalities produce as well as govern, and that they govern productively, often in service of biopolitical projects. In this theorization, time can also form part of the social vernacular or wider disciplinary schemes, to the extent that many temporalities have also been at least partially defined through law itself: constructs such as work-life balance, for example, are inherently socio-legal (Grabham 2014).

A few years ago, however, I began a research project on the temporal concepts underpinning early legal approaches to HIV discrimination in Canada and the United Kingdom. Operating in a climate of persistent fear and generalized misunderstanding about the potential transmission risks of HIV, many people living with HIV in the 1980s and 1990s faced work-based discrimination and dismissal. Activists pursued legal innovation either to secure the continued employment of these people or to obtain much-needed financial compensation where possible. My research involved conducting semi-structured interviews of lawyers, policy-makers, and activists on their experiences of HIV-related discrimination activism and legal claims. This research underpinned my understanding of the legal regulation of disability as broadly a biopolitical endeavour, and legal definitions of disease and disability as what Freeman would term "chrono-normative," remobilizing exclusionary norms of health and the life course through powerful concepts of time.

Yet the legal temporalities that emerged through the interview and documentary research processes were not what I had expected. They included "prognosis," "likelihood," "progression," and "uncertainty," and when they appeared in informants' accounts or in legal and policy documents, first-person written accounts, legislation, and cases, they were more often than not accompanied by "things" and apparently nonlegal technologies: T cell counts, viral load measurements, medical reports, questionnaires. Encountering these things over and over again, I was confronted by a particularly intractable analytic problem that threatened to drag the project into a kind of generalized obviousness and irrelevance: the "thing-ness" of legal time. These temporalities did not seem much like the experiences or interpretations of time I had expected to find. They were too specific and mundane. In comparison to concepts of past, present, and future, for example, or memorialization, these temporalities appeared slightly askew, overly technical, and not "wholly" legal (often being, for example, medico-legal). Even worse, legal time appeared to be just as much about the objects as about human experience, even though the temporalities had immense significance for many people. My understanding of temporal mechanisms, despite having been influenced by approaches to power and social action drawn from governmentality, critical legal studies, and legal geography, could not at that point accommodate processes of creating legal times that seemed to involve nonhuman as well as human actors.

How can a form or an antibody test assist in creating legal time? Isn't it the people who have experiences of time and the objects that are enrolled in these political and legal actions? Approaching legal-temporal mechanisms as biopolitical or even chrono-normative projects helped to conceptualize "likelihood," for example, as the temporal feature of a set of disciplinary mechanisms that constructed HIV as a disability. But it did not, in itself, assist with the question of how to understand the interlinking of law, time, and things (tests, medical reports) as it arose through creating "likelihood" as a concern. The valences, constructions, and shades of time percolating through the research seemed ungeneralizable to the extent that they were attached to very specific things and, moreover, that these things were of different types, were variously "legal" or "medical," and could not articulate themselves, despite having clear effects.

To give one example: in Canadian provincial human rights law, the legal test for covering HIV as a disability was, from the relatively "early" point in HIV infection, that of "manifesting antibodies" (Chapter Two). Yet this legal test could not have existed, and could not now work, without the clinical innovation, shortly beforehand, of the HIV antibody test, which provided clinicians with a means of visualizing the virus and its biological effects. Furthermore, the "manifesting antibodies" legal test could not have wider significance without government clinical guidelines posing a standardized temporal schema – "progression" – for understanding and treating HIV-related illnesses. Only with both the antibody test and the clinical guidelines – and, indeed, the antibodies, but that is another question altogether – did the newly legally significant legal-temporal concept of HIV progression make any sense.

I found myself thinking and writing about tests and clinical guidelines and not, I thought, about time. If anything, despite my having been influenced by theories of temporalization, time remained the ether in which the tests floated. The focus on things often felt as though it actively precluded an in-depth analysis of temporalization: the temptation was to understand the analytic endeavour as either metaphysical or about the things and objects emerging through the research, with time disappearing from view on either account. At best, it might have been possible to conclude that the antibody test created a new legal *interpretation* or *disciplinary production* of time, which was fundamentally a matter of human subjectivity or governance: the human creation of law *in* time. Yet this did not do justice to the production of material and environmental contexts through law.

Following Bourdieu and Freeman, I could understand through the HIV research that the sense of forward motion in time evoked by the concept of "progression" was fabricated and powerful, not metaphysical, and that the linear time it evoked was not "natural," despite often appearing all-consuming. Freeman's concept of "chrono-normativity," in particular, allowed me to understand temporal mechanisms as tactics of intervention with powerful effects in shaping lives and politics. Yet even this, I concluded, did not require an acceptance that human time was the only time that mattered. Such an analytical shift was supported from two angles, unlikely because of their quite divergent disciplinary alignments and influences: the work of the anthropologist Carol Greenhouse and the sociologist Bruno Latour.

Modern Times

Carol Greenhouse has observed that the apparent naturalness of time is itself contingent upon social claims associated with order and legitimacy (1996, 4). Greenhouse positions temporal modes as the provisional result of cultural claims about law and techniques of governance. She reverses the modernist assumption that law exists *within* time to argue that linear time expresses law's effects: "what passes for the natural rationality of linear time is, in fact, a set of cultural claims about the efficacy of law and specific technologies of social ordering" (4). For his part, Bruno Latour argues that, if the time that passes in linear fashion is widely accepted to be transcendent, then it is constructed as such as part of what he views as the project of the moderns, which continually recreates a split between nature and culture (1993, 73). Specifically, he understands time to be brewed in complex relationships between human and nonhuman actors. Linear time is the result of a particular kind of what Latour would term "sorting," a productive process that mixes up a wide range of actors and elements with variegated temporalizing effects.

These accounts have direct consequences for how we imagine and respond to law. They require attention to the world-making capacities of legal temporalities, as much as the subjective experiences of those coming into contact with law (see Chapter One). In Greenhouse's account, linear time expresses law's effects, so that a sense of what "comes next" could be understood as much as a result of governing, as it follows what appear to be "naturally" sequential events in time. In other words, law and legal temporalities assist in the fabrication of "social" and "natural" time. Hence, Greenhouse's work, in particular, prompts us to return, on one level or another, to the specific qualities that *legal* concepts, objects, and ontologies have in instantiating time and temporalities.

Yet what often gets in the way is law's apparent reliance on things or legal form as vehicles of representation: the "legal" drug, for example, or the law in the case report or contract. In my research on the temporalities of HIV law, medical reports, forms, and questionnaires were particularly powerful legal actors in constructing diverse temporalities of HIV. But I had trouble understanding how law created time when legal documents appeared merely to *represent* power, discipline, or social ordering, particularly when they were written and read. At these moments, law appeared not to travel much farther than the text.

The apparent naturalness of time (as diagnosed by Greenhouse and Latour, in very different ways), and its stabilization through legal ordering, depends on at least two other moves: first, reading legal technicalities and legal form as representative of social worlds only outside of law and, second, understanding law as wholly immaterial. Sticking to the first move, the story that the texts and things do not act except to represent law not only keeps Latour's modern split between nature and culture alive; it continually resuscitates an idea of natural, encompassing, metaphysical time, the kind of time that many scholars, including Bourdieu, have repeatedly challenged. By contrast, critical approaches to law might happily (and justifiably, in my opinion) prevaricate around the second move (whether to understand law as material), failing to settle on law's material dimensions, or holding the question in abeyance to follow more closely law's movements and effects.

Yet the problem comes when trying to trace the effects of legal technicalities and form in creating legal time. Hence the approach outlined here returns to the question of how we analyse law. Traditionally law and society scholarship has worked to deconstruct what legislation and cases mean, by which I mean deconstructing the knowledges about law found in written documents, understanding legal texts as representation. Drawing on the work of legal anthropologists such as Annelise Riles and Marie Andrée Jacob, the case studies in this book assess legislation, case reports, and policy documents for their legal and material form, treating these objects as artefacts in themselves that have a certain shape, typeface, and structure, that contain patterned phrases, and that have a performative power (Jacob and Riles 2007; Riles 2006b). Such a shift allows one to analyse, on a pragmatic level, the types of legal person that legal forms enact and the means by which legal assemblages orient themselves temporally. In turn this fortifies an analysis of the nonhuman dimensions of power and governance because it is aimed at understanding, as Heath Cabot (2012) puts it, how "things govern."

If the law in the document is only representative of social worlds outside itself and never also material, if law cannot be instantiated by "things," then time exists outside law and is ineffable and mysterious. This was the problem I faced in understanding the temporalizing effects of legal technicalities and legal documents in the HIV research. If, on the other hand, legal things grant us access to new worlds, as Amiria Henare and her colleagues have proposed (Henare, Holbraad, and Wastell 2007), and if time is "sorted" (as suggested by Latour, drawing on Michel Serres), then legal things and relationships create specific temporal ontologies (Chapter One). Likelihood, progression, and uncertainty, in this account, appear a little less odd. Time is material, apparent, and often close at hand, conjured at least partly through the things we use when we "do law" – antibody tests, for example, and statutory declarations. Linear and other arrangements of time are not either "natural" or "social" but always both, brewed through changing relationships of humans and material forms. For their part, legal temporalities, far from being merely aspects of human conscious experience or social practice, are instantiated, picked over, contested, in relationship with technicalities, things, humans, and legal form.

Brewing Legal Temporalities

Although the concept of temporal mechanisms goes some way to evoking legal time as a constructed process, therefore, understanding legal processes as "brewing" time allows us to pay attention to the assembly of legal temporalities through a range of disjunctive moves and apparently unlikely actors.[2] The political stakes of such a project might not be readily apparent, and, indeed, in introducing a wider range of actors to the analysis of time, might be viewed as obscuring questions of social justice. Yet tracing and understanding the multiple relationships that constitute legal temporalities need not take us away from questions of politics and justice; in fact, I argue, it brings us closer. Following the creation of time in processes of human-nonhuman interaction, the politics of legal temporalities becomes much more alive and close at hand than we might hitherto have imagined. As we will see in Chapter One, Elizabeth Grosz, for example, has spoken of refusing the "neutral immersion of things in a temporal medium" (1999, 4). For their part, Amiria Henare and her colleagues speak of the political stakes of accepting that unfamiliar objects give rise to new worlds, not merely to interpretations of "our" world (Henare, Holbraad, and Wastell 2007). These positions prompt a certain politics of engagement with time. If we understand that our legal actions, arguments, documents, classification systems, mistakes, and innovations have temporalizing effects, and do not merely exist "in time," we can also understand those temporalities, things, and effects as inherently political because they are world-making, and not merely passive. Drucilla Cornell has stated that "[i]nvention is inescapable if legal norms cannot be discovered purely through their mere recollection" (1990, 268). For Cornell, recollection implies a cultural economy of law-making that operates through retrospective appeals to that which has already been decided. Yet, as she argues, the politics of doing law inevitably requires invention, and invention can be radical. By denaturalizing the temporalities that co-produce legal norms, by putting "mere recollection" to one side and engaging in the process of analysing and making time, we encounter and remake questions of justice over and over again.

2 Many thanks to an anonymous reviewer of the manuscript for encouraging this clarification.

Chapter One, then, provides an introduction to the conceptual work of understanding legal time to be "brewed." As I argue in that chapter, an object-oriented approach to time raises the question not just of multiple interpretations of reality, but of multiple realities. Annemarie Mol states that "ontology is not given in the order of things, but ... instead, ontologies are brought into being, sustained, or allowed to wither away in common, day-to-day, sociomaterial practices" (2003, 6). Drawing on the work of anthropologists such as Mol, the question I pose in Chapter One is how to think about multiple legal ontologies of time, multiple ways of creating and practising legal temporalities, rather than plural interpretations or representations of legal time. If time passing is a technique of the moderns (as Latour and Greenhouse argue), then linear time does more than represent a certain type of reality; it enacts it. The challenge, therefore, is how to understand the clusters of people, things, and knowledges that create legal temporalities, rather than how legal concepts of time represent linearity through "past," "present," or "future."

Each of the following chapters engages with a distinct legal temporality or cluster of temporalities emerging through this research. Chapter Two focuses on *progression*, the result of uneasy alliances between clinical models of HIV and the legal concept of disability in Canada in the late 1980s and early 1990s. During the early HIV epidemic, legal activists created a number of temporalizing techniques to respond to the retrovirus and to manage their caseloads, including using the "tools we have now" and redirecting complaints to achieve a swifter resolution of disputes for severely ill people. At the same time, Canadian health authorities' clinical model of HIV articulated a number of defined stages, ranging from exposure to the retrovirus, through seroconversion, to asymptomatic good health, and continuing through the development of symptoms and an eventual diagnosis of "AIDS-Related Complex." In this model, a defining feature of HIV/AIDS was that it could be measured through the absence or presence of symptoms and, crucially, that it progressed. This ontology of progression was taken up and reconstituted differently in distinct jurisdictions in Canada, such that it benefited people making human rights claims and caused more legal problems for people trying to claim income assistance. In provincial human rights law, HIV was articulated as a disability from the point of "manifesting antibodies," yet in provincial welfare benefits disputes in Ontario, an AIDS diagnosis was required, itself a gendered and racialized threshold. In relation to the regulation and clinical use of the new drug AZT, moreover, measuring the progression of HIV became entwined with access to new and badly needed treatments. AZT could be administered only to people with an AIDS diagnosis, forcing clinicians to make difficult and far-reaching decisions about how to assess and categorize a person's illness. In Chapter Two I trace these developments and explore their effects, arguing, among other things, that, in different ways, progression helped to ground HIV as a legally "real" phenomenon.

Chapter Three continues with the focus on HIV, but this time in the UK context. It covers the development of a curious type of medico-legal health speculation, *likelihood*, introduced through the requirements of the United Kingdom's Disability Discrimination Act 1996 (DDA), and then abandoned in 2004. Prior to the DDA, legal claims relating to HIV were confined to unfair dismissal or to other "grounds" of discrimination that a person might have encountered (such as racial or sex discrimination). Legal debates about HIV and employment centred on the lawfulness (or not) of pre-employment HIV testing, HIV-related dismissals, and "pressure to dismiss" cases, in which employers apparently acceded to customers' or workers' demands not to have to associate with people living with HIV. With the introduction of the DDA, and a new route to claiming disability discrimination, however, HIV-related claims were radically temporalized. Using a frame of speculation, with its associated rhetoric, legal practices, and effects, the DDA required people living with HIV to prove that their condition amounted to a legally defined disability before then being able to argue the substance of their case (a dismissal, for example, or harassment). Being what was termed a "progressive condition," HIV could be a legal disability only if it was "more likely than not" that it would result in future impairment. Likelihood thus became the object of significant legal and clinical deliberations, prompting the drafting and circulation of medical reports about claimants' HIV prognosis. Legal representatives argued over whether clinicians had understood the correct legal test for "disability"; disability activists worried about clinicians' ability or willingness to make appropriately grim predictions about future health to assist their patients' legal claims. The relatively rapid adoption of this test, as well as its abandonment after pressure from HIV and other health organizations, provides one example of the contingent and unstable nature of legal temporalities.

With the analysis so far having been on medico-legal ontologies of time, Chapter Four focuses on time's documentary enactment. It analyses gender *transition* as legal artefact or "thing." Engaging with critiques of gender reclassification as a transgender rights strategy, I consider how transition itself is legally materialized. Once reclassification measures are adopted, it becomes necessary to achieve the transition as much as a matter of law as of embodied becoming. Gender transition – for example, through the United Kingdom's Gender Recognition Act 2004 (GRA) – becomes a change in legal status brought into being via specific legal techniques. More specifically, the GRA requires, among other things, that people intending to change their legal gender make a statutory declaration that they intend to live in their acquired gender "until death." Tracing the "career" of this strange provision, Chapter Four considers the policy precursors to the GRA, its appearance in Bill form, and parliamentary debates, and continues by paying attention to the material dimensions and requirements of the standard form statutory declaration. One of a number of requirements, the "until death" provision appeared, largely unexplained, in the earliest drafts of the Gender Recognition Bill, and remained throughout the legislative process, occasionally accompanied by ministerial statements about ensuring gender "permanence" post-transition. Potentially quite a conservative temporal idiom in the context of transgender lives, post-transition permanence nevertheless allowed government ministers to rebuff successive amendments to the draft Bill brought by a conservative peer in the House of Lords aimed at constraining what she termed gender "reversals." Yet the "until death" provision requires an odd temporal commitment of applicants under the GRA, requiring us, in turn, to reflect on the documentary enactment of legal time, its relationship to legal form, and the material-temporal qualities of standardized paperwork.

The final substantive chapter considers the temporal qualities and political rationale of *work-life balance*. The chapter begins with an extended reflection on balance as socio-technical strategy and the right to make flexible work requests as its associated legal technicality. Disputes over the working day and working week have long structured labour politics and labour law, yet work-life balance merges the politics of labour time with the ideology of contract to manufacture an equilibrium, of sorts, between paid work and unpaid care. This "reckonable present," no less a constructed temporality within labour regulation than the artefact of "real time" has been to financial speculation (de Goede 2005), is supported by particular legal innovations. One such innovation, the right in the United Kingdom to request flexible working, achieves a shift in regulatory scale from public obligation to privately managed contractual relationship, specifically via a legislated right to do something that all employment contracts foresee in any case: negotiate. Analysing this legislated negotiation as a type of regulatory "unwinding" (after Riles), I trace the modulated suspension of certainty that allows bureaucrats to ensure that employers and employees have truly negotiated a new working pattern. The highly temporalized qualities of the flexible work request process, on this account, contribute to labour market equilibrium through the management of doubt. Expanding the usual range of actors in labour regulation, I then move on to consider the role of "things" (cars, signalling boxes, and so on) in work-life balance disputes, pulling the analysis of labour regulation, in this small area at least, away from the domain of the purely human to think about balance as assemblage. Tracing the textual patterning of nonhuman actors between case reports, I conclude with comments on the material dimensions of legal citation practices and their effects on our understandings of the temporal orientations of precedent.

My aim, throughout the research for this book, has been to follow the "making of law" as much as the "making of time." Increasing the range of actors in analysing law and time has required drawing on a combination of socio-legal methods, including interviews, observations, and doctrinal and documentary research. The research for the chapter on "progression" (Chapter Two), for example, involved interviewing lawyers, legal activists, and clinicians in Ontario and Nova Scotia in 2012, as well as analysing provincial and federal human rights cases, legal reports, and guidelines, and historical materials (such as biographies and first-person accounts) on the experiences of living through the early HIV epidemic in Canada. Chapter Three, which focuses on the concept of "likelihood," is again drawn from interviews, this time of lawyers and HIV activists in the United Kingdom (mainly in London and the North East) undertaken in 2012 and 2013, as well as historical and contemporary documentary research on the UK experience of the epidemic. I use fairly traditional legal methods, such as an examination of parliamentary proceedings and case analysis, in Chapters Three, Four, and Five, to assist in the task of understanding how legal temporalities are made through the legislative process and through precedent. I did harbour an ambition to observe and interview legislative drafters to understand, at close hand, how time-related provisions are drafted and put together; one element, in other words, of how the formal laws of time are "made." Although this did not happen for the current project, legislative drafters have joined a collaborative research network on law and time that I run with the sociologist Siân Beynon-Jones, and they are providing insights into the technical projects of drafting concepts such as "daytime," "nighttime," the leap year, and commencement dates for legislation.[3] In this way, the research for this book continues to invite further reflection and methodological reorientation.

As we turn to the core chapters of the book, however, it is worth reflecting on the epigraphs at the outset of this Introduction. Frank O'Hara eloquently reflects on "the eagerness of objects to / be what we are afraid to do." Conjuring a set of fairly mundane objects (a can of coffee, a cheap earring), he asks: "what do these things do to us?" (1991, 21). Juxtaposed with O'Hara, we have Carol Greenhouse making an apparently audacious proposition about a bureaucrat with an hourglass, starting and stopping time, the italicized emphasis on *starting* and *stopping* referencing a limit of explanatory force. This book, then, lies somewhere on the edges of O'Hara's and Greenhouse's worlds, trying to account for the eagerness of the hourglass, the timeliness of the bureaucrat, and the point at which law becomes relevant to any of it. I am intrigued by Greenhouse's stating that the bureaucrat started and stopped time; I also empathize with her apparent frustration. The following chapters, then, through case studies, propositions, diversions, and my own emphatic italicizations, explain my journeys through law and time over the past five years.

---

3 This is the "Regulating Time" network, funded by the UK Arts and Humanities Research Council. For further information, see http://www.kent.ac.uk/law/time/.

Chapter One

"Praxiographies" of Law and Time

[T]ime arises not from the ethnographic ground on which it is played out as a relative question but from the temporal assumptions embedded in specific state practices – bureaucratic administration, taxation and the regulation of economic life, and through a variety of executive, legislative, and judicial powers.

– Carol Greenhouse, *A Moment's Notice*

Time doesn't flow; it percolates.

– Michel Serres and Bruno Latour, *Conversations on Science, Culture, and Time*

This book explores the interconnections between law, objects, and matter in the making of time. In this chapter I offer a way of thinking about legal time and temporal legal actions as disaggregated instead of universal, generated as well as generative, and provisional upon relationships between humans and nonhumans. My argument is for an approach to temporalization that is attentive to the world-making capacities of "things" and other nonhumans – in other words, a "praxiographic" approach (Mol 2003). Legal temporalities, in this theorization, are created through the connections between actors in a network or between nodal points in an assemblage. No overarching or "container" time needs to exist for such an account, outside what is generated through the temporal sortings of different types. Human action is important, but not central – indeed, the "human" can be understood just as much as a question of "vital materiality" (cells, viruses, bones, electrical currents, following Jane Bennett (2010)) as conscious embodied subjectivity. For their part, legal temporalities are not only produced by human actions and subjective experiences of time, but inaugurated by vital matter in various forms, modes, and relationships: assemblages of objects, humans, animals, minerals, for example. In this account, "time" and the "legal" are not (merely) the domain of the human, and they are material as much as symbolic.

Reflecting these conceptual moves, then, I begin with a discussion of the temporal approaches of the legal anthropologist Carol Greenhouse, on the one hand, and Bruno Latour and Michel Serres, on the other. Each of these thinkers problematizes a model of universal, natural time acting as a backdrop to human temporalities. Latour and Serres, in particular, conceptualize something akin to the "brewing" of time in networks or assemblages. Adopting what could be termed a posthuman approach to temporalization requires attention to the role of nonhuman actors. Hence the focus then turns to key debates about matter and materiality, drawing on anthropology-inspired accounts of "things," actor-network theory (ANT)-inspired work on nonhuman agency, and theories of "vital materiality." In the following section, I consider some of the ways in which objects and nonhumans have been conceptualized in socio-legal scholarship, especially when what constitutes "law" has not been defined in advance. This requires being able to trace when things enter, leave, or are shaped by heterogeneous assemblages, and it also encourages the researcher to look past what has already been stabilized as the subject of legal regulation. In the final substantive section, I reflect on two identifiable clusters of effects that legal temporalities are observed as having: helping to constitute distinctions between law and nature, on the one hand, and helping to tether law to "reality" or providing an objective "ground" for law, on the other. I also, then, reflect on the dilemmas of understanding legal form as an ongoing material project and the implications of these dilemmas for an account of law and time.

Praxiographies of Time

In the introduction to her ethnography of atherosclerosis, Annemarie Mol proposes an approach to research that focuses on enactment rather than knowledge, multiplying our potential objects of analysis (2003, vii). Mol terms this kind of research a "story about practices," or a "praxiography" (31), which places practices in the foreground, watching for objects to come into being instead of being viewed from different perspectives. "The body, the patient, the disease, the doctor, the technician, the technology: all of these are more than one," she states, referring to the incommensurability of world-making practices in the medical diagnosis and treatment of vascular disease (5).

This book is oriented towards the "more than one-ness" of time – in particular, legal temporalities. Adopting an approach that is friendly to multiple ontologies of time, this and the following chapters attempt to follow time-making practices that are connected with law. Such an approach involves diagnosing time, watching it, and working out where it might have come from, instead of assuming that time is natural and/or metaphysical. When agency is the domain purely of humans, then time is about human history: it is about the forward or circular movement of events or themes, about epochs and narratives. As hardly bears repeating, Latour's task in *We Have Never Been Modern*, for example, is to provide an account of the condition of modernity and to reconstruct the separation between humans and nonhumans to arrive at what he terms the "full constitution" (1993, 14). Part of this task requires taking on what Latour calls the "temporal framework of the moderns" (67), a paradigm characterized by the "arrow of time," definitive temporal breaks, and, most important, the passing of time. Moderns, as Latour puts it, understand the passage of time as if it abolishes all that is left behind, yet they also want to keep, date, save, and display the past. This idea of time's passing irreversibly is, as such, a *technique* of modernity, a "classificatory device" for evacuating the work that goes into keeping the natural and the social separate (73).

Latour's account has the temporal framework of the moderns arising as a result of the expulsion from the field of agency, politics, and action of objects and other types of nonhuman actors (what Latour terms "quasi-objects"). Purification allows the moderns to hold in place two fields of time: an ahistorical field populated by universal and necessary things or forces of nature, and a much more contingent field of human history, detached from things. In challenging "natural" time and the temporal framework of the moderns, Latour's perspective is not unique, as we have seen already in the Introduction. Carol Greenhouse, from a very different perspective, argues that "all formal temporal representations, not just linear time, involve modernist assertions" (1996, 219). Greenhouse's account emphasizes the role of power, law, authority, and culture in the construction of modernity as an epoch and "period" of time: "modernity is not an epoch in time but a temporal situation in relation to configurations of political power and cultural diversity. The modern habit of viewing modernity as a period of time is only testimony to the long-standing self-legitimating claims of sovereigns and nations in the West which draw on the past" (219).

According to Greenhouse, therefore, time is created and naturalized in the West through specific legal modes. As we saw in the epigraph to the Introduction, she writes of the bureaucratic appropriation of time from God: "The bureaucrat with the hourglass did not just keep the time; he *started* it and *stopped* it. He literally created time and ended it with each intervention of the advocate" (22). Yet Greenhouse's bureaucrat raises a conundrum: how is it possible to start and stop time with an hourglass? This, I argue, requires an approach to temporalization that allows nonhuman actors to exert shades of agency. Reading Latour and Greenhouse together, we might say that the way we normally talk about time, as a container or a given, posits natural time as existing separately from human time, and grants nonhuman actors ("things") little or no agentic capacity. But if, for whatever reason, we leave the concept of linear, container time to one side, or at least view it as only one of a number of temporal modes, then we have a strange problem: how to think about the creation of time by humans in connection with nonhumans (such as Greenhouse's hourglass) and various forms of matter. This, in turn, requires understanding the relationship between time, agency, causation, and materiality in new ways.

Latour refers to a process of "sorting" through which temporalities are created out of elements belonging to different times. He proposes that identifying "sorting" processes can lead us to a fuller account of the role of nonhumans not only in political life but also in sustaining particular understandings of time:

> We have never moved either forward or backward. We have always actively sorted out elements belonging to different times. We can still sort. *It is the sorting that makes the times, not the times that make the sorting.* Modernism – like its anti- and post-modern corollaries – was only the provisional result of a selection made by a small number of agents in the name of all. If there are more of us who regain the capacity to do our own sorting of the elements that belong to our time, we will rediscover the freedom of movement that modernism denied us – a freedom that, in fact, we have never really lost. (1993, 76)

In these temporal propositions, Latour clearly has been influenced by Michel Serres. In a well-known set of interviews Latour conducted with Serres in 1991, Serres elucidated his proposition that "all authors are our contemporaries" – even authors such as Pythagoras or Lucretius. This holds because of Serres's disaggregated definition of time and, hence, the "contemporary": "What things are contemporary? Consider a late-model car. It is a disparate aggregate of scientific and technical solutions dating from different periods. One can date it component by component: this part was invented at the turn of the century, another, ten years ago, and Carnot's cycle is almost two hundred years old. Not to mention that the wheel dates back to neolithic times" (in Serres and Latour 1995, 45).

Serres's proposition means, furthermore, that the past is not frozen or out of date, and that we are not at the cutting edge of time. The Enlightenment, in categorizing nonscientific truths as outside reason, did so through the temporal mechanism of consigning such truths to archaism, stating not that they were false, but that they were "out of date." In this way, a temporal rupture, as Serres puts it, acts as a "dogmatic expulsion" (Serres and Latour 1995, 49–50). Much more, Serres argues, can be gained by thinking about time through frames of disorder and proximity that we see, for example, in chaos theory: "Time does not always flow according to a line … not according to a plan but, rather, according to an extraordinarily complex mixture, as though it reflected stopping points, ruptures, deep wells, chimneys of thunderous acceleration, rendings, gaps – all sown at random, at least in a visible disorder … Once you understand this, it's not hard to accept the fact that time doesn't always develop according to a line and thus things that are very close can exist in culture, but the line makes them appear very distant from one another" (57).

Through the Serres-inspired metaphor of "sorting," then, Latour introduces a project of following the temporalities occasioned by the meetings, connections, and juxtapositions of a wide range of elements and agencies, human and nonhuman. The "extraordinarily complex mixture" that we might wish to trace in analysing law and time, instead of acting as a backdrop to human action, is constantly percolating, folding in on itself. Time does not push these percolations forward. Instead, out of teeming, knotted clusters of human and nonhuman connections, new temporalities emerge, act, and have effects.

Temporalization beyond the Human

In effect, I am arguing for an alternative account of what we might otherwise understand, following Bourdieu, as temporalization: the practices that go into making time. Temporalities are confabulated and do not exist as ethereal, nonmaterial "forces." There are many analytically productive consequences of holding time in this way as a set of techniques constituted by and within a network, not as a given (Bhandar 2009). But more than this, temporalization takes place not merely through human subjective action, but as a result of a wider set of agencies and interactions. It involves understanding human experiences of time in relationship with nonhumans: things, or "vibrant matter" (after Bennett). In turn, it requires some understanding of, first, the kind of agency that things and other nonhumans exert and, second, the temporalizing features of this nonhuman agency.

The Agency of Things

Thingly concerns are widely shared across a number of contemporary disciplines and currents of thought. For example, ANT (actor-network theory) encourages researchers to move slowly and to hold many aspects of enquiry in a state of productive tension. As such, this body of work suggests increasing the number of actors and following their agentic effects. ANT scholars try to avoid explaining social phenomena by resorting to "social forces," being interested instead in tracing associations. Any "thing" that modifies a state of affairs is taken to act. Allowing objects various degrees of agentic effects, furthermore, means that the space can be filled in between short-lived local interactions and durable social ties. As Latour puts it, "there might exist many metaphysical shades between full causality and sheer inexistence" (2005, 72).

These metaphysical shades, and their lively actions, might also be thought of as what Jane Bennett terms "vital materiality." Bennett (2010) has turned her attention to nonhuman matter – stem cells, electricity, metals, trash – and its lively effects. She asks what politics would look like if the vitality of nonhuman entities were taken into account. Specifically, in proposing an account of "thing-power," she draws on Spinoza's concept of *conatus*: a tendency to persist, shared by all bodies, human and nonhuman. Vibrant matter, in this account, is an "active, earthy, not-quite-human capaciousness," and matter, far from being automative or mechanical, is vital, possessing what Bennett terms a *conative* force (2010, 2). Her account of materiality differs from Latour's, yet she retains a similar concept of distributive agency, through which agency is conceived as a "human-nonhuman working group" (xvii).

Taking a slightly different approach, however, Amiria Henare, Martin Holbraad, and Sari Wastell explore a methodology in which things themselves might "dictate a *plurality* of ontologies" (2007, 7). Their key proposition is that objects need not merely point beyond themselves to concepts or epistemological frameworks, but instead might open up new worlds. Such an analysis works at the far "posthumanist extreme" of approaches challenging the human/thing distinction (Holbraad 2011, 11). Drawing on the work of Marilyn Strathern and others, it involves troubling the very distinction between objects and concepts, and undermining the idea that objects are distinct from their meanings: "Rather than accepting that meanings are fundamentally separate from their material manifestations (signifier v. signified, word v. referent, etc.), the aim is to explore the consequences of an apparently counter-intuitive possibility: that *things might be treated as* sui generis *meanings*" (Henare, Holbraad, and Wastell 2007, 3).

This type of research, in effect, reverses what anthropologists have done for a long time through ethnographic fieldwork. Instead of providing the focus for theoretical reflections, things are permitted to "dictate the terms of their own analysis" (Henare, Holbraad, and Wastell 2007, 4). Such an approach to things echoes a concern among many anthropologists about the tendency of Western anthropological approaches to assume that one world underlies a variety of cultures, so that what is required is to understand these diverging accounts of a common ontology. Hence the adoption of a stance that recognizes the radical implications of different "worlds" or ontologies: "If we are to take others seriously, instead of reducing their articulations to mere 'cultural perspectives' or 'beliefs' (i.e. 'worldviews'), we can conceive them as enunciations of different 'worlds' or 'natures,' without having to concede that this is just shorthand for 'worldviews'" (10).

Henare, Wastell, and Holbraad argue that, if anthropology has been the study of diverse epistemologies, then, within humanist approaches, matter and things have been viewed as coterminous with one "reality," juxtaposed with a plurality of *interpretations* of that same matter. On this account, if someone were to tell an anthropologist that powder is power, an inquiry would still be needed into the content, context, and meaning of that interpretation of matter. Yet what is required by the ontological turn is to accept, first, that powder is power and, second, that the anthropologist really does not know what her interlocutor is talking about (Henare, Holbraad, and Wastell 2007, 12). Indeed, Henare and her colleagues argue that this is the only way of taking difference seriously – the goal of anthropology being to work out not how other people think about the world, but what anthropologists must do in order to conceive other worlds (15). Things are concepts in this account, and they open up new worlds instead of new interpretations of one world:

> We start with the ordinary (representationist/epistemological) assumption that concepts are the site of difference. Then we argue that in order for difference to be taken seriously (as "alterity"), the assumption that concepts are ontologically distinct from the things to which they are ordinarily said to "refer" must be discarded. From this it follows that alterity can quite properly be thought of as a property of things – things, that is, which *are concepts* as much as they appear to us as "material" or "physical" entities. Hence the first answer to the incredulous question of *where* "different worlds" might be, is *here*, in front of us, in the things themselves. (13)

Henare, Wastell, and Holbraad quite self-consciously distinguish this "radically essentialist" approach from the perspective of Latour. Where Latour aims to include things within human-nonhuman hybrids that destabilize the distinction between object and subject, their proposition is that things themselves can "dictate a plurality of ontologies" (Henare, Holbraad, and Wastell 2007, 7). Latour, they argue, presents a unifying theory of things, whereas their approach could generate multiple theories of things. Yet it is possible that their argument does not take account of ANT's subtleties in relation to empiricism and material lives. In tracing associations, ANT-inspired research, including Latour's, explicitly requires open-mindedness about what form objects take when the distinction between natural and social is undermined (not what *knowledges* are required about those objects, as such) (Latour 2005, 111). Embedded within this approach is an acknowledgment of potential multiplicity, not only of interpretations of formerly stable "natural" or "social" entities or things, but also ontological status. Specifically, what is required by ANT's altered approach to formerly settled ontological/epistemological distinctions is the recognition of multiple ontological fields and a movement towards, instead of away from, materials and material lives:

> Everywhere, the empirical multiplicity of former "natural" agencies overflows the narrow boundary of matters of fact. There exists no direct relation between being real and being indisputable …

> Empiricism no longer appears as the solid bedrock on which to build everything else, but as a very poor rendering of experience. This poverty, however, is not overcome by moving *away* from material experience, for instance to the "rich human subjectivity," but closer to the much variegated lives materials have to offer ... The great chance of ANT is that objectivity's many folds become visible as soon as one moves a bit *closer* to where agencies are made to express themselves, namely scientific laboratories. (Latour 2005, 112)

The act of understanding objects, therefore, does not merely require interpretation of a "new" epistemology, but the work of "conceiving" the distinct world of the object-concept. This is the only way, according to Henare and colleagues, that anthropological and other scholarly methods can respond fully to alterity.

Things, Matter, and Time

Following the broad trajectory of this work, my argument is that objects and vital materiality can be seen to conjure *sui generis* agencies and ontologies, not merely alternative interpretations of human action. This requires acts of conception, not merely interpretation, on the part of the researcher. Within legal assemblages the question, then, is not so much how to *interpret* legal things, but what worlds (including what legal worlds) material actors conjure or invite us to access through their conative actions. The enquiry remains, however, how to conceive of the temporalizing effects that objects (or object-concepts) have. It is to this extent that investigations of becoming (Elizabeth Grosz) or conatus (Bennett) can illuminate not only the actors that have previously been excluded from the domain of many social theories of time because they have been viewed as inactive or inert, but also their lively, temporalizing actions.

In Elizabeth Grosz's work, we find an analogous refusal of the temporo-ontological project of the moderns to that found in the work of Latour and Serres, but one with a distinct philosophical outlook. Grosz engages with Darwin, Nietzsche, Bergson, and Deleuze, all of whom, she argues, articulate themes of opening up and difference. As Grosz proposes, drawing together her theories of becoming, each of these thinkers rejects commonsense understandings of time as progress and lineage, for example, and, crucially for this inquiry, each refuses the "neutral immersion of things in a temporal medium" (Grosz 1999, 4).

Time, as a "materializing if not material" force, thus links the world, consisting of human and nonhuman actors, with the generation of specific temporal modes in diffuse and diverse ways. Against the logic of causality, time "unfolds ... with its own enigmas and impetus" (4).

This is a posthuman ontology of time, in which the time of the cosmos or the natural world that frames human consciousness and experience (different epistemologies of time within an overarching framework) is juxtaposed with the unpredictable generation of new temporal modes through and against new material forms. As Grosz puts it, "time is dynamized, seen as a virtual force and as that which builds, binds, contains, and transforms all relations, whether natural, cultural or personal while also ensuring their dispersal, their development beyond current forms and parameters" (1999, 5). The attention to generation that Grosz pursues in her critical engagement with Deleuze and Darwin, in particular, also requires scepticism of any clear distinction between life and nonlife, the organic and the inorganic. Such scepticism results in deliberations over the ontological status, for example, of viruses; Grosz asks whether we should define them as self-reproducing organisms or biochemical programs: "How can any clear line be drawn in any case, such that material objects are characterised by inertia and by temporal self-containment (i.e., by being) that the organic world enlivens (through becoming)?" (23). The temporal significance of this kind of question resides in the extent to which we perceive material phenomena, such as viruses, to be lively or inert. Many foundational definitions and distinctions that order the modern world are, in this way, achieved through temporal distinctions. What is seen to be capable of agentic or semi-agentic movement or action – the growth of a plant, for example, or a geological shift, compared to the movement of an animal or human being – depends upon a perception of concerted action in time or actions upon a wider environment.

Jane Bennett, for her part, purposefully flattens distinctions between humans and matter, adopting alternative accounts of agentic action (for example, the electrical power grid as "agentic assemblage"; the concept of conatus) and, crucially, its temporal relations. She draws on Manuel de Landa, for example, to think about the emergence of bones through mineralization, and Vernadsky to think about humans' role as two-legged forms that redistribute oxygen (Bennett 2010, 11). By shifting the temporal frame, Bennett argues, the aliveness of matter sometimes can be better perceived. For example, by adopting the "long view" of evolutionary, rather than biological, time, it is possible to perceive a "mineral efficacy" through which mineral materials are active and human beings (our bones, for example) are understood as effects (11). In other words, the ability to shift between temporal registers is key to understanding, perceiving, and accounting for vital materialities: the time of minerals, the time of metals and chemical reactions, for example.[1]

This is a different account in which time, again, is not (or not only) aligned with intention, agency, subjectivity, and history, but instead can be seen to be mobilized or "brewed" through the interactions of agents of different types and at different scales within tangled assemblages (humans, metals, bones, for example). Bennett's (re)constitution of the political requires a sort of distributive agency familiar to scholars of ANT, through which the active powers of nonhumans are recognized within the context of lively assemblages. Once again, we see the avoidance of a containing type of linear time in favour of a flat ontological field in which matter can become alive or, despite being perceptibly inert, can operate in ways that elide distinctions between the human, the mineral, and the biological, for example. Bennett's attention to matter has much to tell us about time, including that there is nothing more special or distinctive about human temporalities, and there is nothing less interesting about the temporalities of rocks, seasons, plants, or cells. In this "active, earthy, not quite human capaciousness," the inauguration of temporal schemas need not be attached to a thinking mind, intentional relationships, or any form of agency we have come to recognize so far. Furthermore, to the extent that such capaciousness becomes active through assemblages, it is the temporalities of assemblages themselves, or meshworks (De Landa 1997), not only single, disaggregated actors, that could be the focus of analytic attention.

The Materialization of Law

The approach to temporalization I have outlined above permits attention to nonhuman actors and their lively, time-creating actions. Importantly,

1 Importantly, however, we need this shift only when adjusting the status of human actants to vital materiality, and human power to thing-power. In other words, the reason for reframing human temporalities is not to extend the project of humanism or to put human time better into the context of an overarching "natural" time, but instead to conceive of the electricity of our neurons, for example, as "lively and self-organizing, rather than as passive or mechanical means under the direction of something nonmaterial, that is, an active soul or mind" (Bennett 2010, 10).

this approach also requires an open attitude to things, involving acts of conceiving new material worlds and not merely interpreting the meaning of objects, for example. Thinking about the materialization of law similarly requires scepticism of how "law" itself has been defined and stabilized within heterogeneous networks. According to some, there has been a tendency within socio-legal theory to approach material forms through legal categories instead of allowing their specific physical and cultural properties to come through (Levi 2009). As such, this analysis tries not to presume, in advance, what is law and what is non-law, and aims to displace such a distinction wherever possible. As Alain Pottage puts it, we should, by contrast, "begin with materiality rather than 'law,' and, in so doing, we should recognize that the vicissitudes of 'materiality' dissolve the instances – in this case, 'law' – that they are supposed to constitute" (2012, 183).

Within recent work in legal geography and law and science and technology studies, law is often not immediately visible, because the analytic intention is to avoid bestowing upon processes, actors, or objects particular categories such as "social" and "legal" in the first place. As Catriona Rooke and colleagues put it: "The material and its link to regulation are conceived of in a more interdependent way where law is both the result of socio-technical assemblages and becomes part of specific materials, so the 'things' followed during analysis are themselves shaped and defined by the legal and regulatory frameworks that they carry" (Rooke, Cloatre, and Dingwall 2012, 43). Following "legal things" might entail using a concept such as "socio-materiality" to describe the interaction of human and nonhuman actors within performative legal and scientific networks, describing the processes through which theories and material worlds, and a range of actors, are coordinated and co-constituted as "socio-technical agencement," a type of performative material agency (Faulkner, Lange, and Lawless 2012, 10). Or it might involve, for example, analysing the materializing practice of "pedestrianism" (the legal structuring of sidewalks as finite public resources, under threat from specific actors) without recourse, in the first instance, to legal categories such as public and private (Blomley 2011). In these kinds of accounts, regulation in or through assemblages might or might not enact "law"; "legal effects" might be enacted otherwise than through legislation; and the workings of "things" might be key to both potential outcomes.

Emilie Cloatre, for example, has analysed the role of the World Trade Organization's Trade-Related Aspects of Intellectual Property Rights

("TRIPS") agreement on pharmaceutical patents in Djibouti, a country with no pre-existing law or institutions relating to intellectual property (Cloatre 2013). She finds that pharmaceutical patents themselves, although lacking official existence, have exerted significant effects within pharmaceutical networks in Djibouti, partly through packaging attached to drugs imported into the country. As multidimensional objects, or hybrids, patents have had particular regulatory effects, determining the entrance (or not) of drugs into the local market. Patents are "alive" in Djibouti despite the nonextension of TRIPS into relevant networks. Nonhuman legal/pharmaceutical things have survived in these circumstances, acting as what Cloatre terms "silent regulatory tools" (2013, 100). In this way, drugs (and drug packaging) are seen to constitute legal effects.

More obviously, perhaps, for legal enquiry, documents, for example, and documentary processes can also be analysed for their lively actions in legal assemblages. As Annelise Riles points out, documentary practices, including the provision of bus tickets, the archiving of letters, and the completion of employment applications, are constitutive of modern institutions and cultures and are key to understanding bureaucracies, contemporary knowledge practices, and concepts of ethics (transparency and accountability, for example). Yet the study of documents has been largely overlooked (2006b, 5), apart from when documents are viewed as containers of other types of information – vessels as opposed to objects in themselves (Prior 2008). Riles argues that because they are the material outcome of knowledge practices that have helped to create ethnography itself, documents challenge us to study how ethnographers know: "Documents are artifacts of modern knowledge practices, and, in particular, knowledge practices that define ethnography itself ... To study documents, then, is by definition also to study how ethnographers themselves know. The document becomes at once an ethnographic object, an analytical category, and a methodological orientation" (Riles 2006b, 7). Documents, then, bring us face to face with our own world-creating practices as researchers, inviting us to pay attention to the means by which modern practices materialize knowledge.

Tracing the things involved in these examples, whether or not predefined as legal, shows the huge amount of work needed to create and extend legal networks. "Law" and "regulation" play ambivalent roles in these constellations, sometimes failing to extend and survive, sometimes surviving in unexpected ways (as, for example, Cloatre's patents have done in Djibouti (Cloatre 2013), but often requiring other human or nonhuman actors (such as drugs or documents) in order to extend within networks. In this sense, an analysis of regulatory dilemmas and processes, in their various guises, often cannot provide a convincing enough explanation of the actions of things (defined as legal or not) within networks or assemblages (defined as legal or not). This might be because the type of relationship that things, or hybrids, have with legal networks shifts from context to context. In some circumstances, pharmaceutical innovations (medicinal nicotine) have trouble being classified through regulatory processes as particular types of things (drugs), and therefore have difficulty extending into particular networks (being prescribed through the United Kingdom's National Health Service) (Rooke, Cloatre, and Dingwall 2012). Through complex interactions, innovative "things" come off badly or fail to circulate within key networks when put into contact with regulation.

Yet these sorts of enquiries can aid an object-friendly account of law and time. Sticking with the suggestion not to predetermine in advance what is law, we could say that legal temporalities, and their associated actors, become "legal" only in specific orientations and relationships. Law and regulation are constituted through particular processes; they either extend or do not extend into wider networks through concatenations of interactions between actors. As such, although the "law" in "law and time" is already the result of processes of (temporary) stabilization of things and relationships, the "time" or "times" are provisional upon actions, meanings, and states of matter. Both things and temporalities can change the status and significance of legal interventions.

Temporal "Hinges," Legal Effects

The approach that I propose in this chapter therefore rests on three broad conceptual moves. First, displacing the ontological split between nature and society unmoors the idea of one overarching time and the necessity of time's *passing*, as such. If we increase the range and types of actors beyond merely following humans and our interpretations of time, then it is easier to hold the idea of universal, natural time, *as distinct from* social time in productive critique. Time as such need not be an overarching principle or universal ontological ground on the one hand, nor merely an experience on the other. Instead, time is the identifiable result of a provisional hooking together of elements into something that, in modern terms, looks cohesive. Second, the linear passage of time as a classificatory device or technique, which accompanies the moderns' purification of nature and society (after Latour), and which results from law and specific modes of social ordering (after Greenhouse), is no less real for being achieved. In other words, it is not necessary to state that there is no ontological grounding for time just because time is not natural, as such: the ontological status of new classificatory devices of time should point us in the direction of multiple ontologies of time. As Mol puts it, "if reality is done, if it is historically, culturally and materially located, then it is also multiple" (1999, 75). Third, temporalities are the result of human and nonhuman relationships, so that, if these relationships shift, new temporalities emerge.

Yet we have seen that Greenhouse reaches a limit of explanation when she states that the bureaucrat with the hourglass started and stopped time. Does this not accord the bureaucrat far too much power? Stopping time itself sounds like something out of science fiction. Accepting that linear time is an arrangement like any other and that time is generated through diverse relationships between humans and nonhumans produces worlds of disjunctive temporal possibilities in which objects such as the hourglass participate. Bennett terms the force of such nonhuman participation "conatus." In this kind of account, the hourglass has conative force in starting and stopping time as a matter of law. The question remains how nonhumans and their shades of agency help to constitute legal temporalities in relationship with human action.

What does a nonhuman object or, for that matter, a human do to assist in the creation of legal time? How, in other words, is it possible to speak of an object-oriented form of temporalization, one in which humans act in concert (or tension) with other humans and nonhumans to create legal effects? It is possible to describe the juncture at which human actor meets object or form, specifically, as a kind of "folding," through which legal time is created as an effect. In a piece entitled "Where Are the Missing Masses?" Latour addresses the phenomenon of delegation. A door is persistently left open at his place of work. A technological device – the hinge – initially performed the work of allowing the door to be opened and closed. However, the hinged door, when left open, also allowed cold into the building. Briefly put, the door-closing issue could be solved by delegating to a human groom or porter, who would be relatively expensive and require some discipline to work consistently. In the midst of this discussion, Latour raises the different temporal dimensions of delegating to nonhumans (hinges, for example) and to humans (porters): "The first one evokes the past perfect ('once hinges had been installed ...'), the second the present tense ('when the groom is at his post ...'). There is a built-in inertia in the first that is largely lacking in the second ... A profound temporal shift takes place when nonhumans are appealed to; time is *folded*" (Latour 1992, 234).

Latour refers, then, to a "profound temporal shift" occasioned by the innovation or use of the hinge. He does not provide any further explanation of the folding metaphor in this piece, but it is likely that it comes, again, from his productive engagements with Serres. As Serres puts it, time "can be schematized by a kind of crumpling, a multiple, foldable diversity" (Serres and Latour 1995, 59). What Latour does with the door metaphor is to bring this theory of multiple, crumpling times into his flat ontological field populated by human and nonhuman actors. Latour's assertion that time is folded in the appeal to nonhumans is not merely a statement about the human *experience* of interacting with objects and nonhumans, but, rather, in the context of his wider understanding of temporalities, a specific assertion about relationships and connections, or about how time occurs within human-nonhuman assemblages. Folding is just as much down to the hinge as it is to the people going through the door. It is in this way that a new temporality, or temporal mode, is materialized.

In what might be a counterintuitive move, I use the idea of "folding" to analyse the materialization of *legal* temporalities. In other words, my approach is to engage with topographical concepts of time in analysing law and legality. Latour states that the hinge evokes the past perfect ("once hinges had been installed"), whereas human action appeals to the present ("when the groom is at his post"). Because humans and nonhumans appeal to different temporal modes, time is folded in their interaction. My argument is that accounting for the role of nonhumans in the creation of new strains, or genres, of time requires attention to the ways in which objects open up new legal as well as other worlds. Informed by fieldwork and in conversation with a wide range of scholars, my analysis, then, lands in an area that might otherwise be termed the "folding" of time in and through *legal* assemblages.

Latour's subsequent writings on law explicitly discourage such a move. He does not view law in itself as having the same capacities to fold relations and time as would the hinge in his own example above. In his ethnography of the Conseil d'État, Latour specifically distinguishes law from other techniques, arguing that it cannot have the same effects in relation to human action as a range of other nonhuman artefacts. As he puts it, "law ... never manages to *fold* space-time, to replace its injunctions by another matter. The humblest technique – this lamp, this ashtray, this paper-clip – mixes periods, places, and totally heterogeneous materials; it folds them into the same black box, causing those who use them to act, by diverting the course of their action. Law is incapable of that ... [L]aw, unlike other techniques, is neither folded nor delegated. It has meaning only if it is unfolded, deployed, spread out" (Latour 2010, 272–3).

There are very good reasons for Latour's attention to law's specific style of recursivity, its apparent inability to imagine a world outside of itself (Pottage 2014). Yet there are also good reasons why we might contextualize Latour's argument and assert that, in certain circumstances, law can and does, as he puts it, "fold space-time." The analytic direction of *Brewing Legal Times* focuses on how law is implicated in confederations of agencies (following Bennett) that are associated with multiple ontologies (following Mol). As such, what we choose to stabilize as law does not have to have the kind of status or effects that Latour perceives in his own ethnographic work in order for it to co-produce new temporalities through "folding." If assemblages are viewed dynamically, it is not always necessary to name some relations as legal and also *for that very reason* unable to fold time.

In *The Making of Law*, however, Latour seems to position law in some ways as immaterial, even as he continues to argue for an approach to time that challenges splits between nature and culture, the same splits that assign time to nature, away from the workings of mundane objects or technological innovations. As we have already seen, a wide range of work in legal anthropology and law and science and technology studies ("law and STS") encourages analytically productive ambivalence about whether, when, and how law is material. Pottage (2012), in particular, has argued for beginning with materiality rather than law; some things, objects, or material forms, in other words, become materialized specifically as law. We can also draw on object-oriented anthropology to challenge distinctions between law-as-object and law-as-concept (Henare et al. 2007) that would otherwise evacuate both law and time to the realm of relative epistemologies.

My suggestion is that law and legal objects are associated with the kind of temporal "folding" that allows objects to gesture to new worlds, and that is not attached in advance to particular distinctions between law and matter. A more appropriate verb for these diverse actions might be "brewing," because it evokes a process of fermentation that leads to material transformations. Law brews time in the sense that legal rationales and technicalities often transfer problems and functions to nonhuman actors and do something very similar to Latour's description of folding: they transform a present problem into the past perfect ("once hinges had been installed," in Latour's language) or into another temporal register. Nonhuman actors also have effects in brewing legal time, whether or not they have been explicitly invited to do so by legal actors or processes. As my research suggests, once the HIV antibody test became widely available in the late 1980s in Canada and the United Kingdom, it became necessary to decide legal dilemmas relating to HIV and disability differently and with new temporal ontologies. The development of the HIV antibody test in the late 1980s inaugurated the legal artefacts of asymptomatic status and progression in varying forms, and with distinct effects, in the two countries (Chapters 2 and 3). Similar effects can be seen with evolving clinical classification systems relating to HIV.

The crucial point is that no legal-temporal register exists outside of what is materialized in diverse ways through confederations of human and nonhuman actors and, furthermore, that what is created through these processes is a cluster of very material times. Chapter 4, for example, shows the processes associated with the United Kingdom's Gender Recognition Act's delegating to a standard form statutory declaration the work of managing a transition in legal status, with significant subsequent bureaucratic and experiential effects. Once again, folding is not necessarily an inaccurate description for this. Without the hinge, we would need a human porter to close the door. Without the standard form statutory declaration, we would need repeated bureaucratic acts to certify that a person intends their transition, with all its legal and experiential effects, to be a permanent state of affairs. But more than that, the legal time of permanence is an object-concept coterminous with the form, just as the past perfect is enunciated through the hinge. As such, the legal ontology of permanence *is* the form. This temporal ontology – this permanence – does not have to be metaphysically outside the generic legal object; it is co-extensive with and materially enacted via the form.

"Legal Temporalities"

It is possible to understand legal objects and legal relations as having something similar to what Latour would term "folding" effects in relation to time. But this only works if we draw on a wider range of intellectual resources – for example, Bennett's approach to vital materiality, socio-material approaches in law and STS, and new approaches to objects in anthropology. If we allow materiality a similar status to law in our analysis, then what is materialized as law can fold or brew ontologies of time in a wide range of ways. In the final substantive section of this chapter, I argue that the resources already exist within legal studies, particularly in the work of Alain Pottage, Javier Lezaun, and Annelise Riles, to support these propositions. More specifically, through a praxiographic approach to temporalization, it is possible to identify at least three areas of concern for enquiries into the roles and consequences of brewing legal temporalities. These temporalities can be seen to mark the point at which law and nature dissolve into each other. They also seem to have effects in creating essential fortifying links between law and reality. In a different register, however, legal temporalities, such as those that emerge in the present book, remind us of the work we need to do as researchers to denaturalize the apparently merely discursive and immaterial significance of legal technicalities.

Dissolving Law and Nature

As we have already seen, law is understood to have world-making capacities; it is closely associated with the dominant temporalizing practices of the moderns, in particular, and might be understood within human time as purely cultural. Yet what have come to be understood as legal forms of time – legal temporalities – also participate in marking and dissolving distinctions between nature and culture. This is possible when juridical forms develop in relationship with biological ontologies – in other words, when law becomes indistinguishable from life. Alain Pottage, for example, has investigated how the time of inheritance has been articulated through legal and political debates over genetic patrimony. In particular, he focuses on a petition created by two parliamentary members of the Council of Europe in May 2000, protesting the European Union's Directive on the Legal Protection of Biotechnological Inventions. The protestors argued that this directive authorized the patenting of human gene sequences and that instead, it should be recognized that "the human genome is the common patrimony of humanity," hence no patents on the genome should be granted (Pottage 2004, 249).

As Pottage shows, the phrase "common patrimony of humanity" blurs complex interactions between legal institutional practices and scientific concepts, which recur specifically within bio-ethical accounts of genetic research. The French legal tradition of inheritance underpinned the wording of the petition. Within this system, the assumption is that material wealth could and should be conserved and passed on; that past arrangements of wealth could be transferred into the future within a fund, the transmission of which would be handed to an executor. On this logic, genes, like a fund, are not for individuals or corporations to commodify. Yet appealing to genetic patrimony in this fashion, Pottage shows, obscures law's own roots in early modern botanical taxonomies. Inheritance law both draws on and informs the construction of genealogies through which inheritance is traced by means of co-sanguinity. In such a way, Pottage illuminates the co-construction of cultural time – heritability, governed through law – and the time of plants and biological change. As he puts it: "In the case of legal technique, the difference between law and life is dissolved into a single institutional compound; biological life is always already institutional" (Pottage and Mundy 2004, 255).

Furthermore, and this is Pottage's second key point, these temporal questions become all the more interesting when we bear in mind that the study of genomics is changing. Earlier accounts of genetic inheritance held that gene action caused DNA to constitute the material body of the organism (or phenotype): genotype determined phenotype. Yet, within scientific accounts of gene action, arguments against the concept of genetic patrimony have become almost ubiquitous, and have begun to undermine this economy of whole and part. As Pottage puts it, recent research questions ideas of linear gene action and instead suggests a model of cellular epigenesis, in which proteins have a role in activating DNA. Within this science of proteomics, legal models of patrimony become unstuck because, in effect, the heirs are creating the fund (Pottage and Mundy 2004, 269).

More particularly, with Pottage's argument that distinctions between law and life can be dissolved and that biological life can be "always already institutional," it becomes much harder and arguably much less necessary to propose, as Latour has done, that law cannot "fold space-time." The implication of Pottage's analysis is not that there is anything more or less "natural," as such, about the genetic fund, but instead that understanding such a fund requires challenging distinctions between law and nature. Part of such an endeavor involves following the multiple temporalities of genes and genomics and their juridical entanglements. In other words, there is temporal "folding" in Pottage's analysis, but it relies on an ability or a commitment to trace the co-materialization of law and life in a way that I have already described as "brewing." There is, for example, the time of the already-juridical genome, constructed through a notion of patrimony, apparently linear, but more specifically legally created as time-less (despite legal inheritance inaugurating multiple temporalities). In this world, the genotype, as species, is a fund to which juridically constructed persons/humans (organisms or phenotypes) owe their allegiance and in conjunction with which they gain human dignity. There is also, however, the time of epigenesis, in which genes' regulatory functions are themselves conditioned by cellular metabolism: not merely an inversion but a radical displacement of the previous ontologies of genetic authority. In this world, organisms are their own cause, and through ontogenesis they help to bring the genome into being (Pottage and Mundy 2004, 268). Patrimony is an inadequate descriptor for such a self-generating process; Bennett's concept of conatus seems all the more relevant here.

Pottage's analysis of gene activism helps to underscore the extent to which legal temporalities, such as inheritance, once interrogated, can dissolve ontological splits not only between nature and culture, but also between human and nonhuman. This is all the more interesting given what Pottage terms the "already institutional" shape of biological status (Pottage and Mundy 2004, 255). Bennett's proposal to open political engagement to the question of vital materiality, as a response to the ongoing splitting off of human and material agencies, engages with this sort of conundrum. More specifically, Pottage's approach to law and life helps to explain the difficulties we might have in understanding how cells, tests, and symptoms, for example, might be legally powerful, as we will see in Chapters Two and Three, in particular. In this account, law can "fold" time to the extent that it is constantly materialized in new forms of life and matter.

Making Law "Real"

Yet it is also possible to trace the mobilization of specific legal temporalities in fortifying otherwise fragile links between law and "reality." Legal temporalities, in other words, can help ground the objectivity of legal concepts and projects. Again, law and legal objects here can be seen to have effects that "fold" or "brew" time. As Javier Lezaun shows, fabricated legal "things" – reference materials – can act as transitional objects for law in approximating the "real world," allowing regulation to extend into wider networks (Lezaun 2012). To the extent that these reference materials are temporally limited, each through a specified "shelf life," we can begin to understand how legal-temporal constructions assist in the work of creating and maintaining connections between law and objectivity.

Lezaun undertook ethnographic research at the Institute for Reference Materials and Measurements (IRMM), an organization in Geel, Belgium, that produces the materials that allow EU legislation to function. Without these materials, which promise a temporally limited and, as such, stable reference point for other substances, EU law would not be a "force capable of ordering our material world" (Lezaun 2012, 23). Lezaun gives the example of Commission Regulation (EC) No. 1881/2006, which prohibits (among other actions) the commercialization of milk that contains with more than 0.020 milligrams of lead, and which is standardized, and gains viability, through Certified Reference Material BCR-063R, a vial containing 50 grams of milk powder with the relevant amount of lead, certified for one year (22). He shows how paperwork creates law's material reference points, through certification practices, instructions, and documentation, all in accordance with international standards, in such a way that it is possible to discern the creation of a reference material out of a mass of text. Furthermore, techniques of "handling stuff" allow technicians to create usable reference material through drying, grinding, and creating protective environments for matter, and through a "deep familiarity" with tools (for example, the glove box) (28). According to Lezaun, the value of these highly manipulated reference materials in connecting law with "reality" does not lie in their "purity" as such (because, through intervention, any objective of purity is lost), but in their capacity to resemble natural matter, which is a different standard. The closer the fit of the reference material, the narrower the scope for avoiding the material standard. This happens largely through reconstitution, the re-creation of naturalness through highly skilled processes. Technicians in charge of producing reference materials choose a particular "idiom of realism" (33), and make sure their techniques fit, through attention to fabrication, rather than to preservation as such: "The pragmatic sanction of materials is thus never a matter of *applying* a legal principle to a singular object, of fitting the abstract ideal to the mundane exemplar. Nor is it a mere attempt to *embed* a value – legal or otherwise – in a piece of matter. It is, rather, the manufacture of *radically original legal substances*, substances that allow the law to become *of the world*" (38).

There is a striking resonance here with the work of Henare, Holbraad, and Wastell on the ontologies of objects. In this piece, Lezaun discusses the processes by which legal things are brought into being. As he so convincingly demonstrates, these reference materials do not evoke a particular epistemological stance as much as inaugurate what Henare and colleagues would call a legal/scientific object-concept. These are legal materials or substances that, in order to work, *have* to be *of* the world (to use Lezaun's phrase), not a particular perspective *on* the world. Henare and colleagues talk of asking "the incredulous question" of "where the worlds might be" in an approach oriented to ontological, rather than epistemological, inquiry. They answer the question by proposing that the worlds are right here in front of us, in the objects themselves (Henare, Holbraad, and Wastell 2007, 13). In this vein, it is no more strange to propose that the (power of) law can be found in Lezaun's reference materials than to propose that "powder is power," as Holbraad has done, for example. In Lezaun's analysis, the outcome of technicians' dogged fabrication of legal objects renders law, thing and concept, for a specific time at least, analytically inseparable and powerful.

Lezaun's example has particular salience for the current inquiry into "folding time" because of the temporal connections between a reference material, the "real world," and the law. He asks of the milk vial, for example: "Why the peculiar temporality of the qualities ascribed to the material, the precise duration of IRMM's guarantee?" (Lezaun 2012, 22). If the reference material is, as Lezaun suggests, the limit of law's reach, then my argument would be that the period for which the material is guaranteed (the "shelf life") modulates such a limit: it is the outer reach of the outer reach, the final boundary, and/or a means of constituting the boundary itself and deciding when law slips back into immateriality. As such, the shelf life acts, as much as anything else, as ontological lubricant for decisions about the status of law, matter, and presence. Outside the shelf life, the link between law and "reality" that the reference material encapsulates is unstable. The shelf life helps to constitute the temporally significant modes of preservation and "infinite permanence" (36) that animate much of the technicians' work in this area, responding to vibrant, radically fluid, material life by pinning substances down, even if only temporarily (with "temporariness" being key here). As Lezaun puts it: "Reference technicians treat *all* materials as if they were living matter. They are constantly attuned to the plasticity of substances and the temporality of any of their forms … This is a world in continuous 'degradation' or 'decay,' a process reference technicians strive to interrupt, if only provisionally, by fabricating unusually homogeneous and stable versions of worldly stuff" (37).

If radically original legal substances – reference materials – are created through temporalized guarantees (the certified period of one year, for example), then what questions might we ask of other objects/things enrolled into legal assemblages? It is possible that this form of ontological enquiry does not require such a "strong" case, in which legal objects are fabricated explicitly to connect law with the world, for us to think about the role of legal temporalities in tethering law, through things, with variegated "realities" or worlds. Whether or not in a particular instance things are created *as* legal objects, it should be possible to think about the reconstitution of both "law" and "time" in these and similar projects. As such, Lezaun's work provokes useful questions about the ontological status of law and the implication of time in projects of world-making through the fabrication of "legal things." Again, with an approach that focuses on the materialization of law, it is possible to view these processes and objects as "folding" or more specifically "brewing" times. In the coming chapters, I return to this line of analysis, considering the means by which temporalities of progression, prognosis, and likelihood attach legal dilemmas about a person's "disabled" status in law, for example, to the "reality" of a retrovirus and its physical effects (Chapters Two and Three), or how gender recognition laws adopt statutory declaration forms and promises of gender permanence to instantiate the "transition" that materializes a legal change in status (Chapter Five).

The Power of Legal Form

As we have seen from the discussion so far, it is possible to argue that legal concepts (such as inheritance) and legal objects (such as reference materials) inaugurate and deploy particular types of time in managing law's ambivalent ontological status. Through the materialization of law, or law's implication in biological ontologies, we can get to an account of law "brewing" time. However, a difficult question that remains is the status of legal form in these enquiries. How "material" is legal form? Positioning legal form as the object of inquiry challenges the prevailing tendency in social science research to view technicalities and documents as "mute evidence" or "non-reactive" (Prior 2008, 823). Instead, it is in the chosen or fabricated form of law – the particular discursive and material shape of the contract, for example, or the orientation and wording of the contractual term – that we can discern much about legal rationalities, actions, effects, and relationships, as well as about our own practices as researchers.

The difficulty with legal form is that it seems to occupy both a particular material shape (being a property, at the very least, of documents, whether contracts, legislation, or reports) and the realm of the immaterial (being apparently also to do with legal principles and sources of law). Contractual terms, for example, are features of documentation as much as they express formal legal principles. If we allow that vital matter and other nonhuman elements can have conative effects in legal assemblages, then the clusters of words, references, text, paper, and meanings that contribute to formal legal technicalities (such as a contract term) participate in assemblages with at least a degree of agency. What might it mean, then, to think of a contract term, and the formal technical qualities of such a term, as having the capacity to "brew" temporal relations between actors in a network? As Riles has shown, legal documents, being the result of modern knowledge practices that themselves have constituted ethnography, invite us to study how ethnographers know. Treating documents as ethnographic objects, in other words, requires pulling back from the temptation to see them purely as vehicles of some other legal meaning, and focusing, also, on their material form. In the legal context, this might require focusing on legal technicalities, their materialization through documents, and their temporal effects.

Through an ethnography of Japanese derivatives markets in the late 1990s and 2000s, Riles discusses the temporalizing features of one innovated contractual term that acted as a temporal "placeholder," resolving uncertainty about a legal dilemma in order to allow the contract to function. The term was about the posting and holding of collateral. Uncertainty – for example, the threat that one party will go bankrupt – is usually managed in the swaps market through posting collateral (cash or bonds) with the other party, to be held until the swap date. If a party fails to fulfil their side of the swap, the collateral is kept. Japanese financial workers experienced difficulties over the question of rehypothecation, or the ability of the pledgee to use the collateral up until the date of the swap. In US law, rehypothecation rights had been legislated, meaning that pledgees could use the collateral, but no such legislation existed in Japan. Yet the standard form documentation of the International Swaps and Derivatives Association (ISDA) contained a clause simply allowing the pledgee to use the collateral. Riles describes this apparently simple technical solution as a "placeholder" – a means through which both parties could act as if the pledgee already had rights that were not yet legislated in the domestic law of a given state, such as Japan. As she puts it, "one of the interesting features of the placeholder is where it puts our attention – on the provisionally settled present, and on the near future. The assumption is that all we can really know at the moment is this near future. We will leave final outcomes to unfold as they may" (Riles 2011, 169). The ISDA clause, as a legal technical solution, worked in and with time, demonstrating the "temporality of legal technique" (175). Instead of imagining the present as open ended, the placeholder, a technical legal fiction, treated the key ambiguity as if it were already resolved, creating a short-form approach to the future, a close horizon. Similarly, the placeholder was not concerned with developing a permanent solution to a risk, but merely held that the dilemma had been resolved "for now." Placeholders were "private constitutional moments" (177) because they created and required that a certain group be held, for the duration, by an "as if."

It might be tempting to understand this temporalizing process wholly as a matter of legal technique, but, as Riles shows, the material form of the contract documentation was also significant. Legal routines associated with "making" the contracts relied heavily on the ISDA form itself, which required backroom financial workers to engage in specific behaviour, circling here or filling in a blank there (Riles 2008, 620). The act of "contracting" was hence much more responsive to the standard form documentation than Riles had expected: "What ISDA members, through the battalions of documentation people I studied were busy making were not rules, not norms, not sources of law, but documents ... Legal scholars have read such contracts for their meaning – they have treated them as texts that entextualize particular sets of norms. But such forms are often meant not to be read, but to be *completed*. That is, ISDA documents are technologies that compel a very specific kind of activity, form-filling" (620). The contractual term or placeholder had a particular textual appearance within the contract, and a specific technical role. As technicality, it helped to create a specific cluster of legal temporalities (the "near future," "for now") oriented at the pragmatic resolution of a dilemma of possession among a newly defined group of actors. Legal form, fiction, and technicality, the placeholder was neither wholly material nor wholly immaterial in terms that we might otherwise understand.

As the coming case studies show, legal technicalities have conative force within wider networks of human and nonhuman actors, referencing questions to do with the *source* of law (dilemmas over the use of contract or statute in Chapter Five, for example), the temporalizing effects of legal technicalities (the "until death" provision in Chapter Four; the "likelihood" test for disability in Chapter Three), and law's diverging material forms. In particular, the changing legal-temporal technicalities associated with requesting flexible work, addressed in Chapter Five, indicate shifting bureaucratic and government approaches to the unpaid care burden. Focusing on changing formal approaches to timelines and process in UK labour law, we can understand the interconnections of temporalized legal technicalities with attempts to "responsibilize" employers and employees.

Concluding Remarks

So far, therefore, we have a set of propositions that denaturalizes modern times and human temporalities. Materiality, nonhumans (including objects), and lively assemblages of various sorts are integral to the work of scholars writing in quite distinct philosophical areas, including the feminist philosophy of Elizabeth Grosz, but also extending into the vital materialism of Jane Bennett and the critical approaches to modernity of Carol Greenhouse, Annemarie Mol, Bruno Latour, and Michel Serres. Greenhouse suggests that time is a result of particular forms of social regulation and law, not the other way around. Time, following Serres and Latour, is created through sorting, instead of itself acting as the backdrop for human action and "natural" temporalities. Within complex assemblages of human and nonhuman actors, people, artefacts, and matter of various types interact, "brewing" or "percolating" time. Thinking about "things" in the context of law and time, it might be that actors engaged in the process of percolating legal temporalities do not merely cause new or alternative shades of interpretation, but fresh questions of ontology. Seeking to understand the conative force of objects and other nonhumans, we can access not merely new interpretations of the "world" (as provided by previous anthropological stances), but "new worlds" themselves.

Not only are temporalities created through relationships between humans, things, and matter, but the strange qualities of legal time produce specific effects. Inheritance, the shelf life, and the placeholder are all reference points at which legal relationships, in their various guises, have acted temporally and indeed, have generated new temporal modes. In turn, legal temporalities have specific effects in dissolving distinctions between law and nature, and in strengthening ontological ties between law and reality. Studies of law and time will continue to generate new vocabularies with which to speak, enact, and conceive legal temporalities in their various material forms. It is to these questions that I turn in the following chapters.

Chapter Two

Progression

What is called AIDS is generally understood as the last of three stages – the first of which is infection with a human immunodeficiency virus (HIV) and early evidence of inroads on the immune system – with a long latency period between infection and the onset of "telltale" symptoms.

– Susan Sontag, *Illness as Metaphor and AIDS and Its Metaphors*

The medical evidence given by Dr. McLean was that the entire HIV infection should be thought of as a continuum from the individual being exposed to the virus, to being seropositive but asymptomatic, followed in many instances by the development of ARC or AIDS where the person would have a medical condition in which the symptoms would be apparent and would require medical treatment.

– *Biggs v Hudson*

As we saw in Chapter One, it is by now a familiar move for scholars working in a range of disciplines to follow nonhuman actors of various types – drugs, patents, documents, for example – in addition to our familiar legal friends, humans. Yet this kind of work also inevitably shifts how we understand law and time. If we expand what is often termed in science and technology studies the "cast" of actors, then we must grapple not only with temporalities that operate in the domain of human legal consciousness and subjectivity, but also with those temporalities that are co-produced between legal actors of different types, species, and registers: human and viral, for example. Shifting our understanding of law and time in this way means engaging with ongoing ontological splits between law and nature.

This chapter follows the actions of HIV-related drugs, clinical tests, and a range of documents through Canadian law in the late 1980s and early 1990s to better understand the medico-legal temporality of *progression.* At that time, therapeutic and epidemiological classification systems in Canada and other countries for understanding HIV and AIDS used the idea of disease progression to tabulate a patient's relative health and to make decisions about drug and other treatments. A person's status was understood to "progress" from infection with the HIV virus, through a sero-positive but asymptomatic phase, to the first signs of symptoms, and from the symptomatic status to "full-blown AIDS." Symptoms were not just read on their own as singular indicators of disease, but had explanatory force predominantly within a series of stages through which initial infection led to compromising the immune system via a decrease in T cells, with patients succumbing eventually to opportunistic infections.These classification systems became significant within legal networks during the same period, with vastly different effects. In some contexts, as we will see, people living with HIV were able to assert legal rights from the point of infection, whereas in others they had to show progression to a relatively "late" stage of the disease. Different legal areas, legal practices, and legal techniques all contributed to distinct enactments of HIV temporalities in Canadian law.

More specifically, however, I argue that the achievement of progression and the performance of "progression work" have been central to the creation of medico-legal objectivity around HIV. The modulated progression of HIV infection through asymptomatic to symptomatic states in Canada in the late 1980s and early 1990s was just as much legally as medically accomplished. Furthermore, the significance of progression to Canadian law on HIV (in various areas) was closely linked with the need to establish the "reality" of the disease. As such, legal tests and practices that engaged with clinical classification measures were intended to ground legal responses objectively in what was perceived to be a new and challenging medical "problem."

The first section of this chapter provides some background to the debate. Drawing on interviews of legal activists, lawyers, and clinicians working on HIV in Toronto, Ottawa, and Halifax in the late 1980s and early 1990s, I trace the inauguration of "urgency" as a temporal-ontological phenomenon during that period. This is followed by an analysis of how HIV appeared as a legally defined disability in distinct fields of Canadian law, again drawing on interviews of lawyers and clinicians, and paying particular attention to differences across legal areas, the effects of antibody tests, and the newly emerging field of "asymptomatic status." In the final section, I relate a "story" about one HIV case in particular – *Thwaites v Canada*, from the early 1990s – that provides some ways of understanding the efficacy of (legally defined) drugs and their interactions with classification systems in producing legal temporalities.

The following discussion, then, engages with multiple types of legal ordering that determined how HIV and HIV-related issues were conceived, shaped, legally mobilized, and adjudicated in different areas of Canadian law. In my fieldwork, it became apparent that clinical temporalities of progression were key to the highly mediated means through which legal processes in distinct areas of law were able to account for a new virus and imagine it as a disease or a disability. In the context of an epidemic that created "uneven urgencies" depending on race, First Nations status, and gender, people claiming income assistance on the basis of HIV had to show, by virtue of Ontario provincial law, that their illness had progressed to a much later "stage" than was required under provincial human rights claims. Poverty law concerns around HIV, in other words, become entangled in a set of debates about whether a person had reached an AIDS and/or what was then known as an AIDS-Related Complex (ARC) diagnosis, marking a degree of disablement that was much "later" and more complex than the "manifesting antibodies" test required for the definition of disability under provincial human rights law. This was all the more a problem because the fraught process of determining the progression of a person's illness to AIDS was itself gendered and often delayed for racialized claimants. Such debates inevitably were structured through questions of what we might call, for want of better terms, "jurisdiction" or "area of law." To say that an area of law – welfare benefits law, for example, or human rights law – can be temporalizing, and vice versa, suggests that legal worlds or plural legal orders are enacted through distinct processes of doing time. For these reasons, I argue that a "praxiographic" approach to law and time, by increasing the range of analytic concerns and remaining attentive to the productive power, for example, of things in the constitution of distinct areas of law, provides essential ways of understanding how time is implicated in processes of social injustice.

Uneven Urgencies

From the outset of the epidemic, tropes of "emergence," "urgency," and contagion structured legal and political actions around HIV/AIDS in countries across the global North (Patton 1990; Sontag 2001). "Emergence" both accompanied and constituted the "newness" of cases of what was called GRID (Gay-Related Immune Deficiency) in the early 1980s, with its distressing opportunistic infections (Kaposi's sarcoma, a rare form of cancer not usually found in healthy young people, and *Pneumocystis carinii* pneumonia, or PCP), relatively high morbidity, and unclear etiology. It also accompanied and provided the context for developments during the 1980s and 1990s establishing the epidemiology and etiology of AIDS, as well as the politics of treatment, described so painstakingly in Steven Epstein's 2009 book, *Impure Science*. The "crisis" traced by media reports on the virus in North America was heavily racialized, focusing on the effects of the virus on white gay male communities and neglecting AIDS cases among black gay men, injection drug users, and women (Cohen 1999; Treichler 1999). In Canada, members of Haitian, immigrant, and urban First Nations communities were particularly affected by HIV transmission and difficulties in accessing treatment and care (Bastow 1994).

In this context, temporalities of crisis and urgency were inaugurated through small-scale legal strategies, practices, and activist work around HIV and AIDS in Canada in the late 1980s and early 1990s, responding to the "new" temporal frames occasioned by the retrovirus: illness, decline, shortened lifespan, and "early" death (Rayside and Linquist 1992). Some of these strategies addressed the slow time of a "failure of urgency" on the part of government actors. Legal activists sensed inertia on the part of federal and provincial government departments, accompanied by unpredictability. As this advisor put it: "Because HIV was new (when I started we still talked about GRID and ARC), government departments had no cohesive policy about anything. So everything was very ad hoc and unpredictable."

As is well documented in much of the literature on the politics of HIV and AIDS in the 1980s, activists treated the epidemic as an emergency that required innovation and immediate action. Yet there was a perception that government and regulatory bodies in Canada and the United States (including those regulating research and licensing drugs), if convinced that the epidemic was a social problem at all, treated it as a different kind of emergency, requiring slow and careful steps (Cohen 1999; Rayside and Linquist 1992). This HIV policy worker describes what they felt was the tension of articulating the epidemic as a crisis in the face of hysteria: "That tension has been there from the beginning, the very beginning of the epidemic, where you had horrible fear and stigma that

[you] had to fight against, [and] at the same time you had the demand. This is a serious crisis. Government needs to respond. Money needs to be mobilized. How do you keep sounding the alarm about something without having all of your public policy being infected by alarmism?" Legal activism, therefore, took the shape of "sounding the alarm," which meant alerting governments to the need for more funding not only for legal services, but also for HIV drugs and services, without feeding into widespread panic about the emerging epidemic.

It is worth remembering that this activist sense of "urgency" itself took shape within a productive network of clinical evaluation, epidemiological measurements, early AIDS activism (Cohen 1999; Crimp and Bersani 1988), reports produced by the Centers for Disease Control (CDC) in the United States, and, in Canada, federal health policy on HIV emanating from the Health Protection Branch of the federal Department of National Health and Welfare. HIV tests became available in Canada only from the mid-1980s, which meant that many HIV-positive people had already developed AIDS by the time they were diagnosed, and were in what came to be called the "late stages" of illness. What previously had been viewed as a condition in its own right then became the "final stage" of a longer-term infection, "lateness" being complexly articulated with "urgency" through new forms of techno-scientific intervention. Yet effective treatments were still not available. As one HIV clinician working at that time in a Canadian hospital put it, "We were faced with essentially no good treatment options for the HIV itself. Because of that and because it was still pretty early in the epidemic, we were seeing people at late stages with HIV infection. We were faced with an extremely poor clinical prognosis in terms of HIV."

In his diaries, white Toronto queer activist Michael Lynch recorded his thoughts about the politics of the lifespan during the late 1980s. Ann Silversides reports in her biography of Lynch that sometimes the quick death of a friend or acquaintance of AIDS would raise feelings of embarrassment – from 1985: "You get embarrassed when someone dies before you've even heard they're sick" (Silversides 2003, 92). At other times, an otherwise normal social encounter would reassert differences between straight and queer expectations about the future. For example, after attending a straight party in August 1986, Lynch wrote: "They all still expect, assume, rely on themselves and their friends, with the odd exception, living a long time ... I really don't expect more than a few years, I realized on the way home" (108).

At the same time, a key moment for black gay and lesbian activism was the realization that racialized groups were disproportionately highly affected by HIV and AIDS in Canada and the United States. Cathy Cohen, for example, quotes Gil Gerald, former executive director of the (US) National Coalition of Black Lesbians and Gays speaking about his reaction to a CDC report in the spring of 1983: "Here is the report from the Centers for Disease Control, and it is the Morbidity and Mortality Weekly Report. I had never seen one in my life … [It] showed that blacks were disproportionately affected by HIV and by AIDS … I just looked at it and just as a lay person it jumped off the page at you. I knew that, as blacks, we were only 10–20 percent of the population, but [here] we were disproportionately affected. I think we were 20 percent. Like, it was crazy at the time, and so that became the first real evidence to me personally" (Cohen 1999, 95).[1]

With different life expectancy in Canada following diagnosis between women and men, First Nations and white people, and low-income and higher-income/professional workers, urgency itself did not constitute a smooth terrain of political action, but instead was striated by gender, race, settler colonialism, and class (Bastow 1994). By the end of 1983, around a quarter of the one hundred people who were found to have AIDS were of Haitian background (Rayside and Linquist 1992), and even by the early 1990s women were dying up to three times faster than men following diagnosis (Bastow 1994). It is clear even from these short references to much richer and more detailed investigations in Canada and the United States that not only was the crisis experienced, and constituted, differently in the two countries, but also that these differences manifested in reports, figures, and death rates, as well as in subjective experiences. In other words, a significant aspect of the epidemic was that clinically measured "stages" of HIV and designations of "poor prognosis," themselves produced through gendering and racialized processes, contributed to temporal experiences of foreshortened life associated with HIV.[2]

1 By the early 1990s, a new dimension of HIV racialization and activism concerned the forced HIV testing and incarceration of Haitian refugees at the US base at Guantánamo, Cuba, with those testing positive being refused entry to the United States (Chávez 2012).

2 Government reporting on HIV, race, and ethnicity has been in place in Canada only since 1998, and at the time of writing Quebec still does not provide statistics on race and ethnicity; see Canada (2013, n5).

Such uneven urgencies were accompanied by a genre of inexperience or emerging expertise across legal and clinical fields. Inexperience was sufficiently widely reported through interviews to be described as a professional stance, associated specifically with HIV, responding to and conjuring clinical and legal techniques as "new." Legal workers active in HIV networks during the 1980s spoke of the significance of being "honest" about their lack of knowledge regarding the retrovirus and associated legal issues and about their subsequent efforts to educate co-workers, tribunals, and courts. As one human rights lawyer on what later became a significant HIV-related case put it, referring to her (lack of) knowledge at the time about relevant legal arguments, "I'm bright and I'm hard working and I will do my best, but I don't know anything about human rights law." Another legal worker spoke of the reason they were given a job in an HIV legal organization: "[Name of boss] told me this years afterwards. He said, I gave you the position because when I asked the question, what do you know about HIV, you honestly said, not very much. You said, I know this and this and that's about it. He hired me because I was up front and honest about my ignorance [laughs] ... He's the one who taught me about sero-conversion and a window period[3] and all of those things. Those were things that the general public was completely ignorant about." A clinician who later acted as an expert witness in an HIV claim also spoke of being "junior" and lacking in experience in the late 1980s, despite having a relatively senior role: "I was a good, solid, average HIV care provider, but I was not one who was going to be writing the treatment guidelines or the latest review article on the pathogenesis of HIV. I sort of felt ... I'm very junior."

"Honesty" about both legal and clinical ignorance regarding HIV is positioned in these accounts not only with a certain degree, perhaps, of retrospective deskilling, but also as a threshold moment, a stage in professional development constituting the retrovirus as "new," as requiring innovation. In this way, the epidemic appeared as "novel" in Canadian legal networks, a movement that both prepared the ground for, and justified the development of, "fresh" legal skills and clinical strategies.

3 The "window period" describes the lag between when the virus enters the body and when the body produces antibodies to the virus.

"The Tool We Have Now"

Canadian activists and lawyers developed practical methods of pragmatic legal short-termism, associated with the foreshortened lifespans of claimants. Legal advice organizations, responding to claimants' health conditions and altered future-scapes, produced their own temporalities of urgency through distinct legal strategies, against a background of overwork and high demand for services. For practitioners familiar with poverty law issues, HIV brought a shift in legal priorities from "predictable" benefits work to "pressing" issues of HIV disclosure. As this HIV and poverty law specialist put it:

> The hardest part I think was that, if you work at a poverty law clinic, it was predictable. The people, they are either facing eviction or their benefits are being cut off. That's your bread and butter of a poverty law clinic. When HIV was thrown into the mix, suddenly you had a whole bunch of other more pressing issues, like there were people who were being cut off their benefits, but who cared less about [that] and more about whether or not their social worker knew that they were HIV positive or not and how they could apply for disability without disclosing their status.

Activists and advisors, who frequently found themselves occupying both roles, also spoke of being overwhelmed by the physical hard work of providing legal services and keeping cases afloat. As this HIV legal advisor put it: "It's important I think to remember that in the late '80s and early '90s almost everyone with HIV was dying or expected to die shortly. Some of those people turned out to be long-term survivors and I'm grateful some of the people I met during that era are still alive and kicking. But most are not." Many advisors in poverty clinics, which housed the first HIV legal clinics, were overworked in any case due to the scale of service provision and the local need for advice and representation, but found that the challenges of managing HIV caseloads required considerable technical and administrative innovation. Legal activism and advice became oriented to the fluctuating health conditions and "short" lifespans of people living with AIDS.

A pressing day-to-day concern – that the impairment of immune function occasioned by HIV was leaving many clients open to potentially fatal opportunistic illnesses – not only caused legal "problems" for advisors to address, such as denial of housing, employment harassment, dismissal, and problems with accessing benefits, but also required a speeded-up approach to legal advice and representation. As we will see later in the chapter, as a retrovirus HIV is clinically enacted through specific techno-scientific means (for example, electron microscopy) such that its "presence" within legal assemblages cannot be traced without reference to these conjuring techniques (van Loon 2002). Yet assessing HIV-related legal activism also cannot ignore the multiple conative actions of the retrovirus, however it is scientifically measured or enacted, in co-producing human physical effects and new temporalized subjectivities and in reordering activist and legal strategies. HIV, after all, had physical effects that made people ill and (albeit in complex ways) caused hundreds of deaths at that point, resulting in new temporalities of life expectancy and specific legal problems. Advisors developed specific professional and personal techniques for managing the affective and administrative burden of the very frequent deaths of clients and co-activists, such as avoiding funerals and swiftly closing files, for example: "We weren't the only people doing anything, but sometimes it felt that way. And having people die … I just very early on, very early on, I said, I'm not going to funerals. If a client died, file closed, we move on, because there was just no way" (an HIV legal advisor).

Through a range of decisions, strategies, and responses, advisors who might otherwise have been interested in exploring legal points of principle instead developed a set of pragmatic legal techniques, a politics of expediency and improvisation, that focused more on achieving beneficial short-term results or immediate goals, even if this required a significant degree of compromise. As a worker for an HIV and AIDS legal research and policy organization put it, speaking of the approach at the time, "We need to use whatever tool we have now rather than trying to get what might be in some way the more politically pure or satisfying approach." Using the "tool we have now" involved institutional innovation, finding alternative, nontribunal, and noncourt routes for certain complaints, as well as putting pressure on legal bodies to expedite cases concerning HIV.

Yet these tools were themselves reliant upon networks, institutions, and legal processes. Some legal advisors directed complaints about service provision for people with HIV to professional bodies, rather than to provincial human rights bodies, specifically because of a concern with "timelines" and institutional slowness. This HIV legal activist describes the rationale: "Different legal processes had different timelines. One of the reasons we did a lot of complaints about health professionals to the colleges rather than to the [Canadian Human Rights] Commission was because they were faster and clients would choose that route over the commission one even though they knew they could not get monetary compensation from the college process." Lawyers and activists also lobbied the commission to obtain an expedited process for hearing HIV-related cases on the basis that people were dying before they achieved an outcome in their case. The lobbying was eventually successful, with the 1996 Canadian Human Rights Commission Policy on HIV/AIDS containing a specific section on "complaints processing" that explicitly referred to the temporal demands of responding to the epidemic: "Although people with HIV/AIDS may lead productive lives for many years, unfortunately there is still no cure for the disease. Due to the special nature of HIV/AIDS the Commission will expedite the investigation of complaints based on AIDS/HIV. This will help to ensure that complainants are able to receive the benefits of any redress that may be owed to them in a timely manner" (Canadian Human Rights Commission 1996, section 4). The practical effect of this policy was that commission staff would schedule HIV-related claims for mediation or assign them an investigator earlier than non-HIV-related claims, but because the commission's complaints procedure had turned into what one lawyer called an "administrative quagmire" affecting all cases, this expediting had little useful effect overall.

Pragmatic, short-term approaches to legal strategy also, finally, had as much to do with when not to turn to legal organizations for advice or representation. Treatment activism took hold in Canada through bodies such as AIDS Action Now! and the Vancouver Persons with AIDS Society, which contested administrative inertia in the approval and funding of new treatments such as the early anti-retroviral drug AZT and aerosolized pentamidine (for use in preventing PCP).[4] One aspect of this activism was the stockpiling of AZT donated to local AIDS committees in Ontario by the partners and friends of people enrolled in authorized drug trials in the late 1980s.[5] AIDS committees then distributed the AZT to other people living with HIV (PLWH). In an environment in which

4 See *Brown v Canada (Minister of Health)* 1990 CanLII 1064 (BCSC). The term PCP refers to pneumocystis carinii pneumonia, a specific form of pneumonia associated with HIV. The term is not now in common use, as pneumocystis jirovecii pneumonia has been found to be the human strain. I thank one of the clinical research respondents of this study for clarifying this.

5 I cover these trials, and their associated regulatory regime, in more detail below.

legal activism around HIV was taking hold and proving, to various extents, useful, or at least viable, for PLWH who were contesting housing, employment, and benefits problems, it is significant, therefore, that AIDS committees in Ontario did not turn to legal activists for advice on the legality of these measures. As one legal advisor speculated, this was possibly because treatment activists already knew, informally, that what they were doing was illegal, and the desperation of their and their friends' situations was more important than establishing officially sanctioned routes for obtaining the drug: "I think that was because the people doing the illegal dispensing knew it was illegal and simply didn't care about the consequences, either because they had HIV and believed they too would die shortly or because they felt the urgent need meant desperate measures were called for."

In this way, temporalities of urgency and "crisis" were produced through legal orientations, strategies, and stances around HIV in Canadian legal activist networks in the late 1980s, in relationship with the temporalities of the physical effects of the retrovirus itself and the institutional capacities of legal tribunals and other decision-making bodies. Urgency was just as much about closing files and avoiding funerals, material practices of day-to-day legal activism, as it was about the variegated urgencies of treatment politics. It was created afresh, and in different ways, every time a symptom was enrolled as evidence of a legal disability, a lawyer redirected a complaint to a professional body instead of to a human rights tribunal, or a clinical test established that a client or patient had reached a new "stage" in the disease.

Achieving Progression

If "urgency" defined the field of legal activism and casework in relation to HIV, then "progression" became the temporal ground on which many HIV cases were decided. Progression normally refers to the movement from one position or point in a series to another, with the implication that such movement is oriented towards, or incrementally works to achieve, a specific goal or end state, or alternatively that some kind of improvement is made. As a temporal mode, progression is usually future-oriented. Unlike concepts such as precaution or preemption, which are co-articulated with the management of uncertainty (Scott 2005), progression assumes a future that is already in some senses known. It can be interpreted as an ontologically confident temporal stance, identifying and registering phenomena within a self-referential order. Progression has significant pragmatic world-making capacities, to the extent that it both describes and reinstantiates an overarching teleological directionality that can bring about specific actions and effects *as already understood or predicted,* in contrast to speculation and pre-emption, which co-produce, and manage, the unknown (Amoore and de Goede 2008; de Goede 2012).

A key theme in this chapter, therefore, is how progression has appeared in medico-legal circles, in a manner similar to recent work on uncertainty in legal and bioclinical fields. Dayna Scott (2005) has analysed public health attempts to manage uncertainty about the West Nile virus in Toronto in 2003 through the emerging (legal) precautionary principle. Emma Cunliffe (2011), for her part, has traced the productive effects of scientific uncertainty about sudden infant death syndrome within criminal trials of mothers for the deaths of their children in otherwise unexplained circumstances. In the realm of regulatory science, Tiago Moreira and colleagues have traced how uncertainty was both produced and came to have effects in proceedings of the US Food and Drug Administration (FDA) in tackling controversy over new diagnostic categories for Alzheimer's disease. As the authors put it, uncertainty was essential to the FDA's "knowledge machinery": "[T]he deployment of uncertainty is reflexively implicated in bioclinical collectives' search for rules and conventions, and … the collective production of uncertainty is in fact central to the 'knowledge machinery' of regulatory objectivity … [T]he production and temporary stabilization of biomedicine's knowledge and entities requires continuous 'uncertainty work' in the clinic, laboratory and regulatory forum" (Moreira, May, and Bond 2009, 685). Uncertainty, and the performance of "uncertainty work," therefore, is not so much a by-product of inquiry as constitutive of legal and scientific objectivity; it is something that, as Moreira and colleagues argue, is *achieved.*

Similarly, progression was achieved through legal networks in the late 1980s, and constituted its own genre of medico-legal objectivity, grounding HIV as "real" and enabling it to be legally visible. In Canadian legal networks in that period, HIV was something that, if nothing else, progressed through stages and could be measured through the presence or absence (or not-yetness) of symptoms, whether or not such measurements were easy. AIDS was a further or terminal stage in this series. Clinical tests placed the patient on a continuum for therapeutic and epidemiological reasons in such a way that infection with HIV could not be conceived outside the notion that a patient was at this point and would soon be at that point, with the movement between points (asymptomatic to symptomatic, symptomatic to AIDS) being the clinical reality of the disease just as much as the apparently "bare" fact of sero-positive status. Interacting with this reality were legal tests that articulated symptomatic status (and changes in such status) to access remedies of different types, such that claimants were protected from "manifesting antibodies" in human rights claims and from the point of being functionally unable to work through ARC or AIDS in welfare benefits claims, as we shall see.

Given the subject of study, HIV, it is worth remembering and engaging with some of the problems encountered in tracing and visualizing viruses in another relevant field of enquiry: virology. As Joost van Loon puts it, scientific difficulties of "seeing" the object of study – the virus – were partially assuaged with the early use of the electron microscope in 1939, but he also questions what it means to say that one can "see" a virus through a microscope (or more recent technological innovations) if layers of manipulation and technological innovation are required. Drawing on Annemarie Mol and John Law, van Loon argues that viruses can be read as "virtual objects," entities that are attributed causal force, but that are "'hidden" beneath the dense texture of practices and discourses that we find in, for example, clinical medicine (van Loon 2002, 110). Virtual objects such as viruses are differentially enacted or enframed, depending on the techniques used to visualize them. Such enactments rely on processes of indexicality that create referential relationships: "The relationship between indexicality and the virtual object becomes apparent here. Scientific evidence is based on techniques of 'revealing' and 'enframing' through which particular virtual objects are 'ordered' (both in terms of classification and commandment). The alleged natural relationship between the index and the virtual object (which is often produced by laboratory experiments) is based on already existing indexical associations between the sign and the referent" (111). Understood in this sense, the reliance of legal processes, as we will see, on repeated enactments of HIV progression could be understood as a means of legally revealing the virus as virtual object in Canadian law.

Yet the enactment of progression happened differently depending on which legal area was concerned. The stages had distinct meanings, symptoms were articulated in diverse ways, and the entry of law in the guise of legal rights, or at least the ability to fit within a legal definition, varied. In law and society scholarship, the concept of jurisdiction refers to the alignment of law with a geographically, territorially, or politically situated exertion of power (Braverman, Blomley, and Delaney 2014; Valverde 2015), so that, for example, we can speak of federal and provincial human rights law and understand that these constitute distinct orders of legality, diversely oriented, containing different standards, preoccupations, and content, the boundaries between which are carefully mediated. What I found in my research on Canadian legal engagements with HIV in the 1980s and 1990s was divergences in legal temporalities depending on which area of law was engaged. Although the distinctions between these legal areas were not straightforwardly territorial, they were jurisdictional in the sense that distinct types, orders, and strains of law were engaged.

What might therefore be termed the jurisdictionalization of legal time resonates with Mariana Valverde's (2015) concept of legal "chronotopes," which refers to the co-articulation or co-thickening of temporal and spatial modes of legality. Mikhail Bakhtin devised the idea of the chronotope for analysing the co-relationship of spatial and temporal governance and living. Valverde suggests the chronotope can be deployed, for example, in analysing land-use law – for example, the legal doctrine of the "character of the neighbourhood" (Valverde 2015). The value of Valverde's deployment of the chronotope concept is that it productively theorizes clustered relationships between time and space, and is not a theory of space-time as such. As such, reading jurisdiction through the co-thickening of time and divergent interests of provincial and federal law in the regulation of HIV reminds us of jurisdiction's multiple logics and potentialities. What happens, however, when bodies and viruses, diseases and disability, and not territory, scale, terrain, or land, are under analysis? Specifically, what happens when different legal ontologies of disability do different things with the temporality of progression, depending on jurisdiction or area of law?

A conundrum in my documentary analysis and fieldwork ran as follows: why did respondents in even the earliest provincial and federal human rights claims concede HIV to be a disability for the purposes of relevant legal definitions (meaning that no further argument on this issue was required), while HIV and AIDS still had to be carefully and vigorously enunciated and proved as a qualifying reason for access to welfare benefits? The most obvious explanation would be: well, they are different kinds of law, aren't they? Within different jurisdictional paradigms, it was surely inevitable that HIV would emerge as a distinct legal object. One lawyer's explanation of the tension between benefits law and human rights law in Ontario better illuminates this tension:

> I can distinctly remember colleagues in the AIDS community, when I talked about benefits allowances and [so on], … would start trying to tie the two together, saying … their refusal to grant this person benefits is discriminatory, because they are disabled under the Code and they are bringing a different standard to the table in terms of granting benefits. I would go, well no, they are not bringing a different standard to the table … because the statute says you have to be unable to work, and so it's a factual enquiry about work. They would want to make an argument – well, their factual enquiry is biased by their internal fears and hatreds, which was, I believe, completely true [laughs].

In the passage above, an Ontario-based poverty lawyer talks about the experience of mediating not only the vastly different standards attaching to HIV claims in different legal orders, but also other activists' expectations of what could be achieved for distinct groups of claimants. Human rights claims for HIV-related disability discrimination under federal and provincial law, attractive perhaps for their aspirational potential in establishing new legal and social norms, were less relevant to the concerns of low-income people in the late 1980s and early 1990s. More specifically, these claims were *inappropriate* to the mechanics of welfare benefits decisions because they related to a different area of law entirely. Most relevant to poverty law practices at that time was the goal of establishing HIV as a disability for the purposes of providing access to (provincially regulated) income assistance. Making such a claim mobilized a set of arguments about a person's capacity to work, and if he or she were refused income assistance, then in-depth arguments were required about how much the person's health had deteriorated.

In the following sections, I argue that the temporo-legal artefact of "progression" was the product of the coming together of the techno-scientific and clinical innovations that went into the antibody test with the legal capacity to designate even asymptomatic HIV as a field of legal intervention. Through these actions and relationships, progression became an entirely different temporality in welfare benefits law as it was in human rights law. At work were legal knowledges reminiscent of, but not quite wholly described by, the concept of jurisdiction. What resulted was something, again, reminiscent of, but slightly askance from, Valverde's productive deployment of the chronotope for socio-legal theory.

Manifesting Antibodies

I begin with human rights law. The 1988 British Columbia human rights case of *Biggs v Hudson*, concerning the termination of a tenancy due to the tenant's "ARC" status, was the first reported federal or provincial human rights case on HIV or AIDS. *Biggs* set a standard in Canadian human rights cases such that HIV would, after that point, overwhelmingly be accepted to constitute a disability for the purposes of provincial and federal human rights law. Because of the novelty of the issue in this case, the BC Human Rights Council took care to explicate current clinical knowledge about the disease in significant detail, referring to the early and recent history of the virus, up-to-date epidemiology, transmission, and development of symptoms. In doing so, the council used a medico-legal language of disease progression that would later reappear in other fields of law with very different consequences.

The *Biggs* decision drew heavily on expert testimony given by Dr Harry McLean, a consultant in communicable diseases in the Vancouver health department and, among other positions, member of the Advisory Committee-Cancer Control Agency of BC. In a section of the decision titled "The Disease," the Human Rights Council established basic points about transmission relevant to the landlord's fears concerning Biggs's ARC status, yet it is the statements about the nature and characteristics of HIV and AIDS that are the most useful for the purposes of this analysis. In this case, the concept of an HIV/AIDS continuum was first legally articulated for the purposes of a human rights complaint. As the council put it:

> Clinical signs and symptoms appear as on a continuum in people who are exposed to the virus. There is the eventual conversion from negative to positive and then there is the asymptomatic period when one is infected but there is no evidence of the virus in terms of a person's health or anything noticeable in a medical examination. Dr. McLean stated that the largest group of the infected population are HIV infected and asymptomatic ...
>
> The medical evidence given by Dr. McLean was that the entire HIV infection should be thought of as a continuum from the individual being exposed to the virus, to being seropositive but asymptomatic, followed in many instances by the development of ARC or AIDS where the person

> would have a medical condition in which the symptoms would be apparent and would require medical treatment. (*Biggs v Hudson*, paras 40342, 40352)

In these passages, the council identified three or four successive health stages relating to infection with HIV. First was exposure, followed by sero-conversion, followed by asymptomatic "good" health. Then, as the council put it, symptoms would appear: "Symptoms gradually appear and include persistent generalized lymphadenopathy ..., fatigue, persistent fever, weight loss, diarrhea, and certain neurological conditions. The course of the disease is difficult to predict" (para. 40342). The legal construction of HIV/AIDS (as opposed to HIV and/or AIDS) thereby adopted temporal devices of stages and symptoms from clinical discourse, mobilizing frames of unpredictability and disease progression as legally significant.

Furthermore, the clinical frame of asymptomaticity made a specific intervention in this case, as we can see from the excerpts above. Catherine Waldby has described the preoccupation of biomedical circles during the mid- to late 1980s with the problem of asymptomatic but sero-positive status, such that by 1986 a very long period of latent infection was understood to be possible, leading to fears about unwitting infection of others and increased calls for compulsory HIV testing of high-risk groups (Waldby 2004, 116). In the *Biggs* case, the asymptomatic period, once a techno-scientific and now a legal artefact, was similarly productive, establishing a new field of potential action and a new set of dilemmas, but with very different effects. As a legible frame and temporal marker-point for disease, it helped to stabilize the legal definition of HIV/AIDS as a virus and not (only) the accumulative breakdown of the immune system, with the effect that sero-positive people were legally protected from the point of infection.

Specifically, in *Biggs*, the BC Human Rights Council stated that HIV would constitute a disability from the point of seropositivity, which did not need to involve any measurable symptoms. This was not necessarily surprising as a point of law, given well-established principles in Canadian human rights jurisprudence even then recognizing a diverse range of differently constituted disabilities – the decision cites heart condition, spondylolysis, varicocele, asthma, diabetes, epilepsy, cerebral palsy and blindness (see *Biggs v Hudson*, paras 40353–9) – as well as discrimination on the basis of "perceived" health conditions. But it is the starting point of disability that is of interest. As this slightly confusing passage indicates, legal protection for HIV and AIDS discrimination would ensue from the stage of "manifesting antibodies": "Applying the reasoning identified by our highest court in the cases cited above, I conclude that acquired immunodeficiency syndrome constitutes a physical disability within the meaning of the *Act*. Any person who is seropositive by manifesting antibodies to HIV has a physical disability and, in the absence of a bona fide occupation requirement ... is entitled to the protection set out in the ... Act" (*Biggs v Hudson*, para. 40353).[6]

Such a legal threshold could not have existed without the expert witness testimony of Dr McLean, human rights principles allowing the recognition of a virus as a disability, the biomedical field of asymptomatic HIV status, and, possibly most important, the HIV antibody test, which had been approved and made available in Canada only a few years earlier.[7] The very first HIV tests in Canada became available in August 1984. Initially only 20,000 tests were available, and there was little information about who would be tested. The Canadian Red Cross began screening blood donations for HIV in the summer of 1985 (Robertson 2005). "Manifesting antibodies" was therefore a mediated status, which, while not defined in any more detail in the *Biggs* decision, meant having had a positive HIV antibody test result, an end point in a long process of clinical practices. Waldby (2004, 116) refers to the test as "not simply a diagnostic laboratory practice but ... an entire bio-administrative regime, taking place over several days or weeks." By the late 1980s the standardized test process involved two enzyme immunoassay, or ELISA, tests – a sensitive test that tended towards false positives but that could be interpreted via computer – and a Western blot, a confirmatory test requiring expert human interpretation. Although HIV infection could still be deduced from the presence of a range of symptoms, a positive result in all three of these tests both "proved" and constituted the retrovirus (Waldby 2004, 127).

Contemporaneous literatures on HIV and AIDS from the late 1980s and early 1990s, including social science scholarship as well as legal

---

6 Later in the decision, it was made clear that actionable HIV-related disability discrimination could be taken to have occurred in cases of discrimination against a member of a group regarded by others as especially vulnerable to HIV infection, and against people associating with these groups or with seropositive people (see para. 40360).

7 Many of the earliest people to receive an early positive HIV test – including Simon Thwaites, whose case I cover later in the chapter – learned of their status after having donated blood.

activist work, emphasized the many potentially worrying consequences of the wider availability of testing. Fears focused on the development of mandatory testing practices by employers and public health bodies (Rayside and Linquist 1992), giving rise to dense clusters of research and policy-making advocacy by bodies such as the Canadian HIV/AIDS Legal Network, and eventually to a wide range of policies at both the provincial and federal level on HIV, testing, and confidentiality,[8] continuing through to the late 1990s and early 2000s. A more recent concern has been the development of liability for HIV transmission, with recent case law by the Supreme Court of Canada clarifying that nondisclosure of HIV status prior to sex in circumstances where there was a "realistic possibility" of transmission might lead to criminal proceedings for aggravated sexual assault.[9] These very active fields of law and ethics implicitly rely on the antibody test to mark the boundaries of potential criminality from the point of infection, with possibly devastating consequences for people living with HIV (Grant, Shaffer, and Symington 2013; Weait 2007). Yet in *Biggs* and subsequent human rights cases on HIV/AIDS, infection with HIV was an essential stage in a continuum that allowed people with asymptomatic HIV to gain a measure of legal protection. In this way HIV testing has intensely ambivalent significance in Canadian legal networks: it has allowed some claimants to bring human rights claims for disability discrimination, while subjecting others to criminal liability. Specifically, the clinical enactment of HIV antibodies through testing in the late 1980s also allowed the virus to "appear" in human rights law as a disability at a very early stage in what became understood as the HIV/AIDS continuum.

"Telltale Symptoms"

If the definition of HIV as a disability was hardly subject to further comment in human rights claims after *Biggs v Hudson*, it was a knotty problem to be worked over and proved in provincial welfare benefits cases during that period. Ontario provincial welfare benefits law in the early 1990s did not recognize asymptomatic HIV as a stage of legally

8 This included, for example, a 1989 report by the Information and Privacy Commission of Ontario on "HIV/AIDS in the Workplace," and a recommendation against blanket HIV testing in the workplace in the Canadian Human Rights Commission Policy on HIV/AIDS of 1996.

9 See *R v Mabior* (2012) SCC 47; and *R v D.C.* (2012) SCC 48.

protected disability. Instead, the definition of disability was overwhelmingly co-articulated with an AIDS diagnosis, a relatively late stage on what we might understand to be the *Biggs* continuum. The route to obtaining income assistance was by establishing that an HIV-positive person was either a "disabled person" or a "permanently unemployable person" for the purposes of the Family Benefits Act and associated regulations.[10] These categories were defined by long-term physical impairment and the inability to engage in paid work:

> "Disabled Person" means a person who has a major physical or mental impairment that is likely to continue for a prolonged period of time and who, as a result thereof, is severely limited in activities pertaining to normal living as verified by objective medical findings accepted by the medical advisory board. "Permanently Unemployable Person" means a person who is unable to engage in remunerative employment for a long period of time as verified by objective medical findings accepted by the medical advisory board. (R.R.O. 1990, Reg. 366, s. 1(5))

Having a diagnosis of AIDS was usually enough to qualify a person as eligible for benefits under either of these headings. But such diagnoses relied upon successfully placing the claimant in the latter categories of the three-stage federal government definition of HIV/AIDS progression: (1) asymptomatic status; (2) the development of symptoms and contraction of opportunistic infections (otherwise termed AIDs-related condition, or ARC); and (3) the contraction of one or more illnesses associated with AIDS, resulting in an AIDS diagnosis.

Disability was therefore measured along a scale of HIV progression that posed distinct viral stages, and produced – indeed, required – in-depth legal arguments about the temporal ontology of HIV/AIDS. Karen Bastow, writing at the time about her own and her colleagues' experiences of HIV legal practice, neatly summarized the links between disease definitions, epidemiology, administrative practice, and legal categorization:

> Despite the fact that the Family Benefits Act does not require that a claimant show that she or he has AIDS as opposed to HIV in order to be

10 Disability benefits were provided by the Family Benefits Act (R.S.O. 1990, c. F.2), s. 7(1)(c). Benefits for permanently unemployable people were provided by R.R.O. 1990, Reg. 366, s. 2(5), enacted pursuant to the Act.

> considered "permanently unemployable" or "disabled," administrative practice does – by relying on the decision of the Director who in turn relies on the diagnosis of the doctor. The medical definitions employed by doctors are created by the government, primarily to ensure accurate epidemiological records. The government definition essentially determines when HIV status (assumed to be non-debilitating) becomes AIDS (considered a disability). (Bastow 1994, 181)

At the time Bastow was writing, the "progression" from infection with HIV to death from AIDS usually took around five to seven years (175). Tellingly, Bastow wrote of the AIDS classification as a device, not as a disease, establishing a "point of no return" by measuring depletion in the immune system. Yet the AIDS classification was also a gendered measure of time. The extent to which physicians were willing or able to accept symptoms as markers of AIDS could vary greatly, and was particularly affected by a general lack of understanding or acceptance, at the time, of specific AIDS-related symptoms experienced by women – for example, cervical dysplasia (179). This was all the more problematic because the federal government definition of AIDS did not include such symptoms – in effect instantiating an androcentric model of disease that resulted in the late diagnosis of women with AIDS or failure to diagnose at all.

Karen Bastow reported a case in which an Aboriginal woman, having contracted HIV through intravenous drug use, applied for family benefits because she was unable to work. Her claim was refused on the basis of evidence from her family doctor, who had not identified cervical dysplasia as an indicator of AIDS, instead linking her inability to maintain paid work with addiction. The woman's lawyers appealed the case to the Ontario Social Assistance Review Board, which found in her favour on the basis of arguments relating to discrimination in the allocation of family benefits. But in making this decision, the board did not refer to legal arguments made on the woman's behalf that the Ontario government's definition of AIDS was contrary to section 15 of the Canadian Charter of Rights and Freedoms, which prohibits both direct and "disparate impact" discrimination by government. Despite the relatively positive outcome for the claimant, therefore, the progression of disease remained generally linked to gendered disease markers, making it more difficult for HIV-positive women to claim they had a "disability" for the purposes of welfare benefits. Gendered symptoms and temporalities of disease progression were, in this way, key to the legal experiences of low-income people with HIV in the late 1980s and early 1990s. These temporalities arose as a result of specific interactions between epidemiological and regulatory classifications, on the one hand, and definitions of disability in provincial welfare benefits legislation, on the other.

A multilayered relationship between legal and clinical ontologies of HIV characterized welfare benefits claims, and this was inaugurated through a type of ontological shuffling on the part of legal practitioners. Sometimes, clinical understandings of HIV were legally mobilized through medical reports as "knowledge" that could be used by law. At other points, often within the same sets of proceedings, clinical object-concepts – for example, drugs – were given greater force through reference to treatment side effects listed in a pharmaceutical digest, establishing the external "reality" of HIV as something to which legal knowledge should adapt. These shifting orientations enacted distinct legal temporalities of HIV.

For example, the case Bastow described centred around the drafting, and latterly the interpretation, of a medical report on the claimant's HIV/AIDS status. Medical reports were key to cases about HIV and welfare benefits, and their negotiation and production was one area in which legal and clinical ontologies of HIV met, causing struggles about the virus, its "progression," and its effect on legal claimants. This was difficult terrain for lawyers and, as we will see, clinicians as well, often resulting in clinical articulations of disease that did not "travel" easily into the legal domain. One poverty lawyer describes the strategies for channeling clinical information into legible legal forms: "The doctors were so bad at producing medical legal reports [that] we always offered to pay and actually designed a questionnaire for them, so instead of writing a letter all they had to do was fill in the questionnaire. The questionnaires were usually more useful than simply ordering the medical reports, although that was not always the case and typically we did both."

Medical reports, which we will meet again in the next chapter, helped to instantiate the virus for the purpose of each claimant in each case. The purpose of medical reports was to provide clinical "facts" on which determinations about disability and capacity to work could be made. As a particular kind of legal form, therefore, medical reports mobilized clinical knowledge as representative of an epistemological position that took shape through being amenable and, in the end, submissive to legal reasoning. To be more precise, the reports mobilized clinical opinions about a person's HIV status, or progression along the HIV-AIDS scale, as a well-informed genre of knowledge, not a *sui generis* or alternative medical *reality* as such.

Yet, as the poverty lawyer above pointed out, reports often also failed in this endeavour. Clinicians strayed from the script, or asserted new and different "realities" of disease, with the effect that the idiosyncratic HIV ontologies they asserted could not travel far within legal networks. This is evident from the fact that reports were latterly accompanied by another innovated legal form, the questionnaire, which says much about the struggle between legal and clinical ontologies of HIV and its resolution through innovations in documentary practice. Questionnaires can be understood in this context as much as a legal-ontological patching exercise as a method of fact-finding, re-establishing clinical understandings of HIV as "interpretations," suturing clinical interpretations of disease to legally relevant categories, and producing a more effective and mobile type of legal-clinical hybrid: disability.

Practices of documentary innovation also exceeded activities surrounding and producing medical reports, extending into legal techniques in tribunal. In this domain, clinical object-concepts were asserted as ontologically distinct, in a manner very different from the use of questionnaires. The same poverty lawyer who described the problems with medical reports above reported later developing a strategy for establishing a claimant's inability to work for the purposes of benefits proceedings. I quote at length in order to convey detail and context:

> I can remember that one of the strategies I developed for government benefits hearings was we would … get the doctors to list people's drugs and … early on there were no combination pills … The drug regimes were quite onerous and extremely difficult to follow and the side effects were horrific, really horrific. One of the things I used to do that was very successful for benefits hearings was, I would get evidence as to what people's drugs were, and then I would make photocopies of the pharmaceutical digest, which lists the side effects that are known with respect to drugs. And then I would sort of haul them out, and I would examine my client and say, are you talking about this drug? And they would go, yes, and I would say, do you experience diarrhea in the morning, and they would go, yeah. Do you have stomach ulcers, and they go, yeah. Do you vomit in the morning? Yeah, yeah. I [would] just go through the list, and then I would hand the pharmaceutical compendium to the decision-maker and I'd go, here. And so, it would convince the decision-maker that, oh my god, the HIV may not be killing this guy, but the drugs are.

Through a five-way conversation between lawyer, claimant, photocopied document, pharmaceutical digest, and decision-maker, HIV was enacted, in this way, not via symptoms but through side effects; not via clinical knowledge in a medical report but through the strategic adoption of an otherwise unwitting pharmaceutical reference document. The digest itself did not know or care about the legal proceedings before it was ambushed: it was novel to the proceedings and therefore a peculiarly independent witness/expert, and it was significant and legally useful for that very reason.

Furthermore, the collected actions described here augmented, or even displaced, questions of "progression" along an HIV-AIDS timeline, with their potential to tangle lawyers in debates about whether the "stage" their client had reached rendered them eligible for benefits. In this alternative strategy, the relevant temporalities were not "stages" of disease, as such, but daily drug regimens and the recurrent side effects that claimants experienced. In turn, the "reality" of HIV was no longer just ascertained from symptoms emanating from within the body, but also traced through physical side effects produced in encounters with drugs: a canny legal-corporeal reorientation. In this new ontology of HIV, it did not necessarily matter whether a person had experienced an AIDS-defining illness, but it did matter that the treatments they were undergoing, and the side effects of those treatments, rendered them unable to work for the purposes of the regulations. It was in this way that an unexpected shift in documentary practices altered the legal-temporal worlds of HIV.

The analysis so far suggests that HIV was enacted in distinctive ways in different legal domains or jurisdictions in Canada in the late 1980s and early 1990s. Medico-legal temporalities of HIV disease progression were differentially constituted in the fields of human rights and welfare benefits law, with significant effects on what claimants could argue, and how. Much of what one can say about these differences relates to relationships between law and time, and distinctions between legal areas, but not directly between law, time, and space or terrain as such. Understanding these diverging processes as spatio-temporal through the concept of the chronotope, in this case, then, meets a challenge in explaining the conative effects of viruses, tests, and emergent legal practices.

Instead, Canadian legal engagements with HIV mobilized temporal distinctions through differential enactments of *disease and disability*, diagnosis and treatments, and complex relationships between legal and medical objectivity. The legal reality of HIV in each frame had much to do with how it was defined as a disability, which itself was constructed in relation to distinct temporalities concerning the presence, or articulation, of AIDS-related symptoms or the side effects of HIV treatments. In these different enactments of HIV, the modes in which the virus became real, its legal ontologies, were productively enmeshed in networks of human-viral behaviour. These in turn helped to sustain distinct temporal ontologies, constituting the subject and mode of legal enquiry, rendering legal frames or "fields" of law separable. And, in the end, they produced a curious set of divergences whereby a "new" clinical health condition was effectively materialized, through disability, as HIV in human rights law, but as AIDS or ARC in welfare benefits cases. HIV had, as Mol (2003) would put it, "multiple ontologies."

Time Travelling through Classification Systems

In the final part of this chapter, I turn back to progression via a different route, that of classification. As is already evident, I am interested in how classification systems assist in the production of legal temporalities. More specifically, I am interested in what happens when temporal ontologies from one classification system meet those of another and the sporadic, but significant, role of law at various points in the relationship. Let's say, for example, that ideas about disease progression embedded in the legal protocol for a drug trial meet ideas about disease progression, health, and capability underpinning, for example, a military personnel classification system assigning a service person's duties and geographic areas of deployment. This is what happened in one situation in particular, the termination of Simon Thwaites's service in the Canadian Armed Forces. In Thwaites's case, the friction caused by the interrelationship between classification systems, itself inherently about diverging ontologies of time, led to his dismissal and a prominent set of legal hearings. By analysing the densely clustered problems, persons, and artefacts surrounding what *became* this case, it is possible to explore further whether and how temporal ontologies travel across different bureaucratic domains of knowledge and how law is implicated at various stages of these interactions.

This is the story. Dr Walter Schlech, a clinician specializing in the treatment of HIV and AIDS and the clinical lead on a federally regulated drugs trial for AZT in the late 1980s, provided a very negative report on a patient's symptomatic status in order to get the patient onto the trial and hence into the first available treatment for AIDS. The patient, Simon Thwaites, was a member of the Canadian Armed Forces (CAF). When the CAF found out about Thwaites's newly "downgraded" HIV status, it began a process to terminate his service on the grounds that, in short, he would be a risk to himself and others on deployment due to his health needs. When this process resulted in his discharge, Thwaites brought a well-publicized claim for disability discrimination under the Canadian Human Rights Act. The case was heard by the Canadian Human Rights Tribunal, chaired by Sidney Lederman. In this way, a careful clinical decision about providing a drug to a patient in the midst of an epidemic found itself at a tribunal in 1992 in an entirely different legal area, the subject of weeks of hearings, clinical expert evidence, and legal debate.

Dr Schlech's actions had been precipitated by the new drug, AZT, which itself was federally regulated in such a way as to be available only to people in the later "stages" of HIV. As such, the drug (AZT), clinicians, federal drug regulations, retrovirus, symptoms, and the CAF all came together across the terrain of one patient-clinician relationship and a human rights case. At the heart of this network, or assemblage, was a telephone (and the failure to pick it up), a form, and two commensurable but diverging classification systems.

The Case

The legal issue at hand in the human rights case was whether the Canadian Armed Forces could successfully use the *bona fide* occupational requirement (BFOR) exception in the Canadian Human Rights Act to discharge Thwaites on the basis that active service took him away from the medical facilities he needed for the treatment and everyday management of his HIV. In effect, their use of the BFOR was in response to Thwaites's claim of disability discrimination under the Act. Significantly, during the ensuing tribunal hearing, the CAF repeatedly, through submissions and medical and lay witnesses, argued its own ignorance about HIV.[11] It coupled this "ignorance defence" with what one lawyer on the case, Peter Engelmann, has termed a paternalistic, "we did it for his own good," argument, which, according to Engelmann, was common to disability discrimination cases at the time across a number of conditions with symptomatic and asymptomatic phases, such as insulin-dependent diabetes and epilepsy.[12] The Human

---

11 Personal correspondence with Peter Engelmann.
12 Ibid.

Rights Tribunal decided against the CAF, however, and its decision was upheld in a later appeal to the Federal Court of Canada.[13]

Thwaites had been a member of the CAF since 1980. He was a trained naval electronics sensor operator, a position classified as "hard sea trade" because it involved mostly seagoing postings, rather than shore postings. This would become highly relevant in the context of discussions about what services could and could not be provided for Thwaites: the CAF's argument was that Thwaites would be put at risk by insufficient health service provision available when on deployment (Grabham, in draft a). Thwaites was also one of the earliest in Canada to be informed of a positive HIV test. We saw in the previous section that the HIV antibody test was first used to screen blood donations in Canada in 1985. In January 1986, the Canadian Red Cross informed Thwaites that a patient who had been given a transfusion containing a donation by him had had a reaction. A further blood sample was taken at the CAF base hospital in Halifax, and Thwaites was informed on 26 March 1986 that he was HIV positive, with the results of a final confirmatory test being communicated to him in late April/early May 1986.

An important feature of this situation, therefore, is how, when, and why Thwaites learned of his HIV status. It would be difficult to say that the antibody tests Thwaites took were set in motion entirely for reasons of individual therapy. The first tests had been conducted by a wide-ranging blood-screening program in a context in which blood transfusion recipients had been popularly represented as more legible victims than other HIV-positive people. Thwaites's diagnosis therefore took place at a point in the epidemic when the clinical and institutional procedures that later produced more widespread testing implicated many HIV-positive people not just as patients, but also as asymptomatic "contaminators."

Despite his recent diagnosis, Thwaites was re-engaged by the CAF in April 1986 and then promoted to acting/lacking leading seaman. He had been reported by a colleague as "homosexual," and in the ensuing months, the CAF undertook an investigation into his sexual orientation, eventually recommending his release on this basis in early 1987. The recommendation was not followed up. Thwaites continued to see his civilian doctors in Halifax, and in October 1987, Dr Lynn Johnston wrote to inform the CAF that she had discussed

13 *Thwaites v Canada (Armed Forces)* (1994) 21 C.H.R.R. D/224.

with Thwaites the possibility of enrolling him in a trial for AZT. The CAF took Dr Johnston's letter to indicate that Thwaites was now symptomatic for AIDS, and began the procedure that would lead to a Career Medical Board Review and Thwaites's eventual release from the CAF in October 1989.

The circumstances surrounding the letter from Dr Johnston, and how the CAF responded to it, were described by the Human Rights Tribunal as an instance of "miscommunication." Yet these events indicate much about how clinical and military ontologies of HIV met and did not meet during the late 1980s, how a decision made in one field could have consequences in another, and how classification systems and their associated temporalities could combine with strange and intractable consequences. To clarify this point, it is necessary to provide a short background to AZT, the first mass-produced drug used in the treatment of HIV and AIDS, its early legal regulation in Canada, and the clinical dilemmas it raised.

AZT: Regulating a "New Drug"

AZT (azidothymidine), the generic name for which is zidovudine, interrupts viral replication in HIV. Produced by the UK pharmaceutical company Burroughs Wellcome beginning in the mid-1980s, it originally was developed in the 1960s by a researcher at the Michigan Cancer Foundation with funding from the US National Cancer Institute (NCI), with the aim of preventing cancer cells from duplicating, but shelved when it had no effect in this regard (Epstein 2009, 192). In 1984, responding to the emerging HIV epidemic, the head of the NCI, Samuel Broder, invited large pharmaceutical companies to send him details of any drug they had that might be effective against a retrovirus. As Epstein relates the story, when Burroughs Wellcome sent AZT to Broder's researchers, it was found to be a reverse transcriptase inhibitor, meaning that it blocked an enzyme in the HIV retrovirus that copied HIV RNA (ribonucleic acid) into the DNA (deoxyribonucleic acid) that would form the basis for creating new viruses. Burroughs Wellcome filed an investigational new drug application with the US FDA, and the results of the phase I trial of the drug were reported in March 1986, indicating that it was effective in stopping the creation of new HIV DNA and, with some concerns, that it passed the safety threshold. Dr Margaret Fischl's later phase II trial had to be ended early when the

National Institutes of Health (NIH) Data and Safety Monitoring Board decided that continued double-blind placebo testing on AIDS patients was no longer ethical due to the drug's overwhelming efficacy.[14]

The worldwide demand for AZT was so intense that Burroughs Wellcome was able to announce on 1 May 1987 that it would supply the drug only to those countries that permitted it to be sold. This meant that any country wishing to obtain AZT had to ensure that its rapid passage through domestic drug regulation and licensing procedures. Canada reacted quickly to the announcement, calling a meeting on 4 May 1987 of representatives of the federal Department of National Health and Welfare and all provincial health ministries, at which it was decided that Canada would purchase the drug.[15]

For AZT to be sold in Canada, however, it had to pass through the usual, federally regulated, new drug approval process. In other words, the meeting decided not to "rubber stamp" the drug without further investigation. The new drug process usually involved submitting a preclinical report that included the provision of all available data on human, animal, and in-vitro studies performed on the drug to the Health Protection Branch of the federal health department. If this report was satisfactory, the health minister would approve the drug for clinical testing under strictly controlled conditions (*Brown v Canada (Minister of Health)*, 7). Once the testing had progressed, the manufacturer could submit a "new drug" submission to the minister containing reports of all safety tests on the drug. Only if this submission was acceptable would the minister then issue a Notice of Compliance pursuant to s C.08.004 of the Food and Drug Regulations that would enable the drug to be sold in Canada. Two exceptions in the regulations enabled limited sales outside this process: emergency release, which allowed a medical practitioner to purchase the drug for treatment of a patient under strict conditions of clinical reporting (s. C.08.010), and sale to qualified investigators for clinical testing regarding safety, dosage, and effectiveness, the so-called investigational drug process (s. C.08.005). On 7 May 1987,

---

14 Of the placebo group, 19 out of 137 patients died during the test period, whereas only 1 patient out of 145 receiving AZT died (Epstein 2009, 198). AZT was approved for use in US AIDS patients on 20 March 1987, and it was announced that Burroughs Wellcome would sell the drug for around US$8,000–$10,000 per year, beginning a long-standing controversy over HIV drug pricing (199).

15 *Brown v Canada (Minister of Health)* 1990 CanLII 1064 (BCSC).

only three days after the meeting of federal and provincial health ministry representatives and merely a week after Burroughs Wellcome had announced it would supply AZT only to countries that permitted sales of the drug, the company obtained a Notice of Compliance, the first time one had been granted under this exception. As the BC Supreme Court put it in its decision about the inclusion of AZT in the provincial Pharmacare program, "Thus AZT is unique for it remained a 'new drug,' subject to clinical protocol while at the same time being granted a Notice of Compliance permitting it to be sold" (*Brown v Canada (Minister of Health)*, 9).

It was this out-of-the-ordinary route to drug approval that enabled the first clinical trials of AZT to take place in hospitals across Canada. As a result of the Notice of Compliance, the clinicians treating Simon Thwaites in Nova Scotia were able to set up investigational testing. Yet it was Thwaites's inclusion in this drug trial that precipitated his discharge from the CAF.

Classifying the Retrovirus

As we have seen, Thwaites was diagnosed with HIV in the spring of 1986, one year before AZT was given its Notice of Compliance by the federal government. During this period, Thwaites was under the medical care of Drs Schlech and Johnston of the Infectious Diseases Clinic of the Victoria General Hospital in Halifax, Nova Scotia, both of whom were in regular contact with Dr John Smith, the base doctor at Canadian Forces Base Halifax. Dr Schlech was the provincial coordinator for the Maritime provinces in clinical drug trials conducted in conjunction with Burroughs Wellcome Canada Inc., relating to the long-term safety of AZT as a newly defined "investigational drug." He held this role, which put him in charge of administering and distributing the drug, until AZT gained full approval in 1990. Dr Johnston would later become the physician lead for the HIV/AIDS clinic at Victoria General Hospital in the early 1990s.

Once again, clinical classification systems were of relevance in the way Thwaites was treated as a patient and as a legal claimant. The Human Rights Tribunal's decision refers to two successive classifications, which shifted from relying on "stages" to tabulating "signs and symptoms" of HIV infection. The first, "rudimentary" system, placed HIV-positive people in one of three stages: asymptomatic; AIDS-Related Complex; and Full-Blown AIDS. This was replaced by the classification from the US Centers for Disease Control, which grouped HIV/AIDS patients in four ways:

- GROUP 1: acute infection;
- GROUP 2: asymptomatic infection;
- GROUP 3: symptomatic infection, for example, persistent generalized lymphadenopathy; and
- GROUP 4: development of symptoms consistent with impairment of immune function and development of opportunistic disease (*Thwaites v Canadian Armed Forces* 1993, 8).[16]

As the tribunal's decision put it, among the many reasons for using these classificatory systems was the need to determine the point at which a patient had arrived "in terms of HIV progression" in order to make decisions about prescribing an investigational drug (*Thwaites v Canadian Armed Forces* 1993, 9). Yet this measure did not need to be seen to work in all instances for it to retain its value in diagnostic and clinical terms. Furthermore, the tribunal's own summary of the expert evidence presents a complicated picture of how it and the medical experts on whom it relied thought of HIV "progression," showing that the tribunal accepted that the disease did not need to progress in a linear fashion through the stages in order to be classified as a disability: "The disease does not necessarily proceed through each of the four stages. Some individuals never experience the acute infection of Group 1. Some go

---

16 As detailed in the tribunal's decision, these classifications had the following meanings:

> Group 1 includes people who show signs of recent infection and who have antibodies to the HIV virus. Within a month after exposure, many individuals experience acute flu-like symptoms which usually resolve themselves.
>
> Group 2 includes those who have been infected with the virus for some time but who are asymptomatic. Those within Group 1 and Group 2 appear healthy and can maintain a normal lifestyle.
>
> Group 3 includes those who have a persistent generalized lymph node enlargement that lasts more than three months but who evidence no other outward signs or symptoms.
>
> Group 4 includes those with varying outward symptoms of the disease and they are described as having AIDS. Symptoms include wasting syndrome, dementia and other neurologic diseases; opportunistic infections such as PCP; or certain forms of cancer such as Kaposi's Sarcoma, a skin cancer. (*Thwaites v Canadian Armed Forces* 1993, 8)

directly from being outwardly asymptomatic to having a life threatening opportunistic infection without going through any intermediate stages. Some manifestations of Group 4 may be early manifestations of HIV infection unrelated to its subsequent course" (*Thwaites v Canadian Armed Forces* 1993, 9).

Clinical views of the disease described in the classification therefore envisaged a multidirectional progression that could "jump" or "skip" stages, the signs of which could even be decoys (see the reference to "early manifestations ... unrelated to its subsequent course"). This temporal ontology did not easily fit previous classificatory models – indeed, it was partially enacted through another kind of measure, the T cell count, which the tribunal described as the "best indicator of how HIV patients are likely to do" on the basis of emerging medical consensus (*Thwaites v Canadian Armed Forces* 1993, 9). T cell counts effectively measured the body's remaining immune defence capacity in relation to the virus, and T cell depletion, as Epstein puts it, "was the very hallmark of AIDS" (2009, 271).

At the time Thwaites was being treated by Drs Schlech and Johnston, access to the newly available AZT was made conditional upon showing symptoms for AIDS. There was an incentive, therefore, for any clinician wishing to enrol a patient in a trial in order to get access to the drug to be attentive to any possible symptoms in an otherwise asymptomatic patient. Thwaites's clinicians carefully monitored his health for signs of symptoms, and they made a record of his T cell counts, which fluctuated between 220 and 350 from 1986 to 1988. By 1992, a T cell count of 200 and under was taken to indicate that a patient had AIDS.

It was difficult to work out whether reported symptoms and, indeed, fluctuations in T cell counts were the result of a patient's HIV status or of other factors. Lack of sleep could affect T cell counts, and symptoms were always open to interpretation by clinicians and patients. Given this difficulty, clinicians often took care to document as many symptoms as possible, to create a detailed record on which to rely later, if needed. As one HIV clinician recalls, describing the documentation practices of the late 1980s, such notes were not intended for others to read, but in cases such as that of Thwaites, they could become legal evidence and indicate an entirely different state of health from what was intended: "When you are seeing a patient in your clinic, it's important for you to document what's going on. You don't document things thinking that someone else other than the patient is going to find fault with it. You do document every concern the patient has, because you don't know how it's going to play out ... It can look as though someone is a whole lot sicker than they are."

This practice of recording symptoms is significant because, as of 12 November 1987, Thwaites's clinicians decided that, on the basis of reported night sweats and a decreased T cell count, he had become symptomatic. They placed him in Group 4 of the CDC classification system outlined above, which allowed them to enroll him in an investigational drug program under the regime set in motion by the 1987 Notice of Compliance. Thwaites's T cell count was 230, with 300 being the maximum allowed for enrolment in the program. Yet, as the tribunal reported it, the clinicians later accepted that Thwaites was "probably not symptomatic" but that the decision to classify him as symptomatic had given him access to otherwise unavailable treatment: "In hindsight, the specialists who made this determination admitted to the Tribunal that Thwaites was probably not symptomatic at that time. The decision to classify him as being symptomatic was made to facilitate Thwaites's enrollment in the AZT trial program which doctors felt was the only available tool to combat the progression of HIV" (*Thwaites v Canadian Armed Forces* 1993, 10). This admission indicated much about the exigencies of negotiating the regulatory regime surrounding AZT. The need to remain aware of symptoms, itself mobilized through processes resulting from the regulation of supply relating to AZT, precipitated a set of actions on behalf of clinicians that would have a significant effect on Thwaites's employment.

There were differing rationales for the assignment of Thwaites to the symptomatic category, all of which, however, advanced a theory of "patient care." Peter Engelmann, who acted for the tribunal in the case, has described Schlech's actions as a specific form of "exaggeration" associated with advocating for a patient: "[W]hat I recall about [Thwaites] was that his doctor, Schlech, the infectious diseases specialist, actually exaggerated. I don't know if exaggerated is the right word, but he wanted to get him onto the drug therapy. He wanted to get him onto AZT ... So he suggested that Simon was perhaps a bit sicker than he was, because all of the trials that were happening in the late 80s were suggesting that the sooner you got on this drug the better. Here he is, he's a doctor and he's advocating for his client, his patient."[17] Given the potential legal implications of finding that Thwaites's clinicians had not followed Notice of Compliance conditions in relation to AZT, the

17 Personal correspondence with Peter Engelmann.

tribunal also carefully established that this kind of interpretation was the standard of clinical care at the time:

> All infectious diseases clinicians who testified before the Tribunal were in agreement that in 1987, it would have been reasonable to ... categorize a patient such as Thwaites as CDC Group 4A in order to allow the patient to avail himself of the only drug known to be beneficial to HIV positive individuals. In other words, any doubt with respect to symptoms being expressed by the patient would have been resolved in favour of the symptoms being relevant to the patient's HIV status (as opposed to some other cause) and the strict guidelines of this drug's protocol would have been interpreted perhaps more loosely or bent in favour of the optimal patient care. (*Thwaites v Canadian Armed Forces* 1993, 11)

In such a way, an understandable if "loose" interpretation of the Burroughs Wellcome drug protocol was transformed from a matter of potential noncompliance with a regulatory regime into an example of "reasonable" clinical practice.

This being the case, however, Thwaites's diagnosis with symptomatic HIV for the purposes of the AZT trial had its own effects within the CAF, which operated a system of personnel classification, assigning geographical and duties ratings to individuals on the basis of their health. At the time Thwaites's health status was downgraded to symptomatic in late 1987, the CAF was preparing its 1988 HIV policy directive, a key concern of which was avoiding deployment of sero-positive personnel to "medically isolated areas" (Trent 1988, 1130). In January 1988, the CAF assigned Thwaites to category G5, which meant that an individual required specialist medical services, was unfit for sea and field duties, and would therefore be most likely unfit for any occupation in the CAF. The strategic allocation of Thwaites by civilian clinical staff to CDC Group 4 ("development of symptoms consistent with impairment of immune function and development of opportunistic disease") for the purposes of treatment had, through the juxtaposition of these two classification systems, led to his being at risk of dismissal.

It might have been predictable that reaching the most advanced stage of HIV/AIDS[18] classification would translate into the most restricted

18 I use the otherwise discredited term HIV/AIDS to refer to the fact that these two distinct phenomena, the retrovirus HIV and the condition AIDS, were in fact viewed as part of an overarching temporality of illness during that period.

military employment category. Yet just as the HIV/AIDS classification system was changing in the late 1980s, so were the military's policy directives, which initially had been much less onerous in relation to the disease. When Thwaites first tested positive for HIV, he had been classified through the 1985 HIV policy directive in the category G2, meaning fit and able to undertake full duties. By early 1988, just after Thwaites was diagnosed with symptomatic HIV, this was under review. A discussion paper released by the CAF on 2 February 1988 suggested that even asymptomatic service personnel should be assigned to the G3 category, meaning fit for sea, field, medically isolated, and United Nations peacekeeping duties. The finalized medical directive released on 9 May 1988, however, stated that asymptomatic employees would be assigned to no better than the G4 category, meaning unfit for such duties, and that physicians' services would be required. Any sero-positive service personnel experiencing symptoms would be assigned to no better than the G5 category.

"No one … picked up the telephone"

As the Human Rights Tribunal related it, what then happened was a set of interactions among letters, humans, a (possibly metaphorical) telephone, and the form "2088." Dr Johnston wrote to Dr Smith on 22 October 1987 to say that she had discussed with Thwaites the possibility of taking AZT. This was followed by a letter from Dr Schlech to Dr Smith on 12 November 1987 to say that Thwaites had developed some symptoms and that his T cell count was 220, rendering him eligible for the AZT trial. Thwaites began AZT treatment on 14 January 1988. Later letters, dating between 27 November 1987 and 3 August 1988 were, as the tribunal put it, "ignored as to their content." These letters informed Dr Smith how well Thwaites was doing on AZT and, in fact, described his variously mild symptoms and often *asymptomatic* status on the new drug. As the tribunal put it: "Thus, during the period that a decision was taken to restrict Thwaites' geographical rating to G5 and a decision ultimately taken by CMRB [Career Medical Review Board] to release him from the CAF, there was an indication from the treating physicians that Thwaites was asymptomatic and doing well on AZT therapy. Yet for some reason, no one in the CAF picked up the telephone and called Dr. Johnston or Dr. Schlech to discuss Thwaites' condition and the ramifications it may have for his career in the CAF" (*Thwaites v Canadian Armed Forces* 1993, 29).

Both the failure to act on the content of the letters and the failure to "pick up the telephone" were relevant to the legal question of whether the apparent risk of sending Thwaites on deployment had any basis in fact and to what steps the CAF took to ascertain such facts before it decided that the risk level was too high to continue his service. The tribunal decided that the CAF had not taken sufficient steps to clarify Thwaites's clinical condition, its rationale apparently being that assessing risk would have enrolled many of the possible modes of communication available to CAF doctors and staff, including letters and conversations between civilian and military medical staff.

Yet the "fact" of Thwaites's apparently new symptomatic status, in the end, is what travelled most effectively between the civilian clinical and military spheres. Constituted through the CDC system, Thwaites's new health assessment met an evolving military classification system that was attempting to translate tentative conclusions about symptoms into military determinations around risk, deployment, and capabilities. The heuristic force of the CDC system, and Thwaites's position in relation to it, was such that information in "plain sight" about his fragile symptomatic status (and consequent "good health") did not register within military decision-making bodies.

Once the CAF had been informed that Thwaites had begun treatment, he was asked to attend a full medical with base surgeon Major Kenneth Sutherland on 14 March 1988 for the purpose of a hearing by the CMRB, an internal process assessing a service personnel's fitness to continue work. After the medical had taken place, the layered hierarchical ratification of its results took only a matter of weeks, set in motion by a Change of Medical Category Form 2088. On the day of the medical, Dr Sutherland filled out part 2 of the form, recommending that Thwaites's category be downgraded from G2 to G5 because he needed specialist medical services. The form then travelled to the office of the command surgeon, who added on 21 March 1988: "G-5 – requires specialist medical services. Unfit isolation, sea, field duties. For CMRB decision." From there, the form made its way to the offices of the surgeon general in Ottawa, where it was amended with the following wording: "G-5 – requires specialist services readily available – unfit duty outside Canada or U.S." After that, the form made its way back to Thwaites, who was requested to sign part 5, acknowledging his medical reclassification. Having signed the form, it was then sent to the unit base commander, who completed the final part, stating: "[I]n accordance with CFAO 34-30 Annex B, MS Thwaites' newly assigned category render [*sic*] him unfit for continued service in his present or any other occupation in the Canadian Forces. His release is therefore recommended" (*Thwaites v Canadian Armed Forces* 1993, 5). At the resulting CMRB hearing, on 4 August 1988, it was decided to release Thwaites from service on the grounds that he was disabled and unfit to perform his duties.

It is always difficult to set the boundaries of analysis – to work out where a process might be considered to have begun and where it might be said to have ended or, speaking in a less chronological way, where one might place the edges of an assemblage. Interdisciplinary enquiries into legal regulation are wary of beginning and ending with cases. Artefacts of clustered actions and rationales need to be put in context and teased out more carefully: as we saw in the previous chapter, we need to be attentive even to where law emerges as such, without assuming some kind of preordained legality is at play. Following the processes that constituted "progression" through divergent means of classification could provisionally and strategically begin with the successful AZT trials, then move to the temporary stabilization of AZT as an "investigational drug" through the 1987 regulation decisions, and go from there to the AZT trial at Victoria General Hospital. Focusing on the negotiation of clinical and regulatory dilemmas (how to conduct a trial, how to comply with a treatment protocol), we could in turn trace how Thwaites's HIV was measured, classified, and, eventually legally instantiated; how these actions had effects within the military, and how military classifications in turn affected Thwaites's employment. Drug, drug regulation, drug trials, T cell counts, CDC classification, letter, phone call (or lack of), form 2088: these are some of the legal concerns and shades of action that became significant to the changing articulation of HIV as progression, not to mention human collections in the form of Thwaites's clinical team, the CMRB, and the Human Rights Tribunal itself.

Within all of this, what does it mean to say that documents, tests, and drugs had legal effects? Form 2088 was, as Jennifer Shannon would put it, an "actant that sets people into action, as well as an institutional symbol in an existing cultural context" (2007, 235). Highly mobile within the Canadian military bureaucracy and endowed with significant enunciatory force, form 2088 was uniquely placed to travel between layers in the military hierarchy, instantiating action at different levels, and able to achieve the eventual translation of CDC Group 4 (symptomatic status) into category G5 (unfit for service). If a combination of letter writing and the failure to pick up a telephone began this fragile chain of actions, then the form, once set in motion, had the capacity to define symptomatic HIV as a disability. Without the antibody test and its associated human rights protections from the point of "manifesting antibodies," the legal field of asymptomatic status would not have taken hold in the same way. AZT, temporarily stabilized as an "investigational drug," was only on those terms able to enter Canada in the first place. Once regulated under Notice of Compliance conditions, however, it contributed to deliberations over symptomatic status and the corresponding importance of tabulating HIV progression. In turn, AZT was effective in prompting the articulation of a hinge point between stages – between asymptomatic and symptomatic HIV – that was so significant in Thwaites's case.

Concluding Remarks

In this chapter I have told the story of two temporalities, urgency and progression, that effected the early materialization of HIV within Canadian legal networks. Relationships among legal activists, legal technicalities, tribunals, and the virus itself co-produced urgency through a range of means: posing HIV as an emergency requiring rapid government action, directing cases away from human rights tribunals to professional bodies in the interests of speedier "timelines," and developing particular case management methods to cope with the newly shortened lifespans of clients. At the same time, a temporal ontology of progression was emerging – one might say it was being *achieved* – and it was accompanying the entrance of HIV into the legal field. HIV-related law, in varying jurisdictions, relied on clinical tests and concepts that were relatively recent innovations. Legal tests operated in such a way that techno-scientific innovations (antibody tests, T cell counts, AZT), clinical and occupational classification systems, and the clinical fields of asymptomaticity and symptomatic status were significant in rendering HIV legally visible. Indeed, following van Loon and Bennett, one might say that progression was a result of indexing the *conative* actions of the HIV retrovirus in legal assemblages, making the virus legally amenable, and effectively connecting law to reality. This depended partially on the area of law that was engaged, so that, in the field of human rights, HIV was indexed as a retrovirus through the manifestation of antibodies, whereas, in welfare benefits, HIV/AIDS was indexed through the development of symptoms. Both the retrovirus itself and the retrovirus as disability were differentially enacted depending on where an issue arose in relation to the boundaries that mark out legal terrain. For their part, classification systems, and divergences between them, had timely effects, enrolling the conative capabilities of nonhuman actors – drugs, drug protocols, and documents, along the way.

Tracing the emergence of progression in the context of HIV law and legal activism is like tugging on one thread in a web, watching to see what else moves, whether it is human, document, virus, or legal technicality. It requires being open to the possibility that classification systems produce time just as much as they operate with temporal markers or meanings, and it requires following drugs through dense thickets of regulation. Engaging, then, with the problem of visibility and legibility that HIV posed to law in the late 1980s and 1990s, we find a peculiarly nonhuman (or not-just-human) temporal ontology, progression, occupying the interface between law and nature.

Chapter Three

A Likely Story

The absence of any abnormal signs, three years after his presentation to me, provides grounds for some optimism about his future.

– *Mowat-Brown v University of Surrey*

It's interesting, because I think maybe tribunals are a lot more comfortable with speculating about the future than medical experts are. Tribunals have to do that all the time, don't they ... particularly in discrimination claims.

– HIV legal activist

[T]he alignment of speculative practices with statistical measurement and management was neither natural nor unambiguous, but provided an important step in the emergence of a professional domain for financial participants. Charts, graphs, and tables of market activity did not so much represent "financial reality" as transform diverse and contingent credit practices into a coherent and measurable financial domain with a life cycle of its own.

– Marieke de Goede, *Virtue, Fortune, and Faith*

As we saw in the previous chapter, the "new crisis" of what was soon to be termed AIDS first emerged as a public health problem in the early 1980s. The early years of understanding the virus, establishing the link between HIV and AIDS, and scoping testing and treatments were characterized by a number of intense credibility struggles, as scientific teams advanced different explanations for the causes of this new disease, and clinicians and government agencies advanced a wide range of often conflicting responses (Epstein 2009; Patton 1990). Activists were key to the development of new knowledge, treatments, and relationships between clinicians and health populations in the context of a political climate all too hospitable to homophobic and racist fears about the new disease (Cohen 1999).

By the mid-1990s, the etiological link between HIV and AIDs had been settled, HIV antibody tests had become widely available, and new treatments were being developed. This chapter picks up at the point at which intense struggles of a different kind began, this time across the Atlantic. In 1996, UK-based activists saw a new legal remedy become available: the disability discrimination claim. With the field of HIV-as-disability came the legal articulation of HIV as an essentially temporal phenomenon in UK employment law. Specifically, in this chapter, I argue that the introduction of the Disability Discrimination Act (DDA) radically temporalized HIV for the purposes of defining it, legally, as a disability.

As in Canada, HIV was legally enacted in the United Kingdom as a "progressive" condition, but a progressive condition of a different genre and with distinct associated legal practices of speculation. Early legal responses to HIV discrimination in the workplace had referenced the temporality of progression through controversies over pre- and in-work antibody tests and through the figure of the asymptomatic yet infectious worker. These dilemmas arose through debates over the common law of the employment contract and, to an extent, through statutory dismissal law. The DDA, on the other hand, with its attendant debates over the definition of disability, made the task of understanding HIV all about likelihood and prognosis, introducing a curious kind of individuated medico-legal speculation through the requirement to prove HIV as a "progressive condition" in each case. Such a requirement shifted existing legal strategies around HIV claims such that what had been understood as "pressure to dismiss" or "capability" cases in the context of dismissal law were now often mobilized, instead, in the field of discrimination law. Each case, furthermore, began with intense deliberations about whether a person's HIV was "likely" in future to lead to an impairment before the substance of a claim could be addressed.

People living with HIV, buoyed by recent developments in anti-retroviral therapies, found themselves having to argue their own "likely" decline in health in order to gain access to discrimination claims for HIV-related harassment or dismissal. In this chapter, then,

I analyse how legal categories and clinical genres of time came together in the test of "likelihood," resonating with recent work in science and technology studies that focus on how legal timeframes and cutoff points are negotiated across clinical and legal practice (Beynon-Jones 2012). Drawing on interviews of legal activists and advisors working in the field of HIV, as well as case analysis, official reports, and records of official proceedings, the first section of this chapter charts what could be positioned as a "recent legal history" of HIV in the period just prior to the DDA's coming into force in 1996. I cover this in some detail to explain the context in which the temporalizing practices associated with the DDA then took hold. Legal activists, faced with intense demand for advice and support by people living with HIV, wrote specialist handbooks, aimed for swift settlements of cases, and adopted evolving common law arguments against the use of antibody testing. Not yet a legal "disability," HIV was made legally present in UK employment law through arguments about the terms and conditions of employment governing antibody tests and the "fairness" (or not) of dismissals. Tracing the relatively rapid emergence, development, and eventual jettisoning of the "likelihood" test in UK law specifically as it affected HIV claims through the late 1990s and early 2000s, I consider the contingent material conditions in which influential legal temporalities arise and have effects. The fairly swift subsequent disarticulation of the likelihood test from HIV-related claims, as a result, among other things, of policy pressure from HIV organizations, provides evidence not only that these temporalized legal techniques often become the subject of new forms of expertise and knowledge among the policy actors, lawyers, and legal activists who work with them, but also that legal temporalities, through co-constitutive relationships, are also subject to radical transformation. Far from being mysterious or metaphysical, legal temporalities are picked over, contested, and open to change.

Taking the Money and Running

People living with HIV in the United Kingdom during the 1990s had trouble gaining and keeping employment in the context of widespread fears about transmission. They also encountered difficulties obtaining legal advice where HIV-related issues had received relatively little judicial or legislative attention thus far. From the 1980s through to the early 2000s, the Terrence Higgins Trust, the National AIDS Trust, the Immunity Law Centre, and Lesbian and Gay Employment Rights between them provided advice and support for people living with HIV in the fields of housing, social security, and employment law. Their legal centres and help lines were staffed by a mixture of paid and unpaid, qualified and nonqualified advisors. By the late 1980s, the demand for legal advice was already so significant, nationally, that the Terrence Higgins Trust stated to the House of Commons Social Services Committee in February 1987 that advice and counselling centres should be set up in all cities in the United Kingdom, staffed by trained workers.[1] In 1986, for example, the Trust dealt with two hundred legal complaints relating to employment, housing, and insurance.[2] Of the employment cases, none resulted in cases before industrial tribunals, because their proceedings are a matter of public record and, it was reported, people living with HIV were generally unwilling to disclose their status in this way.[3] By 1991, the Trust was dealing with around thirteen hundred legal enquiries a year and the Immunity Law Centre nearly eight hundred, of which only a tiny fraction (less than 0.5 per cent) led to court proceedings (Wilson 1992).

As in Canada, the experience of providing legal advice during the early years of the UK epidemic was characterized by deliberately short-term strategies, volunteer advice, and pragmatic, informal routes to settlements. HIV activists worked with a near horizon, mindful of positive people's circumscribed life expectancy. Many employment problems involved experiences of homophobic and/or racist harassment as much as specifically HIV-related problems.[4] Given these widespread

1 United Kingdom, Parliament, House of Commons, Social Services Committee (Session 1986–87), "Problems Associated with AIDS," Minutes of Evidence, 25 February 1987 [hereafter cited as "Problems Associated with AIDS," Minutes of Evidence].

2 Ibid., para. 427.

3 Ibid., para. 477.

4 Popular understandings of HIV, in newspaper reports in the *Guardian* newspaper, popular books such as Randy Shilts's *The Band Played On*, and at least one article in the medical journal *Lancet*, advanced misinformed views about the supposedly African "origin" of AIDS, stating that the majority of AIDS cases were in central Africa (which was proved far wrong by World Health Organization figures), and postulating the existence of a particular gene type, common to black people in central Africa, that predisposed them to HIV infection (a view published on the basis of unpublished data with unknown participants) (Dada 1990). The connection of HIV and AIDS with "homosexuality" was so strong in the popular imagination that some legal academics felt it necessary to address the association in considering legal implications of HIV discrimination. For example: "This fear of AIDS has spread beyond fear of AIDS sufferers, to embrace HIV infected seroconverts who show no outward sign of the disease,

experiences, HIV legal activists were just as likely to try race and sex discrimination claims as they were to address HIV issues as such.[5] They aimed for continued employment of people living with HIV if that was possible, or extracting compensation for unfair dismissals to provide badly needed financial support to people who were often already symptomatic. As this prominent HIV treatment activist put it, "If you think, you've just had your diagnosis, you've got a CD4 count which is in double figures if you are lucky, you are already getting symptomatic illnesses, you've probably got diagnosed after your third bout of thrush, because nobody knew what it was the first couple of times … An awful lot of people thought the gain was not worth a candle to challenge their employers. So in those cases, we would just try and extract maximum padding for them, as it were."

Advisors were concerned that legal proceedings could negatively affect the time that people had left, and that heightened stress levels could damage clients' already compromised immune systems.[6] A 1992 report written by Petra Wilson in conjunction with the National AIDS Trust shows the scepticism with which advisors viewed formal legal avenues in the context of the stress that clients were already encountering. Wilson states: "The belief that, in general terms, the law was not a very useful tool was evident in all the HIV help agencies interviewed, including those who employed lawyers amongst their paid workers. All, without exception, indicated that they saw the law as an emotionally costly form of dispute resolution with little to recommend it" (1992, 20). As one health activist put it, settling claims out of court was much

---

to people with risky sexual proclivities, and, it would seem, to homosexuals as a class … [T]he suspicion remains, in some quarters, that male homosexuals are invariably infected with the HIV" (Watt 1992, 280). An early business-side legal textbook on AIDS, *AIDS and Employment Law*, furthermore, found it necessary to spell out to employers that calling workers names such as "pansy" or "nancy boy" was unacceptable: "As far as homosexuals or AIDS carriers are concerned, they are likely to be particularly sensitive to offensive remarks about their sexual orientation or infection and staff should be careful not to make insensitive or insulting remarks to them. Personal remarks, such as 'You are a fairy/queer/queen/pansy/nancy boy,' should be avoided at all cost" (Southam and Howard 1988, 71).

5 Many publications considered, with varying opinions, the possibility of using indirect sex discrimination claims, otherwise known as "adverse impact" arguments, as a means of addressing discrimination against gay men as a result of associations with HIV/AIDS; see, for example, Napier (1989) and Wilson (1992).

6 "Problems Associated with AIDS," Minutes of Evidence, para. 477.

easier and made more sense in terms of people's life expectancies: "Most people took the money and ran at a much earlier stage, because they thought, I don't need some kind of legal case that's going to take a year or two out of what is already a very restricted and uncertain number of years that I've got left."

Taking the money and running was a suitable strategy, given the difficulties of bringing a successful legal claim during this period, as we will see. Yet the experiences of people living with HIV were already leading to legal reform attempts. In 1987, on the basis of representations from the Terrence Higgins Trust, Member of Parliament (MP) David Alton supported a draft Bill that attempted to make dismissal on grounds of HIV infection what would now be termed "automatically unfair," which is to say that it would not even count as a "potentially fair" reason under the Employment Protection (Consolidation) Act 1978 and so would not pass the first hurdle for a fair dismissal. When the Department of Employment failed to provide evidence of the type and extent of discrimination against people living with HIV, the Bill was withdrawn. Two years later, a proposed amendment to the 1989 Employment Bill made it unlawful to discriminate in recruitment, terms and conditions, and dismissal on the basis of real or perceived HIV infection, but it was defeated by Conservative MPs (Goss and Adam-Smith 1995, 121).

As well as attempts at new legislation, however, activists also made pragmatic suggestions about potential legal changes to existing arrangements and eligibility criteria. Jonathan Grimshaw of the organization Body Positive, in his evidence to the Social Services Committee in February 1987, suggested allowing industrial tribunal proceedings to be held *in camera* for HIV-related employment cases and, in a more ambitious move, likened HIV discrimination to sex or race discrimination for the purposes of eligibility to make a claim:

> (Mr Grimshaw) I would think one way would be to make advocacy for the person who is being discriminated against available so they can be represented at a tribunal. Another would be to make the proceedings of the tribunal confidential – have them *in camera* so people could go and not have to worry about publicity and so on, and being identified in the community as somebody with the virus. I would also actually like to see the following: I understand that there is a qualifying period before you can go to an industrial tribunal – I think it is two years after you have been employed unless it is a case of racial discrimination – and for sexual

> discrimination there is no qualifying period. I do not think there should be a qualifying period before you can go to an industrial tribunal if you have been dismissed because you have this virus where there is no threat to anybody's health.[7]

The novelty of Grimshaw's representation lay in his attack on the requirement to have been in employment for two years prior to making a claim of unfair dismissal. This two-year work requirement effectively ruled out anybody working in a high-turnover industry, such as catering, in which unfounded fears about HIV transmission were rife in the late 1980s. Wittingly or not, Grimshaw, in analogizing HIV discrimination with sex or race discrimination, where claims could be brought as early as the recruitment stage, positioned HIV-related work problems as an equality issue precisely through challenging temporal requirements that took effect in dismissal legislation but that were purposively absent in equality law.[8] Through arguments about the temporalized edges of legislative protections – eligibility criteria – a legal ontology began to emerge through which infection with a virus was analogized with other, already protected "grounds" of discrimination: sex and race.

Antibody Tests at Work

The overall argument I present in this chapter is that, in the late 1990s, disability discrimination law temporalized legal questions around HIV by characterizing HIV as a progressive condition. After the DDA eventually protected people with HIV, establishing that HIV was a disability became, in effect, a matter of medico-legal speculation. Yet, as we have just seen, by the late 1980s HIV activists such a Jonathan Grimshaw were already advancing arguments about HIV law that positioned HIV as a social justice concern – a matter for equality law, not just the law of dismissal. This was partly because of time-related requirements already existing in employment law that ruled out anyone with less than two years' work for an employer from making a dismissal claim. A further point, however, is that, by the time the DDA came into force, HIV had already become legally, clinically, and socially understood as a progressive disease for some time, even if it was not yet attached to

---

7 "Problems Associated with AIDS," Minutes of Evidence, para. 478.

8 The committee took on board Grimshaw's points, suggesting in its official recommendations that the qualifying time period be reviewed; see ibid., para. 168.

the legal definition of "progressive condition." Through controversies over work-related antibody testing and public health campaigns about "latent" HIV infection, asymptomatic HIV status had already been well established as a legal concern.

Once again, the focus is on what one might term the conative legal effects of a clinical test. As we have already seen, when the newly innovated antibody test came into contact with human legal actors in Canadian provincial human rights law in the late 1980s, it helped to constitute asymptomatic status as a type of disability through the "manifesting antibodies" test. Asymptomaticity was no bar to legal remedies for claimants who asserted disability discrimination in the field of human rights. By contrast, asymptomatic status *was* a bar to low-income people who claimed income assistance, as they needed an AIDS diagnosis instead.[9] In provincial welfare benefits law, symptoms were the standard. In the United Kingdom, antibody tests similarly helped to constitute asymptomatic status as a significant legal-temporal concern, but this time in a different domain: the common law of the employment contract. This came down to a series of debates over the legality of requiring potential and current employees to be tested for HIV and to disclose their results to an employer.

To understand the way antibody testing figured in the United Kingdom in the 1980s and 1990s, it is useful to recall the numerous restrictive public health measures relating to AIDS that were in effect at that time (Goss and Adam-Smith, 1995). Examples of such measures include the Public Health (Infectious Diseases) Regulations 1985, which made AIDS a "notifiable disease" under the Public Health (Control of Disease) Act 1984 and which allowed a justice of the peace to make an order detaining a person with AIDS in hospital if he or she were satisfied that the person would not take "proper precautions to prevent the spread of disease." Very early on, then, the reasonable fear of many who were living with HIV and/or AIDS was that a diagnosis, however achieved, could result in forced incarceration later on. This was the fraught context in which antibody testing became a settled route to HIV diagnosis. In the late 1980s, with the introduction of the antibody test,

9 Among the many legal consequences of antibody testing has been the development of criminal law responses to knowing or unknowing transmission, which have targeted racialized people in particular (Monk 2009; Weait 2007). The legal construct of "reckless transmission" would not be able to operate if it were not possible to know that a person was HIV positive, even if asymptomatic, when transmission happened.

moreover, legislators and policy-makers actively considered universal testing of the population. Recommendations *against* universal testing and general anonymous screening only gained legislators' attention with the hearings leading up to the House of Commons Social Services Committee report in 1987.[10] The fact that testing had become available led to new health governance discussions: clearly, universal testing could not have been achieved without the existence of the test itself, widely accessible and effective as it was.

A further factor, however, was the gradual appearance in the public discourse of a new cultural figure: the asymptomatic, contagious person with HIV – straight or queer – who unknowingly passed on the virus to others. As John Lynch demonstrates in his analysis of UK public health campaigns on HIV and AIDS in the 1990s, one of the most important medico-cultural narratives about HIV advanced a new temporal sequence that equated asymptomaticity (a temporal artefact of the test) with a sort of contagious latent diseased status: "[T]he first [stage] was the body's reaction to the initial HIV infection; followed by a latent period before the development of symptoms of the 'full-blown' condition; and finally inevitable death" (Lynch 2000, 254). This was a different temporal frame from the suffering and terminally ill AIDS patient found in previous government communications. The latter campaigns relied on a representation of people living with HIV as appearing "normal" *and* being potentially infectious.

In one health campaign advertisement published in the mainstream press, a question was posed and answered, in white, on a black background: "What is the difference between HIV and AIDS? Time" (Lynch 2000, 255). As Lynch points out, the ad advanced an essentially closed, monologic understanding of the temporal progression of HIV to AIDS. The ad looked like a tombstone, and effectively translated individual experiences of infection into what Lynch calls "an abstracted realm of supra-human fate" (256). Not only that, but within these narratives the person with HIV was understood through a fear-inducing matrix of "past-transgression, present-agent of infection, future-death (the absence of future)" (257). Public health campaigns thus promoted the fear that seemingly healthy but infectious people would transmit

10 United Kingdom, Parliament, House of Commons, Social Services Committee (Session 1986–87), *Problems Associated with AIDS*, Third Report, paras 10–15 [hereafter cited as *Problems Associated with AIDS*, Third Report].

the virus. In such a way, debilitation did not define the experience and significance of HIV and AIDS as it had previously. Instead, HIV was understood through tropes of latency and progression alongside temporary good health. Once again, these concerns could not have come to the fore without some clinical means of testing for HIV before symptoms emerged. In other words, the antibody test contributed to the circulation of infectious latency as a concern associated with asymptomatic status.

With the cultural shift from the debilitated "AIDS sufferer" to the potentially infectious yet asymptomatic "carrier" of HIV came new work-related paranoia and practices. A recurring fear seems to have been that employers would hire workers with latent HIV infection, who would either transmit it to other workers or become ill. As a result, many large employers began operating screening processes, using antibody tests to avoid employing people with HIV. During the late 1980s and early 1990s, therefore, common dilemmas about HIV and AIDS in employment included the lawfulness of prehiring and in-employment HIV testing and disclosure.

Under the common law of the employment contract, there was nothing preventing employers from requiring HIV antibody tests and disclosure of HIV status prior to recruitment, although there was also no obligation on the part of the potential recruit to be tested. In 1986, however, the Department of Employment and the Health and Safety Executive published a booklet, "AIDS and Employment," that, without citing any legal sources as such, discouraged all employment-related antibody testing and the use of HIV status as a reason not to employ. The booklet stated: "There is generally no obligation on individuals to disclose their infection or to submit to medical tests for the virus. Anything which can be interpreted as an inquisition into an employee's personal life-style should be avoided ... In almost all occupations there is no risk of an infected person passing the virus on to others and this would not therefore generally be a reason for treating them any differently from other job applicants" (United Kingdom 1986, paras 6, 8). Three million copies of this booklet were distributed, and the opinions it advanced were influential in policy terms, being later cited by the *Problems Associated with AIDS* report, for example.[11] The legal basis of its claims was contested by one academic in the influential *Industrial*

11 Ibid., para. 167.

Law Journal, asserting that there was nothing in English law to prevent an employer's refusing to hire someone on the basis of his or her HIV status, as long as the refusal did not amount to sex or race discrimination (in which case, legislation provided a means of challenging recruitment decisions). "English law imposes no limitations on a refusal to employ a person, except where the refusal is on the grounds of sex or race, or time-expired criminal conviction under the Rehabilitation of Offenders Act 1974. And so it follows that unless selection procedures designed to eliminate possible carriers impinge on such standards, the unsuccessful job-seeker is left without remedy. It matters not that such well-informed bodies as the Social Services Committee of the House of Commons has stated that ... employers have no reason for testing for HIV" (Napier 1989, 86).

What is interesting about this divergence of views is not so much that the Social Services Committee might have "got the law wrong," so to speak, but that a joint expression by two official bodies of what an employer's HIV-related practices *should be* inaugurated a conversation about what the law allowed or prohibited. The publication and distribution of the "AIDS and Employment" booklet evidences the exceptional nature of HIV as an official policy concern in this period. If a government department, and later a House of Commons committee, advocated a position not strictly settled in law, the need for "new" responses to the epidemic provided an impetus for innovation in employment policy to take place.

Nevertheless, by the early 1990s, AIDS and occupational health organizations were addressing HIV-related discrimination more vigorously in a range of fields, including work, and this had an effect on wider perceptions of antibody tests both pre- and during employment. Much effort went into engaging with employers. In 1992, the Society of Occupational Medicine launched *What Employers Should Know about HIV and AIDS* (Society of Occupational Medicine 1992). The National AIDS Trust launched the influential *Companies Act!* campaign, advising employers on "equitable" AIDS policies, which, it stated, should address HIV and AIDS separately, insist that anti-HIV or AIDS discrimination not be tolerated, and treat HIV/AIDS in the same way as other progressive or debilitating illnesses. In 1993, the Terrence Higgins Trust produced *Positive Management*, a training package and briefing notes for companies in the private sector that featured examples of "best practice" from IBM, Rank, Marks & Spencer, Unilever,

WH Smith, Allied Dunbar, Esso, and Kingfisher (Incomes Data Services 1993).[12]

More specifically, activist handbooks argued that employers could not test or require disclosure of HIV status in *current* employees (Wilson 1992). Matthew Weait alludes to the importance of handbooks during this period in providing information and highlighting the needs of people living with HIV and AIDs: "'AIDS law' guides and handbooks were critically important in the early years of the pandemic, providing both the means by which [people living with HIV/AIDS] might know their rights in areas such as housing, employment, insurance, and immigration, and also a means by which legal practitioners might be alerted to the particular needs of a new and growing client base" (2007, 1). More than merely advising, however, HIV activist handbooks on employment evidenced a keen legal sensibility and a willingness to experiment with legal technicalities and remedies. In this way, they can be understood in terms of their innovated, quasi-legal, documentary form, circulating through advice organizations and even government departments and helping to instantiate new legal approaches to antibody testing.

One handbook, in particular, stated that requiring current employees to take an antibody test risked breaching the implied duty in employment contracts not to do anything that might undermine the "mutual trust and confidence" in the employment relationship (Richmond 1990). This duty is a term implied "by law," which is to say that it is implied by tribunals and courts into all existing employment contracts and creates the presumption of a general standard of conduct between employers and employees. By the early 1990s, the term had been in use in the lower courts for over a decade, and it was often mobilized as a means of challenging employers' behaviour in matters such as inadequate investigation of a sexual harassment claim,[13] or inadequate

12 For its part, the London-based advice and activist organization Lesbian and Gay Employment Rights published model guidelines for employers' statements on HIV/AIDS that went as far as addressing discrimination on the basis of *perceptions* about HIV/AIDS against gay men, people with hemophilia, and Africans (Goss and Adam-Smith 1995, 65). Furthermore, the 1991 UK Declaration of the Rights of People with HIV and AIDS specifically covered the employment of HIV-positive people, terms and conditions, privacy rights, and testing.

13 *Bracebridge Engineering Ltd v Darby* (1980) IRLR 3.

support in carrying out duties.[14] Notably, at the time advisors were relying upon the term, it still had not been ratified by the House of Lords – that happened only in 1997.[15] Asserting that a required antibody test undermined mutual trust and confidence was therefore still a relatively novel route for HIV legal advisors to use. Nevertheless, it gained traction, being repeated in publications as diverse as textbooks – for example, in *AIDS: A Guide to the Law* (Haigh and Harris 1990) – and policy and research reports – such as *HIV and AIDS in the Workplace* (Wilson 1992).[16]

Arguments such as this indicate the willingness of legal experts aligned with HIV organizations to innovate legal remedies for people living with HIV using the tools and legal forms already available ("the tools we have now"), including evolving common law principles. It also shows the potential creativity of these contractual implied terms, or arguments based on them, in responding to the workplace dilemmas occasioned by the techno-scientific innovation of the antibody test. Even if common law rules of contract apparently proved insufficient for granting *pre-employment* rights to those potentially excluded by antibody tests – which is what equality law would have made possible – using the implied duty of mutual trust and confidence to argue against in-employment testing constituted a new field of protection against unwanted HIV-related surveillance. Moreover, by asserting that there was "no obligation" on people living with HIV to submit

---

14 *Wigan BC v Davies* (1979) IRLR 127.

15 In the case of *Malik v BCCI* (1997) IRLR 462.

16 In yet further instances, posing HIV and AIDS as a health and safety concern led to overreach by business-side texts advising employers on their common law contractual obligation to ensure health and safety in the workplace:

"In view of the potentially fatal nature of AIDS, it would not be difficult to persuade a tribunal that failure to respond to genuine concerns about AIDS has amounted to a breach of the employer's contractual duty to take reasonable care for the health and safety of his employees" (Southam and Howard 1988, 66). This book was published after a range of government and professional reports, including the *Problems Associated with AIDS* report of 1987 and the Department of Employment's "AIDS and Employment" leaflet, that had emphasized that transmission of HIV could take place only through activities such as unprotected sex or needle-sharing. Thus, unless these activities were taking place during the usual course of employment, or unless the employer was failing to advise on the use of standard precautions in clinical work, it is difficult to imagine how an employer could fail to respond to "genuine concerns" about transmission in such a way as to breach this implied term.

to pre-employment testing – which, of course, there was not, unless the person in particular wanted a job with that employer – the Department of Employment and the Health and Safety Executive were able to create the impression of nonlegality surrounding the use of antibody tests as screening devices. Through diverse means – through leaflets and handbooks, for example – and through the participation of different institutional and noninstitutional actors (activists as well as government departments and statutory bodies), the use of antibody tests at work was gradually undermined. Yet in the course of this debate the figure of the asymptomatic person with HIV had been firmly established as a legal archetype, grounding legal responses to HIV within an overarching temporal ontology of progression that continued to exert legal effects.

"Pressure to Dismiss"

As well as anxieties about testing, the harassment, exclusion, and dismissal of people living with HIV were very common. The only obvious legal route to addressing HIV-related dismissals was via statutory unfair dismissal proceedings under the Employment Protection (Consolidation) Act 1978. It was impossible to argue that an HIV-related dismissal was homophobic or disability-related discrimination as such, because there was no discrimination law allowing such claims in force at the time. The effect of the funnelling of HIV issues into the dismissal paradigm was that a range of aggressive behaviours towards people living with HIV was assessed through the question of whether these behaviours impinged on a fair dismissal, not whether in themselves they amounted to what discrimination law would term "harassment" or what colloquially would be referred to as "stigma" or "bullying." It was, furthermore, almost impossible for people with HIV to remain in their job and make a legal claim relating to an employer's behaviour; the paradigm of dismissal in effect meant that the job already had to have been lost.

The EP(C)A had a two-stage test for the fairness of dismissals, requiring them to fit within one of the "potentially fair" reasons for dismissal (including conduct, capability, and "some other substantial reason"), after which they were also required to be *procedurally* fair. Some publications covered HIV dismissals as potential "illness" dismissals, allowable under the EP(C)A as "potentially fair" if a person's HIV was, to all intents and purposes, symptomatic, and if the employer had followed the correct procedure for ascertaining the effects of the illness on the person's ability to do the job (Wilson 1994). As in Ontario welfare benefits law, symptomatic status in such cases signalled inability to work, meaning that the employer could not use capability dismissals with regard to an asymptomatic employee. Sero-positive status without symptoms would not have allowed an employer fairly to dismiss an employee with HIV for lack of capability as such.

So far, so good: asymptomatic status did not provide grounds for dismissal. Yet much of the legal commentary and at least three early cases concerned a different question: how should employers respond to fears exhibited by co-workers or clients about an employee's HIV status? – the "pressure to dismiss" problem (Watt 1992). Tangling symptomatic and asymptomatic people and those "associated with" HIV alike within its reach, "pressure to dismiss" mobilized a complex mix of emotions, knowledge, and employer strategies, many of which could be articulated with sexuality and race. As this HIV legal activist put it: "[P]eople were being dismissed or discriminated against simply because it became known that they were HIV positive. It was nothing to do with the way that HIV was impacting on their life or affecting them in the workplace in terms of being able to do their jobs."

Employers argued that these dismissals were potentially fair under the "some other substantial reason" clause of the EP(C)A. Two cases in the late 1980s, *Cormack v TNT Sealion*[17] (concerning a chef) and *Buck v Letchworth Palace Ltd*[18] (concerning a cinema projectionist) allowed dismissals on the basis of unfounded and misinformed fears about HIV; another, *Philpott v North Lambeth Law Centre,*[19] in a reversal of this position, upheld the dismissal of two solicitors for spreading rumours about a co-worker's status (Watt 1992; Wilson 1994). For this reason there was no clear route for employees to challenge "pressure to dismiss" scenarios legally: any industrial tribunal (as they were then called) potentially could follow either the *Philpott* or the *Buck* line of reasoning, and lawyers and activists advised people living with HIV accordingly.

"Pressure to dismiss" registered not the physical effects of the virus on an employee's body, but wider affective responses to fears of "contagion." It encompassed employers' own hostile or paranoid views about HIV, as well as their reaction to the ill-informed fears of their workers.

17 Unreported: COIT 1825/126.

18 Unreported: IT 36488/86, EAT 388/87.

19 Unreported: IT 11212/86.

As Petra Wilson (1994) put it, these scenarios positioned workers living with HIV as "viral vectors," not as colleagues or employees. In turn, the very existence of anxieties about "viral vectors" and contagion helped reinforce the importance of asymptomatic status as a legal concern, conjuring temporalities of progression within dismissal cases.

Likelihood

Only a few years later, however, the legal paradigm of HIV claims shifted such that dismissal cases were not the only means of challenging mistreatment at work. Disability rights activism had been growing in the United Kingdom, and after a protracted campaign the Disability Discrimination Act 1995 came into force in 1996. The DDA provided people with disabilities with a legal remedy for discrimination in a range of settings, including employment. Relevant discriminatory acts might include refusing to offer someone a job because of a disability, sacking a person when a disability was discovered, or failing to adjust working practices in such a way as to make it possible for a person to take up or continue in a job. The DDA made all of these things unlawful. There was, however, a catch. To make a claim, a person had to prove – and still must, in most cases – that he or she had a disability for the purposes of the legislation. Specifically, the claimant had to show, under section 1 of the DDA, that he or she had a "physical or mental impairment which ha[d] a substantial and long-term adverse effect on [his or her] ability to carry out normal day-to-day activities." The DDA also required people living with HIV to show that their health status fitted within a schedule to the Act covering "progressive conditions." An employment tribunal (the new term for an industrial tribunal) often would determine this issue at a preliminary hearing.

The legal test for disability had been discussed in some detail in the parliamentary debates preceding the enactment of the DDA in 1995, and acknowledged as potentially excluding the majority of people with HIV.[20] As MP Alan Howarth put it: "My right hon. and hon. Friends used to intimate, as an objection to anti-discrimination legislation, that it would provide a field day for lawyers. Schedule 1, by using expressions such as ... 'circumstances in which ... an effect which would otherwise be a long-term effect is to be treated as not being an effect,' will

20 See, for example, comments during the second reading of the Disability Discrimination Bill on 24 January 1995 by MPs Liz Lynn, Roger Berry, and Alan Howarth.

be a positive paradise for lawyers, and, by the same token, infernal for disabled people ... I am particularly concerned that the definitions in the Bill will not protect from discrimination ... people who are HIV positive."[21]

MP Robin Corbett referenced concerns in the House of Commons on 28 March 1995 about potentially allowing employers to "discriminate early," before the manifestation of AIDS-related symptoms (or symptoms of other analogous conditions):

> This may be a misunderstanding that the Minister can clear up, but my reading of the Bill gives me the impression that it encourages the employer who suspects that someone who has a progressive condition to get in with discrimination early because the person is not covered until he or she exhibits the symptoms of that disability. I find that offensive.
>
> We are talking about people who have been diagnosed after a medical test, who are in the pre-symptomatic state and whom we know will suffer the sad consequences of the conditions over a period of time, which will vary with the individual and the conditions.[22]

Corbett's worries about presymptomatic discrimination were based on the fact that, at the time the Bill was being debated, several large companies (such as Texaco, British Airways, and Harrods) were still conducting pre-employment HIV tests. Yet the objections of Corbett and others to the requirement to prove HIV as a disability were not enough to change the draft legislation, and the Act came into force in 1996 with the requirement intact.

Fairly soon, as predicted, employers took to disputing the legal status of a person's disability as a matter of course, causing added work for legal representatives and added expense for claimants, especially in HIV-related cases, incurred by obtaining reports from medical experts to establish disability. As one legal activist put it: "Respondents would always dispute disability, even in the most obvious cases, even with people who were symptomatic and very ill with their HIV or other conditions ... I think cynically they knew it was quite difficult to obtain medical evidence and the proof that the tribunal would want to see."

21 HC Deb 24 January 1995 col 207.
22 HC Deb 28 March 1995 col 876.

Not only that, but the requirement to advance complex arguments about the nature of disability and its effects on a person's life often seemed contradictory to claimants' intentions to carry on working. One prominent health activist put it like this: "We'd have to make out – it was this ridiculous cleft stick where actually ... there was nothing wrong with people's ability to do their jobs, so it was outrageous that they should be ... hindered in doing it. In fact, we would have to make out they were a little bit ill in order to be eligible to actually get any traction. It was just this bizarre midway point. It was like trying to balance in the middle of a seesaw."

People living with HIV had two main problems fitting within the definition of disability, both of which related to how the United Kingdom's own particular medico-legal artefact of "asymptomatic status" interacted with the legal construct of "impairment" in the new DDA. The first problem was that, if they had no symptoms at all, they would be unable to show "impairment" and therefore would not be covered at all by the DDA. However, once the Act came into force in 1996, this problem usually could be countered in legal proceedings by referring to even very minor symptoms associated with a person's sero-conversion illness (which people often experienced as something like a very bad cold).

The second problem was that, even if a person had experienced symptoms, he or she then had to fit these symptoms within the provisions of the DDA that covered "progressive conditions." Schedule 1, paragraph 8, of the DDA said the following about progressive conditions, mentioning HIV specifically:

> Where – a person has a progressive condition (such as cancer, multiple sclerosis or muscular dystrophy or infection by the human immunodeficiency virus), as a result of that condition, he has an impairment which has (or had) an effect on his ability to carry out normal day-to-day activities, but that effect is not (or was not) a substantial adverse effect, he should be taken to have an impairment which has such a substantial adverse effect *if the condition is likely to result in his having such an impairment.* (emphasis added)

In other words, the DDA allowed for a relatively minor impairment associated with a progressive condition to trigger the legal definition of disability if the condition was likely in the future to lead to a more substantial adverse effect on a person's ability to carry out day-to-day activities. The influential Employment Appeal Tribunal case of *Dr G A Mowat-Brown v University of Surrey*[23] provided the key guidance in this area. *Mowat-Brown* concerned a music lecturer who, in 1995, began to experience symptoms of what would later be diagnosed as multiple sclerosis. He was dismissed in 1998 and later brought a disability discrimination claim. The university, predictably, made an argument that Dr Mowat-Brown was not disabled for the purposes of the DDA. Evidence from his GP was used to establish that his symptoms were few, that "his disease seems to have troubled him very little," and that his multiple sclerosis seemed "quite quiescent." The GP further stated: "Presently, he is not disabled by the condition and is fit for work. Unfortunately, it is not possible to give an accurate prognosis for any individual with multiple sclerosis because of the variable nature of the condition. The absence of any abnormal signs, three years after his presentation to me, provides grounds for some optimism about his future."[24]

I will later return to the reluctance of clinicians to give a prognosis, but the employment tribunal accepted the GP's opinion, and concluded that Dr Mowat-Brown was not disabled for the purposes of the DDA. Dr Mowat-Brown's lawyers then appealed the finding to the Employment Appeal Tribunal, which found in favour of the university, making the following often-cited statement about how to establish a progressive condition as a disability:

> The question to be asked is whether, on the balance of probabilities, the claimant has established that the condition in his case is likely to have a substantial adverse effect. It is not enough simply to establish that he has a progressive condition and that it has or has had an effect on his ability to carry out normal day-to-day activities. *The claimant must go on and show that it is more likely than not at some stage in the future he will have an impairment which will have a substantial adverse effect on his ability to carry out normal day-to-day activities.* How the claimant does this is up to him. In some cases it may be possible to produce evidence of his likely prognosis. In other cases it may be possible to discharge the onus of proof by statistical evidence.[25]

---

23 Official transcript of Employment Appeal Tribunal proceedings, reported as *Mowat-Brown v University of Surrey* (2002) IRLR 235; references in this chapter are to the official transcript.

24 Ibid., para. 14.

25 Ibid., para. 21; emphasis added.

The *Mowat-Brown* case put to one side the question of probabilities of future impairment, rendering "likelihood" the key test in this area. For its part, the temporo-legal ontology of disability did not reside simply in the fact that a condition was progressive. It now meant something more specific and speculative – "more likely than not" – and envisioned the use of prognosis or statistical evidence, mobilizing fraught relationships between lawyers, clinicians, medical reports, and HIV-related tests such as viral load and T cell counts. "More likely than not" was a layered or concertina-type of futurity that read "present" impairments paradoxically as evidence of future "long-term effects" of a progressive condition. It required a to-and-fro movement, deciphering relevant symptoms and projecting the significance of these symptoms, as impairments, simultaneously backwards and forwards in time. This was a very different kind of temporality from progression, which was inaugurated through *stages* of illness: manifesting antibodies, asymptomatic status, onset of symptoms, ARC, and AIDS. What mattered instead with likelihood were the curiously time-travelling, recursive impairments: evidence of a future state of health that would determine a person's ability to claim the category of disability in the present.

Siân Beynon-Jones's (2012) study of the clinical demarcation of "later" abortions shows that clinical decision-making over when abortions fit within the available legal regime is strongly related to specific understandings of pregnant women's and fetal subjectivity and their intersecting temporalities. Similarly, the way lawyers understood and mobilized clinical knowledge relating to HIV, as well as understandings of prognosis and the life course, created a specifically clinically oriented legal genre of time that had significant effects in constituting (or not) HIV as a disability. As one HIV activist put it, indicating that person's own awareness of key clinical terms and their legal relevance, "[i]n HIV it tended to be, are you on treatment? Have you got a CD count below 200? Have you had an opportunistic illness?" These deliberations were often very stressful for the person whose disability was being investigated, and required difficult conversations with people living with HIV about their future health. HIV legal activists were careful in raising these questions: "It's not a very nice conversation to have with someone, particularly in the earlier 90s, I think, because … maybe it was just starting to be seen as a chronic, manageable condition … [I]t was still accepted that you would probably have, if you weren't going to die in five years, that you would die earlier than that."

HIV as disability was therefore difficult to demonstrate in UK law, often requiring complex arguments in preliminary hearings and the commissioning of joint medical reports. Constitutive of a particular type of medico-legal speculation, these practices demonstrated considerable faith in the potential for medical examinations and reports to unravel the "truth" of a person's condition. The test in section 1 of the DDA required, in every case, an element of speculation to the extent that claimants had to show their condition had a long-term effect. Disability, as such, was both waiting to be discovered as a matter of scientific objectivity and also, in the end, subject to legal determination.

As foreseen in the parliamentary debates, this created extra work (a "field day") for lawyers. Perhaps with less gusto than Parliament had predicted, HIV legal activists and employers' representatives developed an entire field of expertise in creating draft questions for clinicians that would elicit the desired response. They also spent a considerable amount of effort arguing, between parties, about which questions should be posed. As one legal expert on HIV put it:

> So the process was ... you'd assert your client was a disabled person in the ET1.[26] You would say why. The respondent would dispute or say we are going to put the claimant to strict proof that they are a disabled person. You would start out by obtaining medical evidence from the claimant's own GP or consultant. You provide that to the other side. They usually say that's not good enough. It doesn't ask or answer, you haven't answered the right questions ... Or they would say, it's biased, it's tendentious because this person is the claimant's own GP who is on their side ... Usually what would happen is that they would say, no we want a joint expert report.

Before they were even written, expert medical reports had significant effects as material legal actors. Structured through negotiations between legal parties over which expert to use, how to instruct them, and how to understand the features and prognosis of HIV generally and the treatments available, each report then had to address the question of *this* HIV in *this* claimant, as we will see below. The adversarial processes leading to the instruction of clinical experts led to some anxiety about

26 An ET1 is the statement of claim form claimants use to commence legal proceedings in an employment tribunal.

what they would say, resulting in an intense focus on educating experts about the relevant legal questions. The widely used text, *Disability Discrimination Claims: An Adviser's Handbook,* featured headings such as "How to obtain a useful written report from a medical practitioner," and cautioned that "[a]n adviser who simply writes to the applicant's GP or specialist asking for a report on the applicant's condition is likely to get only a brief report or letter in return" (Casserley and Gor 2001, 50). Such was the difficulty of drafting letters of instruction to medical experts that the handbook also contained a sample letter of instruction, with a list of specific questions about the nature of a (fictional) client's disability, tailored to the DDA test.

Lawyers managed the tension of negotiating legal/clinical ontologies of HIV via medical reports through what was colloquially referred to by one disability lawyer as "spoon-feeding": "You had to be very careful about how you instructed medical experts, because sometimes they found it difficult to grasp what they were being asked to deal with … You had to really spoon feed them and also you had to use the guidance as well." Yet however interested they were in "spoon-feeding" experts the correct legal approach, lawyers remained wary that employer-side instructions would attempt to lead the same experts into making a statement about the legal status of the person's disability (or lack of it) – a question that was understood on usual legal principles to be firmly a matter for the employment tribunal itself. Claimants' lawyers resisted these attempts, but not always successfully. As this HIV legal activist put it: "[T]here would be a wide range of good and bad chair people in [a] tribunal. Some would see that for what it was. Some would say, 'well, that's settled then, isn't it? And this expert said that this person doesn't meet the definition of disability. That is the end of the case.' That was difficult."

Clinical expertise, imported into legal proceedings to provide evidence relating to a person's disability status, often had the effect of eliding constructed boundaries separating legal "truth" from medical "evidence" (Fassin and d'Halluin 2005), and claimants' representatives were on guard to ensure that this did not happen. One lawyer put it as follows, with disarming clarity: "Ultimately, it was a legal question, and it wasn't a medical question." Nevertheless, through medical reports, and the tensions and discussions that produced and surrounded them, fields of clinical and legal knowledge, and the imagined overlap between them, were produced and fortified.

Contested "Technical Imaginaries" of Time

It was envisioned by the case law on "likelihood" that introducing evidence about a person's HIV *prognosis* could help to establish whether it was "more likely than not" that a claimant would have a future impairment with a significant effect on day-to-day activities. Prognosis thus emerged as a target for clinical articulations and evaluations of time. More specifically, if it is correct to describe "likelihood" as a form of medico-legal speculation, then prognosis was central to such an endeavour.

Generally, prognosis refers to the mixture of statistics, survival rates, and other factors that help predict the course and outcome of a given condition. As a socio-technical invention, prognosis creates fields of power through the articulation of probabilities based on statistical measurements, clinical conjecture, and understandings of the life course. As such, it interacts with other socio-temporal concepts such as "decline," "crisis," and "recovery." Sara Lochlann Jain (2007, 81) has argued that prognosis has a double effect, "causing and evacuating the terror of a potential future" through a logic which is at once incessantly future-oriented and abstracted. When mobilized in legal settings, prognosis co-produces diseases such as cancer and, in the current case, HIV, as objects of legal knowledge. Yet, in Jain's own study, prognosis was not necessarily enough to establish a legal claim. Cases against clinicians relating to "lost chances" of survival, where they were allowed by courts, were successful only if the claimant suffered more than a 50 per cent loss of survival, bringing a claimant from more than a 50 per cent chance of survival to less than a 50 per cent chance. The staging indices usually used in prognosis (for example, the size of a tumour) often did not provide enough specific information to allow this kind of determination (85–8).

Clinicians and legal activists in the realm of HIV discrimination in the late 1990s were similarly beset with temporo-legal problems around prognosis, albeit with very different rationales and effects. Clinical ontologies of HIV progression were created by placing a patient's test results on a normative scale, determined with reference to the techno-scientific artefacts of viral load and T cell count (Persson 2004, 50). Viral load referred to, and materialized, the extent of HIV infection in the body. Clinicians normally viewed (and still view) an undetectable viral load as indicating therapeutic success and "exponential viral replication" as a decline in health (51). As we saw in the previous chapter,

T cell (or CD4) counts measured specialized immune cells targeted by HIV, so they indicated retained functionality in the immune system. In this way, techno-scientific practices of tracing, counting, and interpreting cells and viruses simultaneously enacted HIV and its corporeal effects across clinical and legal fields.

In DDA cases in the late 1990s and early 2000s, furthermore, the disability of HIV-positive claimants was legally established with reference to an individual's own prognosis, not to an understanding of what this condition might usually do in the majority of situations. In other words, what activists reported was an articulation of scale and individuation, which prioritized a legal subject's personalized prognosis and lifespan over a population-level understanding of the progression of disease based on statistical likelihood. As this legal specialist put it: "[T]he definition of likely was more probably than not. That gave rise to real problems ... Even if you can show that more than 50 per cent of people with [HIV] go on to develop a substantial and long-term adverse effect from it ... that didn't necessarily help you, because the tribunals and the courts were saying, 'well, we don't just want to know whether statistically that condition leads to that, is likely to lead to that. We want to know in the case of your client, does your client fall into the 51 per cent who will go on to have substantial and long term effects or are they in the 49 per cent?' "

Likelihood, "more probable than not," was a legal invention, established through the interaction of definitions within the DDA, case law, and clinical expertise, which instantiated the potentially disabled legal subject as temporally distinct and distinguishable specifically through prognosis. This constructed distinctiveness or individuation signalled a relationship, of sorts, between legal and clinical ontologies of disease, managed through the novel temporal orientations materialized in the medical report.

One way of understanding this relationship is through Catherine Waldby's concept of the "shared technical imaginary." Waldby analyses the new relationships of equivalence that emerged between quite distinct domains of biomedicine in the mapping of AIDs, and argues that one feature of this coming together, or equivalence, was a process of schematization:

> In the case of AIDS we have on the one hand a concern about T and B cells, lymph, tissues and glycoproteins, and on the other patterns of sexual practice and alliance. These diverse phenomena can be made to coalesce

> precisely through their transformation into a shared technical imaginary which is characterized by a maximum of schematisation. Wherever possible, pathological processes in both bodies and the population are quantified and mathematicised, rendered into units which can be graphed, plotted, counted. Such mathematicisation places the divergent spheres of clinical and epidemiological medicine into modular and compatible relations with one another, allowing a relationship to be expressed between each of the phenomena so rendered. (2004, 97)

In the context of legal arguments in the late 1990s about HIV as a disability, prognosis functioned across legal and clinical fields, distributing knowledge about T cells, viral load, decline, or recovery, with varying effects. This process relied on a schematic approach to the constructed, internalized, "truths" of the body, creating a shared, or at least co-articulated, temporal order linking the legal concept of likelihood with the realm of projected clinical outcomes. The resulting technical imaginary of time mobilized T cell counts, viral load measurements, and pharmaceutical innovations as much as it drew on claimants' own (temporal) narratives of health and (dis)ability.

The temporalized effects of cells, their functions and measurements, were quite distinct within the co-articulated technical imaginary of HIV time in the late 1990s. Waldby, writing with Melinda Cooper, has traced how the temporality of the cell has been reoriented through the stem-cell industries, so that, in the context of regenerative medicine, cells are no longer defined by their lineage and committed to a future of "progressive differentiation," but instead are entered into cycles of indefinite regeneration outside the organism (Waldby and Cooper 2010, 16). As nonhuman actors, viral load measurements and T cell counts in UK disability discrimination cases contributed to a specific genre of HIV temporality based on viral and cellular replication, through which the purportedly generative function of T cells or the virus (respectively) was instead mapped back onto the future of the body-as-organism/legal claimant, as well as the potential success of the case. On this logic, crudely expressed, as the number of T cells fluctuated, so the potential lifetime attributable to the human legal actor changed, meaning that both a growing number and a high number of cells lengthened and improved a person's prognosis, and made a finding of future impairment, and hence disability, less likely. Similarly, on this logic, a growing or high viral load, indicating exponential generation at the level of the virus, reduced and worsened prognosis, making a legal finding of disability more possible.

In this way, cellular and viral processes, and the actions of lawyers and clinicians, influenced legal determinations of prognosis, evidencing a level of temporal co-articulation that accords with what Waldby identifies in her analysis of scientific knowledge relating to HIV. Indeed, Waldby perceives this type of co-articulation as being very smooth, a "seamless reciprocity" between knowledge relating to individual symptoms and knowledge relating to epidemiology (2004, 97–8). A degree of fit and exchange was established and maintained between clinical and legal understandings of HIV temporalities through various means: legal activists acquainted themselves with key medical terms and concepts in order to educate employment tribunals that were making decisions on the question of someone's disability; and medical experts, carefully chosen and carefully instructed by lawyers, provided what they thought to be the most rigorous and appropriate assessments of a claimant's current condition and future medical outlook within the legal guidelines they had been given.

Yet the machinery powering this "seamless reciprocity" also broke down at times, resulting in fractured or contested imaginaries of time that were still, in many senses, "shared." We have already seen the frustration with which lawyers and legal activists approached medical questions and some expert reports. Despite the apparent reliability of their own T cell and viral load measurements for treating patients and/or undertaking medical research, when faced with the task of making a prediction for legal purposes, clinical experts often did not give the level of specificity that lawyers wanted. Legal activists interpreted this as signifying an uncomfortable relationship with prediction, if not a stubborn unwillingness to give vital information about a claimant's future health. One HIV lawyer stated the problem as follows: "It seems to me that the medical experts are always reluctant to really go out on a limb and give anything other than a vague, well, this could or this might happen." The reason for this, as a respondent with wide legal experience across a number of disabilities stated, could have been that the expert's role as a clinician involved communicating prognosis in terms of life course to patients:

> This was a thing I think that came up particularly in the context of cancer. I suspect it also came up in the context of HIV, although we didn't see as much of it at the [name of organization]. With the reluctance of physicians to say that it was more likely than not that it would progress, certainly in the context of cancer, they just didn't want to say it. They didn't want to

> say that it's likely this is going to come back and it's going to get much worse. They didn't want their patients to think that that's what was going to happen, yet that was [what] they had to say in order for them to fall within the definition.

It is also possible, as the activist quoted at the outset of the chapter asserted, that clinicians viewed using prognosis for legal means as an unpalatable type of speculation. Clinical experts resorted to what they thought was a more acceptable or even more concrete temporal outlook: uncertainty. Professionally, what Fred Davis (1960) would term "functional uncertainty," consciously or not, would have served to deflect difficult discussions and emotional encounters between clinician and patient around prognosis, and would not have equated directly with clinical uncertainty as such. Disclosing uncertainty has varying effects and motivations among clinicians, signalling rigour and discretion in some circumstances, but sometimes also being feared as an admission of lack of knowledge (Gerrity et al. 1992), and any of these factors might have been at play in individual cases.

As we also saw in the previous chapter, uncertainty can be understood in biomedical terms as an accomplishment, constituent of – instead of undermining or reversing – biomedical knowledge production. Taking the enunciation of uncertainty seriously, it is possible in these cases that medical experts, wittingly or not, were engaged in the task of creating a distinctly clinical or scientific genre of what otherwise would be a legal temporality of progression when they expressed reservations about providing a confident prognosis regarding future disability. The resulting uncertainty was often sufficiently unlike a personal prognosis delivered to a "patient" to be understood in wholly therapeutic terms, but it also refused to accede to the requirements and temporal ontology of the DDA. As such, it was perhaps much less unlike speculation than clinicians perhaps wanted it to be. Yet to the extent that uncertainty can be viewed as a productive scientific orientation, it is also difficult to imagine an encounter between legal and clinical fields on the subject of HIV in which the medico-legal temporality of likelihood could be articulated as entirely *distinct* from uncertainty. "Likelihood" was both uncertainty and speculation.

Beyond Likelihood

By the time it was in use, the likelihood test itself was in some senses already belated. The test was more suited to an earlier era of HIV and

AIDS treatment and activism, when a core concern was the debilitating and often immediately life-threatening complications associated with HIV infection and an AIDS diagnosis. By the late 1990s, however, the newly widespread availability of antiretroviral combination therapies had changed the stakes of HIV infection such that HIV infection was now understood to constitute a chronic and not always life-threatening condition. Julian Gill-Peterson's oral history of New York's ACT-UP treatment activist scene reflects on the shift that new treatment technologies provoked from the time of the epidemic to the time of *endemic*, proposing that the endemic required a different and distinct type of politics and ethics (Gill-Peterson 2013, 296).

Ironically, it was only in 2004 that an amendment to the Disability Discrimination Act rendered HIV a disability from the moment of diagnosis. This move had been recommended in the final report of the Labour government's Disability Rights Taskforce, having also been a prominent feature in submissions to the All-Party Parliamentary Group on HIV and AIDS in 2001. As the National AIDS Trust put it in its memorandum on the draft Disability Bill 2004, commenting on the previous test: "This flawed definition of disability disregarded the fact that being HIV-positive and asymptomatic may not diminish a person's physical capacities but can nevertheless substantially limit that person's ability to work or access goods and services as a result of the prejudices and negative assumptions of others in relation to HIV" (National AIDS Trust 2004). Requiring people living with asymptomatic, or marginally symptomatic, HIV to establish their disability before proceeding with the substance of a claim made it more difficult, the National AIDS Trust argued, to address what they felt was the "prejudice" element of HIV workplace problems.

With the 2004 amendment, UK equalities legislation got to a point similar to that achieved in Canadian human rights law in the 1988 case of *Biggs v Hudson*, when a provincial human rights court protected those with HIV from the point of "manifesting antibodies." What are we to make of this apparent temporal (if cross-jurisdictional) lag? If anything, what happened around "likelihood" in the period between 1996, when the DDA came into force, and 2004, the date of the amendment, indicates the productive force and uncanny effects of innovated legal temporalities. Set in motion by the concept of "progressive condition," which in many ways had already occupied employment law through debates over antibody testing and dismissal, tribunals, representatives, medical experts, their reports and tests then brewed variegated types and genres of "likelihood," a plural medico-legal temporality that enrolled prognosis, uncertainty, and future impairments in the work of gauging and reconstituting HIV as a disability.

This chapter, the story of likelihood – a "likely story," even – demonstrates the power of legal innovations to set in motion new temporal ontologies and then to abandon, transform, or reframe them. More specifically, one might say that this "likely story" shows the co-constitution of temporal ontologies with innovated legal form. For a brief moment in the late 1990s and early 2000s, contested technical imaginaries of time not only defined the legal realities of HIV as a disability, but, through "likelihood," brought about entirely novel legal modes of articulating disease and discrimination. This could not have happened without antibody tests and viral load counts and more mundane processes of legal documentation and evidence. Yet in such moments of transformation we can discern the percolation of legal form with what Bennett (2010) would understand as the "active, earthy, not quite human capaciousness" of viruses, T cells, impairments, symptoms, and medical reports. Not quite wholly human, "likelihood" helped to constitute new legal domains of action, forcing lawyers and clinicians alike to re-evaluate the boundaries of their respective fields.

Chapter Four

Transition

We are used to filling out forms with certain questions. We rarely question how we came to be asked for those particular pieces of information and not others except in moments when we personally have a hard time figuring out which box to check off.

– Dean Spade, *Normal Life*

Sex is something that the documents themselves enact, and sex becomes performative in the sense that the *m* or the *f* on the document does not merely report on the sex of its bearer but becomes the truth of and bestows the bearer's sex … Sex is not private property, but rather property *that belongs to the state itself.*

– Gayle Salamon, *Assuming a Body*

A statutory declaration is a written statement of facts which the person making it signs and solemnly declares to be true before a witness authorised to administer oaths. You are required to provide a statutory declaration making several statements about your circumstances and your application. This is to ensure that you meet the criteria for the grant of a Gender Recognition Certificate. You are required to state that … [y]ou intend to live in your acquired gender until death.

– HM Courts and Tribunals Service Form T451

In 2005 the UK's Gender Recognition Act (GRA) came into force, inaugurating a new route for transgender people to obtain legal status in their "acquired gender." Having considered a number of potential mechanisms, the then New Labour government settled on a procedure through which transgender people are to make a formal application to a specialist tribunal (the Gender Recognition Panel) providing evidence of a "successful" transition. The panel is then required to grant a Gender Recognition Certificate if all of the conditions in the Act are met. In turn, a successful standard track application under section 2 of the Act requires that the applicant: (1) be over eighteen years of age and have, or have had, a diagnosis of gender dysphoria; (2) has lived in the acquired gender for two years; and (3) intends to continue living in the acquired gender "until death."

This chapter focuses on the third key requirement in the GRA – that of gender permanence, post-transition, "until death." Transgender legal concerns often evoke questions of temporality (Conley 2008). As we saw in Chapter One, furthermore, the assumed significance of death as a universal concern in Western legal orders helps to ground time in the realm of the "natural." Carol Greenhouse refers to death as a metaphor or archetype of power: "Death is the West's master metaphor of control and power; it is the law that presses against the seeming relativities of time in particular situations" (1996, 4). Pressing against the apparently new legal "relativity" of gender, the "until death" provision fits with an administrative paradigm, familiar to transgender legal activists, that emphasizes gender stability (Cowan 2009; Currah and Spade 2007). Within this paradigm, if legal subjects are to "change gender," then their transition should be final, irreversible, and sanctioned by the state through applicants meeting a number of pre-agreed criteria.

As a governmental regime that seeks to ratify "acquired" gender, the GRA contrasts with other possible legal responses to the problems associated with binary gender classification systems. In the United States, for example, law and policy on transgender recognition varies by state and often between administrative departments, a situation that is disastrous for many transgender people (Spade 2011). In Spain, a national law allows transgender people to change their name and sex on all documents, but does not meet wider social demands by activists (Platero 2011). Despite the apparent benefits of the GRA's reclassification model, Dean Spade has argued that promoting such systems in response to the legal and bureaucratic problems encountered by transgender people elides the more challenging question of why governments use gender to classify in the first place (Spade 2007, 804). Indeed, the question of classification becomes all the more pressing given a rich array of scholarship showing that reclassification models and logics produce as ideal legal subjects economically productive and otherwise normatively gendered workers, as much as they ratify gender transitions (Hines 2013; Irving 2008; Sanger 2008).

Yet as long as they are with us, reclassification models also have timely effects. Specifically, reclassification forces the problem of how to achieve gender *transition* as a legal as much as corporeal or social fact. In this chapter, I consider how "transition" is legally achieved through the GRA. In common usage, the term "transition" refers to the passage from one state or stage to another or to the period during which the transformation or shift takes place. "Transitioning" also refers to a range of experiences and material practices associated with experiencing a livable gender, mediated, as these practices are now, by administrative and legal requirements associated with gender recognition and transgender health care provisioning (Davy 2010). As Salamon puts it, the transition is "rather a shorthand designation for a constellation of acts" (2010, 179). But the idea and practice of the "transition" comes more sharply into view as an object of bureaucratic concern when government responses to transgender issues are framed around "gender recognition," with its associated temporal questions about when status should change and when rights and obligations should shift.

Indeed, transgender experiences of time throw into sharp relief the continued force of dominant temporal ontologies. Chrono-normativities of various shades are clearly of relevance to a wide range of transgender people, marginalizing racialized and low-income trans people (Spade 2011), requiring constant unpicking of damaging cultural and commemorative forms (Halberstam 2005; Lamble 2008), and prompting the retracing of what, borrowing from Nguyen Tan Hoang, we might term the transmission of transgender experience, activism, and pedagogy outside heteronormative kinship models (Dinshaw et al. 2007, 183). A queer orientation to law and regulation can uncover and register the temporal experiences of suspense, delay, and surprise often involved in transgender people's interactions with government agencies (Currah and Moore 2009). It also might begin to account for the gendered bureaucratic violence visited on transgender people by post 9/11 security initiatives such as data pool comparison practices (Spade 2011) and the Secure Flight Program (Currah and Mulqueen 2011), together evoking what Amoore and de Goede (2008) have termed "banal preemption": the targeting of data on ordinary transactions as evidence of potential future terrorist activities. Loosely clustered, these tactics, practices, and programs – temporalities co-articulated with the management of life – as we have seen, can also be understood as "temporal mechanisms" that "produce bio-political status relations" specifically through the creation and modulation of new temporal orders and orientations (Freeman 2005, 57) affecting transgender and non-normatively gendered people.

Yet queerly thinking about legislative initiatives such as the GRA might also reference the "transition" not only as an object of medico-legal regulation, intervention, and negotiation, but also as a temporal-legal artefact in itself. Engaging with the apparent obviousness of transition as a legal and bureaucratic concern, this chapter traces its documentary materialization through the UK gender recognition process. Transition emerges not merely as the description of a psychic and embodied process of becoming or change in one's legal status, but also as a legal temporal "thing" in its own right.

I begin by examining the "legislative career" of the "until death" provision. Tracing the "meaning" of the legislation in this way pays attention to law's representative function, in the sense that we might say that the legislation "represents" something ministers and MPs wanted to achieve. The following section of the chapter then returns us to the administrative logic, textual features, and material presence of the statutory declaration form, reflecting on the inauguration of legal temporalities through documents themselves. More specifically, as we will see below, transition in UK law is *inseparable* from the statutory declaration form that the GRA requires as evidence of intention to remain in gender "until death." Transition emerges, here, not only as a paradigmatic and forceful legal temporality governing transgendered legal subjects in the United Kingdom, but also as a legal artefact, with specific orientations and timely effects.

The Legislative Career of "Until Death"

Don Brenneis (2006) has traced the material histories shaping the text and margins of academic funding report forms, as well as the "evaluative life" they live through meetings and stages of administration. Writing of the "very real presents" of forms, Brenneis focuses on their animating qualities within bureaucratic practice. As he puts it: "[F]orms have very real presents, moments in which they are filled out and subsequent moments in which they are read, cited, and evaluated. As they move from one reading and writing event to the next, these forms have … careers, being animated by and animating meetings, contributing to specific and consequential outcomes for individuals and for scholarship" (2006, 65).[1]

Just as alive and malleable (for a time) as forms, legal provisions are animated by political debate, drafting procedures, and suggested amendments before being formally enacted as legislation and brought into effect. My aim here is to trace the "real presents" and the career of the "until death" provision and its associated temporal logics, watching its appearance, changing shape, significance, and materiality through successive stages of the policy and legislative process leading to the enactment of the GRA. Paying just as much attention to moments when the provision appeared above scrutiny or beneath interest as to when it was the focus of debate or contestation, this short "legislative career," or "biography," aims to unravel the thickly braided threads of policy innovation, argument, and political jostling that contributed, in the end, to what became a self-evident legal-temporal requirement: making a statutory declaration of one's intention to remain *permanently* in an acquired gender.

Such a purposefully dogged description of successive legislative and policy "stages" relies on a wide cast of documents and documentary artefacts, including parliamentary reports, written submissions, draft legislation, and the strange oral-textual-legal archive that is *Hansard* – the almost verbatim report of proceedings in the UK House of Lords and House of Commons – in which peers and MPs respectively debated what was then the Gender Recognition Bill. As such, the research that has gone into constructing this account has itself been largely textual. Whereas Brenneis is able to juxtapose successive versions of a form and hence follow its material and textual evolution, my approach instead traces the shifting meanings and tactics associated with the "until death" provision as legal technique. What emerges is a divergent and sometimes problematic set of temporal genres: from the indeterminate and not-necessarily-settled gender identities changing over time, as envisioned by the Interdepartmental Working Group on Transsexual People in 2000, to the rhetoric of gender "permanence" used by ministers in the Department for Constitutional Affairs from the first stages of drafting the Gender Recognition Bill in 2002, to the appearance of the "until death" wording, a logic of administrative certainty advanced by the Joint Committee on Human Rights, through various challenges mounted by Conservative peers and MPs

1 Here Brenneis cites Richard Harper's (1998) ethnography of documents in the International Monetary Fund.

in the parliamentary debates about "gender switching" and "reversals" in early 2004, culminating in the eventual wording of the standard form statutory declaration, featuring its own temporal twist.

This focus on documents does not mean that transgender people's experiences are not relevant to the brewing of legal temporalities, or that the legal-temporal mechanisms and genres uncovered should be taken as unchanging or unproblematic. As we know from the work of Namaste (2000) and many others, social and cultural research contributes to the erasure of transgender people through specific heuristic stances and practices. Hence the importance of studies, like those already cited, as well as the work of Flora Renz (in progress), that recentre transgender people's experiences, subjectivities, and world-making practices through, among other techniques, grounded engagements with transgender legal consciousness and activist strategies. Focusing on documents, on its own, does not work to challenge the erasure of transgender people's experiences, but can be taken as part of a wider set of engagements with legal paradigms and techniques. My aim here is to draw documents into social justice approaches to law – to focus closely on what legal and legislative drafting techniques do with transgender lives in order to contribute the material presence of law to an understanding of what transition becomes in legal reclassification measures. If the results of this enquiry seem constraining, oppressive, or merely strange, that might provide us with more grounds, first, for understanding the multiple legal ontologies of time that transgender legal reform strategies can inaugurate and, second, for forging ongoing political engagements with legal, bureaucratic, and documentary worlds.

"Permanence"

We begin, then, in 2000, with a set of governmental initiatives precipitated by decisions in the European Court of Human Rights that held the United Kingdom in breach of the European Convention on Human Rights for failing to recognize transgender people in their "reassigned" gender and for failing to allow trans people to marry.[2] The first significant

---

2 See *Goodwin v United Kingdom* and *I v United Kingdom* (2002) 35 EHRR 447, engaging European Convention on Human Rights Article 8 (right to private and family life) and Article 12 (right to marry). See also the decision of the House of Lords in the case of *Bellinger v Bellinger* (2003) 2 WLR 1174, which declared UK law incompatible with ECHR Articles 8 and 12 for failing to recognize as valid the marriage of a trans woman to her husband.

administrative step towards a legal reform project was the Home Office's 2000 *Report of the Interdepartmental Working Group on Transsexual People.* This group's purpose was as follows: "to consider, with particular reference to birth certificates, the need for appropriate legal measures to address the problems experienced by transsexual people, having due regard to scientific and societal developments, and measures undertaken in other countries to deal with this issue" (United Kingdom 2000, preface).

The report identified three options: leave the current situation as it was; issue birth certificates showing the person's new name and possibly "reassigned" sex; or grant full legal recognition of the "acquired" sex, "subject to certain criteria and procedures" (United Kingdom 2000, 26). Part Four of the report discussed some possible preconditions for granting legal status, including sterility and dissolution of marriage, but it did not raise or cover any need for applicants to intend to live in their acquired gender "until death" (21–2). By contrast, in its conclusion, the report envisaged a wide range of transitional outcomes for transgendered people:

> 5.1 Transsexual people deal with their condition in different ways. Some live in the opposite sex without any treatment to acquire its physical attributes. Others take hormones so as to obtain some of the secondary characteristics of their chosen sex. A smaller number will undergo surgical procedures to make their bodies resemble, so far as possible, those of the acquired gender. The extent of the treatment may be determined by individual choice, or by other factors such as health or financial resources. *Many people revert to their biological sex after living for some time in the opposite sex, and some alternate between the two sexes throughout their lives. Consideration of the way forward must therefore take into account the needs of people at these different stages of change.* (25; emphasis added)

In other words, far from proposing that an intention to remain in the acquired gender "until death" should be necessary for a legal response to transition, the Working Group's report suggested that future policy and legislative initiatives should encompass people at various stages of gender transition, *including* those who "alternate between the two sexes throughout their lives." This statement, and the approach it evidenced, was to have effects later on in the legislative process, as we will see.

In the meantime, the Department of Constitutional Affairs was given responsibility for producing draft legislation. Moving swiftly away from the wider definition of transition found in the Working Group's report, the department began using the language of gender "permanence," post-recognition, in ministerial statements. For example, on 13 December 2002, MP Rosie Winterton stated that the government would publish a draft Bill "to give legal recognition in their acquired gender to transsexual people who can demonstrate that they have taken decisive steps towards living fully and permanently in the gender acquired since they were registered at birth" (Winterton 2002). Lord Filkin used the language of permanence in his statement announcing the publication of the Gender Recognition Bill on 11 July 2003.[3] By now, the newly published Bill provided that a Gender Recognition Panel would have to grant a Gender Recognition Certificate if satisfied that the applicant: "a) has or has had gender dysphoria; b) has lived in the acquired gender throughout the period of two years ending with the date on which the application is made (a requirement which is at present usually a precondition for surgical treatment in the [National Health Service]); c) *intends to continue to live in the acquired gender until death*; and d) complies with the evidential requirements imposed by or under clause 2 of the Draft Bill" (United Kingdom 2003a, 25; emphasis added). Such evidential requirements included, under clause 2(4)(a) of the Draft Bill: "c) a statutory declaration by the applicant that the applicant has lived in the acquired gender for at least two years at the date of the application *and intends to continue to live in the acquired gender until death*" (emphasis added).

It is possible that the use of the idiom "until death" originated from within the Department of Constitutional Affairs, being thought of as a technical and even procedural aspect of the gender recognition process. More likely, it originated with the interplay between the legislative drafting team working on the Bill and the department. Whatever the source, its appearance in the Bill at this point, for the first time, alongside the evidential requirement of a statutory declaration, indicates the discursive articulation of gender recognition with the taking of something akin to an oath. Once the "until death" clause was in the draft Bill, it was subject to relatively little subsequent scrutiny. This is possibly because far more controversial debates were at play about the kind of medical evidence that would be needed for a certificate and the effect of a Gender Recognition Certificate on existing marriages (United Kingdom 2003a). But the relative lack of concern also indicates an emerging consensus position that the "until death" clause was a settled aspect of the legislation, a point to which I return later.

---

3 HL Deb 11 July 2003 c63W.

A draft Bill having been published, the Joint Committee on Human Rights then had the responsibility of scrutinizing the Bill for its compliance with the European Convention on Human Rights.[4] Numerous groups, individuals, and the Department for Constitutional Affairs itself submitted written evidence to the Committee. Once again, while ranging over many other topics, this evidence largely did not discuss the "until death" clause. For example, lengthy submissions from the clerk to the Gender Recognition Division in the Department for Constitutional Affairs did not raise or explain it. Likewise, submissions from nongovernmental bodies – including the Gender Trust, Liberty, the Lima House Group, the Metropolitan Community Church of Manchester, the Northern Ireland Human Rights Commission, and Press for Change – that otherwise were heavily involved in policy and human rights debates about transgender experiences of the law and about the gender recognition process – did not mention the provision and associated statutory declaration (United Kingdom 2003b). One notable exception was a submission from the Discrimination Law Association, a group of progressive lawyers working in the legal equalities field. As the association pointed out, the statutory declaration of living in the acquired gender "until death" appeared superfluous to other, apparently more convincing, evidence, such as having lived in the acquired gender for two years:

> Intention to continue living in the acquired gender until death
> 19. We do not understand how the Panel will assess whether the applicant intends to continue living in the acquired gender until death, other than accepting an honest declaration as to this intention. The Panel will have all the evidence before it going to paragraph 1 (4)(b) of the Bill that the applicant has lived in the acquired gender for two years and there will not usually be any further evidence necessary. We would appreciate clarification of the evidential requirements for this element of the test. (United Kingdom 2003b, 15)

Another group, Post Op Women UK, while taking issue with the term "gender" (and substituting the term "sex" throughout its submission), asserted that "being postoperative should be proof enough of any commitment"

4 The Committee has numerous investigative powers, including the power to examine witnesses, require written evidence and documents, and make reports to both Houses of Parliament.

(United Kingdom 2003b, 64). Two different measures of commitment to gender transition, then, in separate submissions, were taken to show the required level of evidence or commitment to the process: having lived in gender for two years and being "postoperative," respectively.

"A Degree of Certainty"

The subsequent report of the Joint Committee on Human Rights barely engaged with the "until death" clause, apart from advancing an overarching logic of governmental and administrative *certainty* for the processes contained in the Bill. These, by implication, included the clause and its associated evidentiary requirements:

> 49. It is reasonable for the Government to take the view that there needs to be a degree of certainty about people's genders. Gender will affect legal status and a variety of other rights and obligations. Certainty is also needed to protect the interests and rights of people who have dealings, either administratively or in the course of personal relationships, with the person whose acquired gender is to be recognized …
>
> 51. How does the Draft Bill pursue certainty? There are two elements: first, the need for certification by an official body, a Gender Recognition Panel; secondly, the application by the Panel of statutory criteria which, if met, would entitle a person to a certificate, and, if not met, would necessarily lead to refusal of a certificate. The Panel would have to assess the evidence, but would have no discretion. (United Kingdom 2003a, 19)

The Committee's argument in paragraph 51 was that the "until death" clause aimed to "pursue certainty." If it did so, on the Committee's logic the clause also assumed no particular importance, as it was one of a range of measures introduced to this end (also including medical evidence and evidence of having lived in the "acquired" gender). The passage excerpted above refers, for example, to the effect of gender on legal status and the rights of individuals who "have dealings with" transgendered people, and this is supported by later passages in the report.[5] Yet through this passage, the report was also articulating the legal effects on others of gender and gender transitions as *otherwise uncertain* for the purposes of

5 For example, paras 60 and 61, which address the evidential requirements associated with an existing marriage.

assessing the processes contained in the draft Bill. Gender certainty was, on this account, a reasonable governmental and administrative aim, and would protect those interacting with a transgender applicant.

As we saw in Chapter Two, uncertainty is a core aspect of regulatory "knowledge machinery," being something that is achieved as much as simply forming the backdrop for regulatory activity (Moreira, May, and Bond 2009). This is significant, because at a point when the gender recognition framework itself was in early stages (in draft Bill form) and was clearing new ground in the regulation of transgender legal status, the need for gender certainty was positioned as against what would be the "uncertainty" and putative ungovernability of gender transitions outside the proposed legal process. In other words, both certainty and uncertainty were co-articulated with the outer boundaries of legal innovation in this area. Uncertainty also worked with a specific temporal ontology of gender transitions as otherwise quite radically fluid. When discussing the criteria for granting a Gender Recognition Certificate, including the "until death" requirement, and their compatibility with European Court of Human Rights law, the Joint Committee on Human Rights argued against what it positioned as a view that choice of gender should be "reversible": "Some people might say that the choice of a gender should be unconstrained and reversible, but that seems to us to give insufficient weight to the interests of others in knowing the legal status of those with whom they have to deal" (United Kingdom 2003a, 21, 25).[6]

In 2000 the Working Group had been able to envisage a wide range of transitions, including "alternating between the sexes," which "must" inform legal measures. Yet by 2002 the human rights scrutiny body charged with analysing the draft Bill juxtaposed potentially "reversible" transitions with the "interests of others." The legal-temporal ontology of gender certainty was one of the means through which such a shift was achieved.

Reversals

"Reversible gender" appeared through key stages of the subsequent legislative process, with a variety of effects. Describing gender

6 The report then proceeds to discuss the proportionality under European Court of Human Rights law of these measures, including discussion of relevant data protection and privacy laws (United Kingdom 2003a, 22).

transitions as "reversals" is an inherently political move, evoking a binaristic sex/gender indecision that belies complex material and social experiences of gender becoming. As such, the temporality of gender reversals advanced by politicians opposing the Bill was fluid and capricious: it conjured scenes of gender mistakes made and rectified, and ultimately retained faith in the idea of "true" or "final" gender. By contrast, I argue that the temporality of intended gender permanence advanced by ministers, despite its terminology, admitted a degree of openness and nonfixity. Both approaches to gender transition, whatever their political motivation and effects, and to different degrees, evidenced moments of technical and temporal nimbleness, with the government's concept of permanence eventually holding sway.

The version of the Bill introduced into the House of Lords for its first reading on 27 November 2003 used the "until death" wording, in terms of both the requirements for a valid Gender Recognition Certificate and the evidence that would be needed in the form of a statutory declaration.[7] Yet in Lords debates on the Bill, some Conservative peers expressed vehement opposition to the very idea of gender transition, based on their understanding of sex as immutable. As Lord Tebbit put it: "Sex cannot be changed ... Sex is decided by the chromosomes of a human being. If we have XX chromosomes, we are women; if we have XY chromosomes, we are men ... So far as I know, there is no law nor any known medical procedure that can change the sex of a human being. The Bill purports to do so. It is therefore an objectionable farce."[8] These parts of the debate concerned the definition of sex and gender and the possibility of being able to "change sex" at all as a matter of legal process. Here, the concept of permanence operated as something of a long-stop, providing a legal and administrative horizon for what were otherwise positioned as fluid and fictional, or "unreal," transitions. On this logic, furthermore, the "until death" clause can be

---

7 "*Gender Recognition Bill 2003/04 (HL). Bill 56. A bill to make provision for and in connection with change of gender.* 2. Determination of applications. (1) In the case of an application under section 1(1)(a), the Panel must grant the application if satisfied that the applicant ... (c) intends to continue to live in the acquired gender until death ... 3. Evidence. (4) An application under section 1(1)(a) must also include a statutory declaration by the applicant that the applicant meets the conditions in section 2(1)(b) and (c)."

8 HL Deb 18 December 2003 c1304.

understood as relatively open, allowing one legal transition, which was intended to be permanent, but permitting more if the intention of permanence was once again present.

The question of what was called "reversing" gender transition applications came up in debates in both houses. In the Grand Committee stage of the House of Lords on 13 January 2004, Baroness O'Cathain moved an amendment that would have allowed applicants who had "changed their mind" or wished to "resume their original birth gender" to obtain only one further Gender Recognition Certificate if they followed the usual procedure:

> REVERSAL OF APPLICATION PROCESS
>
> (1) Where a successful applicant subsequently changes his or her mind, or decides a mistake has been made, and wishes to resume his or her original birth gender, a further application must be made to the Gender Recognition Panel for the issue of a further gender recognition certificate in the resumed gender.
>
> (2) The Panel may grant the application on the same basis as the provisions set out in sections 1 to 5.
>
> (3) Only one reversal of an original decision made by the Panel may be permitted.[9]

Baroness O'Cathain's statements about the proposed amendment positioned such "reversals" as undermining the rationale of allowing ratified transitions in the first place: the reasons someone might wish to obtain a further Gender Recognition Certificate included, on her account, having been "badly advised," having "come to their senses," or having recognized that "a very big mistake has been made."[10] A further reason for the amendment showed exorbitant concern about what others would term the inherent mutability of gender. Her proposal was to curb potentially rapid and repeated gender transitions, undertaken "on a whim": "The other part of the amendment is based on the sure case for saying that, if a gender recognition certificate has been issued and the person is no longer of the gender into which he or she was born, there must be some block on their being able to change their minds again and again, so they do not go chopping and changing at whim.

9 Ibid., c58GC.
10 Ibid.

I suggest that, under the amendment, we should agree that they can change, but change only once."[11]

Lord Filkin's response barely concealed his frustration, emphasizing the difficulty of transitioning in the manner envisaged by the Bill, both legally and as a social-corporeal matter, and stating that the procedure in the Bill would already allow subsequent transitions:

> I shall seek to be brief. Acquiring a new gender is a long, difficult and painful process. It involves a lot of medical advice and a lot of trauma with family relationships. We do not expect individuals to want to change back, having met the medical criteria and been through the minimum of two years' waiting. Having said that, the noble Baroness is right in saying that a very small proportion of people – perhaps 1 per cent – have asked to go back.
>
> The position is in essence exactly as I hinted to her yesterday. The procedure as set out in the Bill allows an applicant who wants to reverse to apply. All that I would say about that – and I would emphasise this even more strongly in the case of her even more hypothetical situation of a person who wanted to change three times – is that *one duty of the panel is to be convinced that the person is committed to a permanent change of gender.*[12]

Again, the temporal concept of permanence had appeared in an official statement by a minister, but this time in relation to concerns about putative gender "reversals." In Lord Filkin's account, above, the duty to consider a person's commitment to a "permanent change of gender" functioned as a means of regulating multiple transitions, even though the actual wording in the Bill did not include the term "permanence" but the distinct temporal horizon of "until death." This was not enough for the Bishop of Winchester, who disagreed with Lord Filkin's characterization of the Bill, and referred back to the statement of the Interdepartmental Working Group in 2000 that envisioned a wide range of gender experiences and states of transition: "Does the Minister remember the statement on page 25 of the report of the Interdepartmental Working Group? This is a statement of its own rather than a part of the material that it reported others making. The left-hand column on page 25 states: 'Many people revert to their biological sex after living for some time in the opposite sex, and some alternate

---

11 HL Deb 13 January 2004 c59GC.

12 Ibid.; emphasis added.

between the two sexes throughout their lives. Consideration of the way forward must therefore take into account the needs of people at these different stages of change.'"[13] The bishop was clearly concerned that the Bill represented the gender politics hinted at in the Working Group's report, but Lord Filkin responded by reiterating his own understanding of the Bill. When Baroness O'Cathain, Lord Chan, and Lord Tebbit pressed him further, Lord Chan asking for the position to be made formally clear on the face of the Bill, Lord Filkin stated: "I do not believe that we should confuse parliamentary draftsmanship by stating facts that are clear to lawyers. I am happy to state the position on Report and to write confirming it. I do not intend to change the Bill."[14] "Facts that are clear to lawyers" is an illuminating phrase, signalling the reassertion of professional legal expertise and self-evident legal objectivity amid what Lord Filkin positioned as the outlandish concerns of Conservative and other peers. Lord Filkin presumably meant that an applicant could indeed apply more than once for a Gender Recognition Certificate, but that the Gender Recognition Panel had to be satisfied, each time, as to the person's intention to make a "permanent" transition.

Baroness O'Cathain then withdrew her amendment. But she remained preoccupied with reversals. In the House of Lords debate on 29 January 2004, she proposed another amendment, this time limiting a person to two legally recognized gender transitions.[15] On the face of it, the second amendment and her statements in Parliament were again motivated by her concern about the concept of fluid gender identity advanced by the 2000 Working Group report, her own values, and media accounts of people who, as Baroness O'Cathain put it, "wish they had never changed."[16] The second amendment would have permitted the granting of more than one Gender Recognition Certificate, on the basis that persons, having legally transitioned once, might wish to return to their "true sex in law."[17] Baroness O'Cathain explained the rationale of her proposal in the following terms:

---

13 Ibid., c60GC.

14 Ibid.

15 See HL Deb 29 January 2004 c377: "Amendment No 19:
Page 2, line 10, at end insert – (4) The panel must reject an application under section 1(1) if the panel has issued a gender recognition certificate to the applicant on two previous occasions."

16 Ibid.

17 Ibid.

> My amendment would make it clear that reversal is possible at the same time as limiting a person to only two changes. That would allow a person to change his sex to a woman and then back to a man, or vice versa, but he or she could make no further changes after that. Otherwise, of course, it is possible that person could change back and forth throughout life. That would clearly be ludicrous, not to say very damaging for the person himself or herself. I know the Minister will say that the gender recognition panel will always be terribly sensible and it would never allow that, but we cannot be sure under the current wording. If he thinks a person should not be able to make multiple changes back and forth, he should be prepared to see a limitation placed on the face of the Bill.[18]

Describing multiple gender transitions as "ludicrous" and "damaging," and attempting to limit them, the amendment nevertheless envisaged at least one Gender Recognition Certificate before what, in law, would be a much more final transition than anything hitherto proposed. Lord Filkin replied by once again framing the Gender Recognition Panel's decision as being about ascertaining a person's *commitment* to live permanently in the acquired gender: "[T]he noble Baroness suggested that we should put a provision on the face of the Bill to stop people making changes back and forth. I do not think that is necessary. The panel is there with expertise to make judgments. The central judgment it has to make in this respect is whether it is convinced that the person is committed to living permanently in that gender."[19]

Having appeared twice in House of Lords debates, the logic of gender reversals was to appear again in the House of Commons. During the second reading debate, the issue again took the form of questions about people who might want to "change back" once they had completed the gender recognition process.[20] As Conservative MP Andrew Robathan put it, "I have been listening with great care. I do not applaud the Bill. I think it is the most arrant nonsense. However, will the Minister explain what happens if, after someone has acquired a new gender, they decide that they wish to go back to their previous gender?"[21]

18 Ibid.

19 Ibid., c379.

20 HC Deb 23 February 2004 c53. Later media reports hyped up "concerns" about trans people "having regrets" about surgeries (surgeries are not strictly required for a legal transition under the Act); see, for example, Batty (2004).

21 HC Deb 23 February 2004 c53.

David Lammy (Parliamentary Under Secretary of State for Constitutional Affairs) replied that "a very small minority of people wish to return to their existing gender" and that "[t]he panel will be able to consider that request."[22] Mr Lammy referred to the fact that applicants could make further applications as long as they fulfilled the requirements of the GRA. Later in the debate, the following exchange occurred between Conservative MP Andrew Selous and Lynne Jones, Labour MP and supporter of the Bill:

> AS: [W]hat does she [Lynne Jones] say, in relation to the question of choice, about those people – I gather it may be up to 25 per cent – who subsequently change back to their original gender, or wish to do so?
>
> LJ: Not 25 per cent.
>
> AS: Let us not argue about the percentage; unequivocally, there are some people who change back, which seems to belie the Hon. Lady's argument that there is no choice involved.
>
> LJ: Such cases are extremely rare, and 95 per cent of transitions are very successful. It is a recognised, successful medical procedure for a recognised medical condition … The Bill is about recognising that, after transition, people are in what they see as their correct gender.[23]

Once again, the spectre was raised of a high proportion of people gaining gender recognition in one gender and then wishing to gain recognition in another gender at a later point in life. On both occasions, the Labour MP concerned minimized the possibility of "reversals" either by referring the questioner back to the recognition procedure or by quoting statistics in their favour. Lynne Jones, in particular, used an argument about gaining the "correct" gender through the transition process.

As it was eventually enacted, the "until death" provision in the GRA reads as follows:

> Section 2 GRA: Determination of applications
>
> (1) In the case of an application under section 1(1)(a), the Panel must grant the application if satisfied that the applicant –

22 Ibid.

23 Ibid., c64.

(a) has or has had gender dysphoria,
(b) has lived in the acquired gender throughout the period of two years ending with the date on which the application is made,
(c) *intends to continue to live in the acquired gender until death.* (emphasis added)

"Until death" – resonating, as it does, with marriage or citizenship commitments – can be understood as the technical legal expression for "permanently." Here, the event of death provides a carefully drafted long-stop for legal obligations. However, the explanatory notes eventually attached to the Act use the wording of "continuing" in an acquired gender "for the rest of his or her life," rather than remaining in an acquired gender "until death":

Section 2: Determination of application
14. The criteria for a successful application under *section 1(1)(a)* ("living in the other gender") are set out in *subsection (1):* the applicant must have, or have had, gender dysphoria; have lived in the acquired gender for at least two years before making the application; intend to continue to live in the acquired gender *for the rest of his or her life*; and provide the evidence required by or under *section 3* ...

Section 3: Evidence
17. Under subsection (4), an application must also include a statutory declaration by the applicant, stating that the applicant meets the conditions as to having lived in the acquired gender for at least two years and intending *to continue to do so.* (emphasis added)

What can, or should, be made of the alternative use of the language of life and death in the Act and explanatory notes? Are they to be understood as synonyms, such that continued life can be mapped onto an obligation continuing until death? Yet this is the same legal-political assemblage that cannot simply use the word "permanently" in the legislation despite its appearance in ministerial pronouncements. Definitional precision is usually of utmost practical and professional importance to the lawyers who draft legislation. Shades of expression, such as this, illuminate the plural temporal orders that occupy the hinterlands between legislative drafting and political debate.

As we have seen, the concept of permanence appearing alongside the earliest drafts of the Bill, and which was reasserted in parliamentary debates, came to obviate the logic of multiple reversals advanced by Conservative peers and MPs. The government's emphasis was more on the intention to transition permanently (and the legal technicalities associated with providing evidence of such an intention) than on preventing subsequent applications or achieving gender stasis, as such. This was a kind of open permanence, not defined or even mentioned in the Bill, which could admit more than one legal transition while securing "certainty," and which was "clear" without any further explanation "to lawyers." "Until death" was the technical legal expression of such permanence, occupying the legislation in both draft and final forms, yet in the explanatory notes giving way to another temporal ordering: the expanse of remaining life. Using the logic of permanence, ministers and MPs, acting through distinct means (formal statements, active debate) and in different forums, came to achieve a temporal horizon that was discursively closed (enough), yet technically open. The logic of permanence ratified an interpretation of the legal process that allowed multiple transitions: there would be just enough permanence to achieve just the right amount of certainty.

Documenting Transition

As we have seen, Spade's work has engaged the politics and legal strategies associated with the administrative practice of "Documenting Gender" (Spade 2007). Here, by contrast, I focus on the documenting of gender *transitions*, a concern made relevant by the UK's legal framework of gender reclassification for transgender people. Following the legislative career of permanence, then, we end up with the form that apparently achieves gender transition as a matter of law. Section 3 of the GRA requires an applicant to make and submit a statutory declaration to satisfy the Gender Recognition Panel that he or she intends to live in the acquired gender "until death"; the declaration is positioned on the face of the Act as "evidence" leading to a successful legal transition. By analysing the statutory declaration, we can go beyond the discursive articulation of transitional permanence to encounter the material-documentary dynamics of the legal transition itself and the importance of legal form in its technical sense.

The term "form" can be understood as shape, appearance, and function, on the one hand, and generic or innovated legal technique, on the other. As legal technique, the statutory declaration is a means of asserting the truth of a fact when it is not possible to bring other evidence.

Statutory declarations originated with the Statutory Declarations Act 1835, which provided certain circumstances in which the (then) novel legal form could be substituted for an oath, which previously would have been required. Indeed, the preamble to the Act states that its purpose is to "make Provisions for the Abolition of unnecessary Oaths." Oaths had been controversial from at least the seventeenth century onwards because of their ubiquity, public effects, and invocation of a purely Christian divine power (Condren 2006), and because of a waning belief in their capacity to induce truthful testimony (Shapiro 1983). Throughout the seventeenth century, at a time when metropolitan London became increasingly diverse, English courts prevaricated over whether testimony by Quakers, Jews, Hindus, and black Christians had been correctly taken, or could even be allowed, in a manner that echoed legal debates in the colonies (Macfarlane 2013). By the mid-nineteenth century, oath-taking of many forms (including the swearing of an oath on the New Testament) had become required for many public offices and positions of responsibility to such an extent that atheists, Quakers, Jews, and nonconformists were substantially excluded from public service (Macfarlane 2013).

As indicated by the work of legal historians, the innovation of statutory declarations in English law therefore referenced pressing questions about the status of legal fact and the intricate machineries evolving for establishing "truth" through testimony, all in a context of colonial expansion and migration into London and Enlightenment challenges to concepts of divine power. Following the Statutory Declarations Act, all that was needed was for the declarer to follow the correct form, specified in a schedule to the Act: "I A.B. do solemnly and sincerely declare, that and I make this solemn declaration conscientiously believing the same to be true, and by virtue of the provisions of an Act made and passed in the year of the reign of his present Majesty, intituled 'An Act' *(here insert the title of this Act)*" (schedule 1). Since then, statutory declarations have become a ubiquitous aspect of modern law-making, providing evidence of status and facts in areas as diverse as property law, company law, family law, immigration law, land law, and so on. Like oaths, statutory declarations carry with them a requirement of honesty undergirded by the criminal law of perjury, such that (under the Perjury Act 1911, sec. 5), making a false statement in a statutory declaration carries a prison sentence of up to two years, a fine, or both.

My attempts to obtain an explanation from the Gender Recognition Panel, and elsewhere, for the logic of using the legal form of a statutory declaration in establishing gender permanence proved fruitless,[24] prompting reflection on whether it might be a "belt and braces" technique: the use of secular oaths to undergird what might be considered fragile legal representations about gender. Often, legal knowledge is imagined as existing independently, outside the document or legal technique as such, in the minds of individuals who are representing facts or trying to find out the "truth" of a matter. This is especially true of liberal legal theories of contract, in which, as Marie-Andrée Jacob and Annelise Riles (2007) point out, the necessity of the written contractual document is underplayed, leading to a tendency to look "through" the document itself to the relationship beyond. Similarly, it was tempting to look outside the statutory declaration form itself for the reason for the declaration, especially when little explanation was given for this particular legal form during the legislative "career" of the permanence provision. On such an understanding, law's meaning existed elsewhere in the minds of legislative drafters, policy-makers, and politicians.

But it is also possible that the explanation for the use of statutory declarations remains obscure in legal and policy debates because these declarations are essential, taken for granted, and part of the common ground of certifying legal status. It may be that the declaration, in this legal and material form, requires no (or at least, little) administrative explanation because it is so fundamental to the matter of legalized gender transition that it itself constitutes law or, more specifically, the legal transition. All gender recognition applications are to be determined, in the final instance, by the Gender Recognition Panel, meaning that the formalized gender transition happens at a constructed temporal and bureaucratic distance from the applicant's own form-filling actions. Yet, if all statutory requirements are fulfilled, then the panel must grant the application. Furthermore, the central presence of a statutory declaration, with its considerable legal efficacy and history, within the gender recognition process illuminates the productive force of the applicant's legal actions in the final stages of putting together an application. Far from merely *representing* a declaration about gender, it could be that the statutory declaration, among other things, instantiates the legal gender transition as a matter of documentary practice and, furthermore, the fact that it does this is so widely accepted as to be beyond comment. As legal technique and document, the statutory declaration, then,

24 Author's correspondence with Gender Recognition Panel, June 2014.

might have been given scant attention as a means of securing the "until death" intention because, in each case, it is a vital step to enacting the legal transition, not because it "represents" the law of the transition.

"I intend to live full time as a male/female (delete as appropriate) until death"

How, then, is it possible to understand the means by which documentary gender transitions are secured? At the time of writing, HM Courts & Tribunals Service form T451 instructed readers to complete all sections of the statutory declaration standard template, and it then covered the process required to make a valid declaration for the purposes of the Act. This involved filling in the form, then reading and signing it in front of a witness and someone who was authorized to administer an oath:

> When you have filled in the statutory declaration and you are content that it represents the truth, you need to take it to an officer authorised to administer an oath. You will then need to read and sign the statutory declaration in front of the witness who will sign the document to witness it.
>
> The statutory declaration must be made before a person who is authorised to administer an oath. Examples of people who would be acceptable: a justice of peace, a magistrate, a commissioner for oaths, a practising solicitor, a notary public, a licensed conveyancer, an authorised advocate or an authorised litigator. In Scotland a Councillor can administer an oath.[25]

A range of bureaucratic actions, clustered around the proper completion and administration of a standard form, accompanies the legal declaration of intention to remain in gender "until death" (see also Renz, in progress). By attending to the wording, typeface, and form of the standard declaration published as part of form T450 by the Gender Recognition Panel, we can reflect on the quality of action it invites and the temporal enactments at play. Having traced multiple temporal ontologies in the legislative career of permanence thus far, we come to yet another small, but significant, mutation. The statutory declaration that applicants in fact made, if they used the standard form, was not exactly that required by the Act but slightly different. Applicants declared:

---

25 HM Courts & Tribunals Service T451, "Guidance on Completing the Application Form for a Gender Recognition Certificate."

"I intend to live *full time* as a male/female (*delete as appropriate*) until death" (emphasis added). The words "full time" were added to the standard form statutory declaration, where they were not required by the Act or mentioned in the explanatory notes. Whether or not intended by the panel, the eventual declaration made by any applicant using the standard form was qualitatively, and temporally, distinguishable from the "until death" provision. Is this a tighter type of legal promise about gender transition? "Full time" implies that other declarations about permanence have the capacity to dilly-dally around gender. Quite apart from the question of whether the standard form statutory declaration functions to mobilize the promise envisaged in the Act, it is still possible to argue that it added a further layer of obligation, happening in an alternative temporal frame. "Until death" pitches the applicant into a future circumscribed by finality; "full time" is about the quotidian practice of gender, the lived moment-by-momentness of it, arguably admitting less variation or even ambivalence. Ironically, as a matter of strict legal doctrine, failure to *intend* to live up to the "full-time" gender undertaken in the standard form could (albeit in only very strange circumstances), under the law of statutory declarations, amount to the criminal act of perjury.

The question remains: what kind of legal person was and is envisaged by the statutory declaration? Again the focus here is on material and textual form as much as on its meaning. In her ethnography of transplant practices in the United States and Israel, Jacob looks at consent forms in hospital bureaucracies to discern what is "viewable and viewed easily." As Jacob puts it, "the documented form constitutes the person even more than it retains her traces" (2007, 250). She discovers an aesthetic of consistency, reproduced through printed forms, the use of typography, and attention to ergonomics, that creates its own particular type of individuated "legal person": "[T]he person is predicted to react to forms according to such canons of knowledge that posit the relations between man and machine at the center of their calculations, as if these relations were mechanically foreseeable. That makes for the person to be reified. The person is reified as such not as thing or form, but as individual. In fact, the design and format of the consent form also effectively individuate the person, so that the form can be in sync with the individuated person, separated from context, kin, and relationships" (254). Within a transplant unit in a US hospital, consent forms to treatment are carefully drafted, using cases, typeface, and spacing to catch the reader's attention. Jacob's analysis of hospital consent forms renders visible the dimensions of the "consenting person" within bureaucratic processes oriented to guaranteeing patient safety and administrative transparency. Treatment consent forms, as Jacob argues, putatively construct a self-reliant, individual person, but in using the words "Do not Sign this form without Reading and Understanding its Contents," ultimately require a considerable degree of obedience (255).[26]

In such a way, specific types of legal person are created through and within forms. The immensity of the "full-time" promise contained in the standard form statutory declaration is all the more interesting in this context, given that the material shape of the document requires only constrained interaction from the applicant.[27] Yet the textual dimensions of the document, and the actions associated with it, also perform "folding" work necessary for a gender transition to take place as a matter of law. The applicant is led through quite distinct legal representations via numbered statements. Boxes provide limited space for applicants to enter their name, numerical figures to represent the number of years they have lived full time in their acquired gender, and, if relevant, the date on which a civil partnership or marriage was dissolved (to comply with other extant requirements of the Act, some of which have now changed) (Renz, in progress). As concerns the "until death" declaration, all that is required of the applicant is the act of deleting a word in "male/female," before signing, dating, and completing information about where the declaration took place.

Riles focuses on a moment when gender was bracketed out of the proceedings of the Beijing conference on women in 1995. In her analysis, brackets framed time and marked institutional progress (or lack of it): "For the delegates working within the brackets, time and institutional progress (bureaucratic analysis) were bound together like partners in a three-legged race. The bracket was both a unit of time and a unit of organizational gridlock" (2006a, 82). In the standard form statutory declaration, brackets around the "delete as appropriate" injunction help to instantiate a very specific kind of legal temporality: the transition. In other words, the brackets, and their contents, are productive: they mark

26 Yet Jacob's discovery of an illegible consent form in an Israeli hospital provides a no less interesting view, indicating at one point a "frail belief" in documents and bureaucracy and a consent process in which the aesthetic dimensions of the form were not believed to impinge on the quality of consent (2007, 263).

27 On the interactions between humans and forms, see Riles (2006b, 2011).

the point of bureaucratic action at which a peculiarly mundane textual instruction prompts what we might term, following the discussion in Chapter One, the "folding" action that leads to a change in legal status. A solemn undertaking to live in one's acquired gender "full time" and "until death" is achieved by the stroke of a pen: a line through one word (the "old" gender) and not the other (the "acquired" gender). In this way, transition is achieved as a matter of legal technique through human engagement with documents.

Transition as Legal Thing

When we discuss the legal assemblages associated with gender transitions, there is much to be gained by strategically analysing law on its own terms. Gayle Salamon (2010) has suggested that, in bureaucratic engagements with sex designations, sex is enacted through documentation and becomes a property of the state itself. In a similar vein, I have argued that tracing the technicalities of gender recategorization requires sustained attention, at some stage, to bureaucratic rationalities and their material accomplices. The result of the GRA's reliance on transition is that gender is legally produced *as if it is sex* – as if it has been binaristic all along, amenable to particular forms of transubstantiation, rather than expressing gender fluidity as such. Shifts in legal status, legal technicalities, and temporal mechanisms are key to this story. Once transgender social and political issues were conceptualized as a matter of formal gender recategorization, statutory declarations assumed a central role in the gender recognition process. They now constitute transition, with its many effects on transgender people, as a legal matter: the subject of legal intervention, requiring specific documentary techniques and methods of enactment. In such a way, temporalities such as transition come to be materialized through the legal documentary practices we see in statutory declaration forms, for example.

If, as Salamon suggests, sex, or in our case gender, becomes the property of the state, the question remains how, and through what means? In Chapter One, we encountered the work of anthropologists who are trying to trouble distinctions between concepts and objects in such a way that taking on board a new object or thing might also mean accessing new worlds. The work of Martin Holbraad and colleagues raises the ethnographic "problem" of powerful powder as a means of exploring, through our relationship with objects, the alterity that anthropological research produces and the necessity of imagining "many worlds" (Henare, Holbraad, and Wastell 2007, 12). With this in mind, it is useful to admit how much we do not know about a legal "thing" that is so intensely familiar in the gender recognition process as to be almost beyond comment: the statutory declaration form. Encountering this legal thing anew, focusing on its material form as well as its legal meaning and effects, it is necessary to take seriously what the form does, legally, bureaucratically, and for the state. When the legislation states that this form, correctly completed and witnessed, is evidence of intention to live in an acquired gender "until death," the form should give us access to new legal-temporal worlds, as much as meanings. Accepting the ontological status of the form, it may well be that statutory declarations materialize not (or not only) the acquired gender status of the newly transitioned legal person, but the *transition itself*. In such a way, "thinking through things," as Holbraad and colleagues urge us to do, gives rise to encounters with new temporal, as well as material, orders. The document is the transition; the transition is a legal "thing."

Chapter Five

Balance

In today's society, both men and women want to find a balance between work, family and caring responsibilities.

– UK Department for Business, Innovation and Skills

[R]elatively recent "work-life balance" public conversations perpetuate the mystification of the colonization of time by focusing on the actions of isolated individuals, rather than situating the individual in the structural, or political-economic reality that most constrains their ability to achieve such a balance.

– Nichole Shippen, *Colonizing Time*

Sometimes the [railway signalling] box had to be left unmanned.

– *Network Rail Infrastructures v Gammie*

In May 2011, on the back of a pro-"austerity" platform, the United Kingdom's centre-right coalition government announced a new consultation on reforming work-life balance laws. Entitled *Modern Workplaces*, the consultation was pitched as an effort to "create a modern workforce for the modern economy" (United Kingdom 2011). Self-consciously aware of perceived shifts in the gendered arrangements of work and care, the consultation contained extensive proposals to change the administration of maternity and paternity leave, allowing "mothers" and "fathers" to share leave between them. Significantly, in what might appear to be a bold and progressive move, the government proposed expanding the availability of the current right to request flexible work, making it available to all employees, regardless of whether they have a care obligation. These measures are now contained in the Children and Families Act 2014.

It might be surprising that, at a time of redundancies and public sector cuts, a centre-right government expanded employees' rights to negotiate flexible working patterns within the paradigm of work-life balance.[1] Yet, for the past two decades, legal solutions to unpaid care in the United Kingdom have been strongly connected to the goal of labour market flexibility. Successive UK governments, as well as EU institutions, have argued that encouraging negotiations at the level of the workplace enables the labour market to better manage fluctuations in demand and changes in business models (Ashiagbor 2006; Conaghan and Rittich 2005). Within recent policy statements and debates in Parliament, this capacity to withstand fluctuations has been positioned as a strength and, crucially, as a key means of ensuring economic growth in a time of crisis. Specifically, the coalition government took the step of linking balance and flexible work with reducing the deficit and achieving economic growth, as the following passage from the *Modern Workplaces* consultation document makes clear: "For employees, flexible working allows them to better balance their work life with their family responsibilities. In today's society, both men and women want to find a balance between work, family and caring responsibilities. Flexible working therefore has the potential to increase overall levels of participation in the labour market, and so make a contribution to increasing employment and decreasing benefit dependency and thus ultimately to reducing the deficit and promoting growth" (United Kingdom 2011, 33).

"Balance" has preoccupied feminist perspectives on labour regulation for at least two decades. Yet coming as they have done in the midst of wide-ranging cuts in public services, redundancies, and changes to the welfare benefits system, recent reforms, including changes to flexible work, have inspired considerable scepticism among feminists. Flexible work mechanisms remain extremely hard for those in precarious work to access because they overwhelmingly require people to hold employment status to claim rights. This requirement is particularly difficult in a context in which so-called "zero hours contracts" and other so-called nonstandard jobs have become much more prevalent (Fredman 2004), leading some commentators to write of the emergence of a new class of disenfranchised workers, the "precariat" (Standing 2011). Furthermore, these measures also retain other, time-related, eligibility requirements, such as the requirement for twenty-six weeks' work before claiming a

1 See regulation 3 of the Flexible Working Regulations 2014/1398.

right, which have put the new expanded right to request flexible work out of the reach of many working in precarious working arrangements (Grabham, in draft b; Grabham and Smith 2010).

This chapter investigates work-life balance and flexible work as regulatory ideals and legal-temporal artefacts. Measures relating to balance and flexibility contribute to a range of feminist political strategies, disruptions, and events that have attempted to stretch dominant understandings of clock time and to map apparently invisible or unpaid activities by women onto legible units of productive days, minutes, and hours. Gaining access to key economic and political paradigms and systems of measurement has been one aim of this temporal reframing (Adkins 2009b). Other strategies have included demands such as wages for housework (Costa and James 1973), arguments for a compressed workweek (Schultz 2010), and proposals for governments to act as the "employer of last resort" (ELR) (Alessandrini 2014). Together, such strategies have had extremely useful, if contentious, effects in providing practical articulations of feminist concerns with the normative production of value (Alessandrini 2014; Federici 2012; Weeks 2011).

Work-life balance measures, conceived through legal and policy responses to what feminists argue is the unequal allocation and valuation of care, can in some senses be understood as temporal "provocations" (Alessandrini 2014). They challenge some versions of chrono-normativity to the extent that they contest gendered times of work: a working day, the argument goes, which is facilitated by women's social reproduction (Adkins 2009b). Unlike wages for housework campaigns, however, work-life balance rhetoric and practices have enjoyed a relatively high degree of legal and policy legitimacy. Due to their mobilization through negotiation and contractual bargaining, they have left intact current arrangements of work and care in a way that wages for housework or ELR proposals arguably would not permit (Alessandrini 2014), and they are positioned as more achievable and pragmatic as a result. Nevertheless, these apparently progressive legal measures are grounded on specific understandings of the time of social reproduction that are being tested within conditions found in the so-called "new economy" (Adkins 2009a). Furthermore, if allocated only to some classes of women and not others, or if mobilized in economic circumstances in which care is increasingly privatized back into families through government austerity policies, work-life balance mechanisms also have the potential to buttress chrono-normative family, care, and poverty patterns.

A genealogy (de Goede 2005, 108) of work-life balance as a sociotechnical mechanism therefore might trace the interaction of labour activism, feminist conceptions of and challenges to the politics of social reproduction, time-use surveys, and sex discrimination laws and policies in the creation of contemporary social policy goals of equilibrium and adaptation. In the first instance, however, analysing the technical legal measures and policy horizons in this area for the relations they assume and create also requires clearing space for the nonhuman as well as the human actors involved in creating the legal temporalities associated with labour market solutions to the care dilemma. The idea of "balancing" work and care through flexibility has become so embedded in labour regulation conversations and in political and cultural life that it is difficult to think outside of the paradigm, even when analysing it. Yet such legitimacy and ubiquity also make it necessary to bring these temporal rationalities into sharper focus, tracing their material instantiation. For these reasons, among many others, scholars interested in labour regulation might think about expanding our account of who and what acts in the service of labour rights, reflecting on how nonhuman actors, and diverse relationships within assemblages, change our understanding of the status of law.

In this chapter, I take a couple of steps towards such an analysis, focusing in particular on balance's associated legal technicalities and the role of what Ron Levi (2009) terms "material forms": registering the effects of such forms on the legal operation of precedent in flexible work cases, for example, as well as understanding the temporal horizons and functions of flexible work laws. The first section focuses on balance, suggesting that we conceptualize its political ideals and temporal form through Jane Bennett's work on material-human assemblages. Subsequent sections engage in more depth with the time-brewing legal technicalities associated with balance: flexible work requests, and the things that come to act in relationship with people in legal disputes. The final substantive section focuses on the materializing temporalities of the common law practice of precedent. Reflecting on precedent's material dimensions, we can understand much more about how flexibility is created and patterned in relationships of legal decision-making. Focusing on the constitution of legal temporalities brings us back to the political stakes of analysing and "doing" time. As temporal modes, balance and flexibility are neither cohesive nor inherently politically desirable. They are legally achieved through a range of measures and relationships, which themselves have variegated social effects and political consequences. The politics, in other words, is in the practices and relationships, human and nonhuman, as much as in the overarching temporal orientations that we choose to identify as significant policy concerns.

Balance

It is tempting to understand working time and its associated techniques of management and modes of resistance as happening within one overarching ontological temporality: the linear time of the moderns that we encountered in Chapter One. Specifically, the idea of work-life balance encourages us to think of labour happening *in time,* instead of labour and its associated projects of regulation having their own ontologies and temporalizing effects. Feminists have long argued that time spent on care or domestic work is equally valuable to, or productive of, time spent in the formal economy. These arguments have reoriented dominant androcentric constructions of working time, but do not always allow for a praxiographic approach to time as such. In other words, it is possible to maintain an approach to time that works within the linear time of the moderns, parcelling up or comparing different experiences of time, even within feminist critiques of the working day and the working week.

Work-life balance is one logical extension of this approach: if time that has been excluded is to be included in some way, then it must be analogized. As the foreword to the *Modern Workplaces* consultation puts it: "We want to create a society where work and family complement one another. One where employers have the flexibility and certainty to recruit and retain the skilled labour they need to develop their businesses. And one where employees no longer have to choose between a rewarding career and a fulfilling home life" (United Kingdom 2011, 2). The horizon of this kind of temporality is not so much the kind of hedgeable future, constructed through notions of risk, that we find in, for example, many areas of financial practice and regulation (de Goede 2005), but an expanded and reckonable present that stretches outwards and maintains equilibrium through analogizing labour of (apparently) different types. If women experience time stress due to conflicting demands of social reproduction and paid work, the argument goes, these can be reconciled within the natural time of the day and the week, through mechanisms that reallocate activities in time.

Analysing time otherwise means engaging with the variegated means by which temporalities, including legal temporalities such as balance and flexibility, are brewed. Such an approach brings with it various material shades of agency in assemblages of humans and nonhumans alongside the conscious actions of working women and bureaucrats engaged in projects of labour regulation, for example. Jane Bennett's account of the 2003 electricity blackout in the United States and Canada references what she terms the conative effects of "a volatile mix of coal, sweat, electromagnetic fields, computer programs, electron streams, profit motives, heat, lifestyles, nuclear fuel, plastic, fantasies of mastery, static, legislation, water, economic theory, wire, and wood – to name just some of the actants" (2010, 25). It is not just that in this assemblage we might discern the actions and effects of electricity industry workers, or that their actions are part of this complex and shifting assemblage, which is legal as much as anything else. It is that what we term "blackout" is the result of all these things.

What if we were to take a similar approach to "balance" and "flexibility," strategically detaching these legal temporalities from the time of the moderns and tracing their complex material instantiations? Bennett refers to assemblages as "living, throbbing confederations that are able to function despite the persistent presence of energies that confound them from within," which have "uneven topographies" and the effects of which are just as much down to the agency of the assemblage as to its members as such (2010, 23–4). What, in other words, if we were to understand work-life balance as a legal assemblage or confederation, comprising clusters of rights, bureaucratic logics, legal technicalities, material actors, and legal principles (such as precedent), that have distinct temporalizing effects? In such a way, legal temporalities could be traced as the emergent properties not merely of specific legal techniques and relationships, but also of the assemblage acting as "open ended collective" (24).

Work-life balance policies have provided routes for successive UK governments to address the perceived tensions brought about by women's increased entry into paid work (Conaghan 2004). Yet they have many critics. It is often argued, for example, that feminist scholarship and activism on social reproduction have not been mobilized in effective ways through legal and policy interventions on work-life balance, or that balance and flexibility have not sufficiently redrawn the conceptual paradigms of labour regulation. Despite the potential of associated legal initiatives to upset norms of care and work, feminist labour lawyers point out that these mechanisms have instead reasserted gender roles within the family and in work, and have reified the position of women as the key agents for performing the "reconciliation" of work and family life (Conaghan and Rittich 2005; Fudge and Owens 2006). Legal and policy work-life balance measures have operated within an ideological matrix of family, household, and market relationships that reproduces racialized labour dynamics (Lung 2010). The archetypal family intended to benefit from work-life balance policies is middle to high income (Williams 2005) and heteronormative, even as attempts to recognize alternative family forms have become apparent on the face of some legislative reforms (Conaghan and Grabham 2007). In promoting "gender-sharing" or roles for fathers in care, furthermore, work-life balance and flexible work goals can also be positioned among policies that increasingly attempt to restructure normative heterosexuality to maintain a concept of privatized social reproduction, instead of working towards a more critical or transformative approach to the governance of care (Bedford 2009).

Balance has been presented as an alternative to "pendulum politics," in which political initiatives lurch between engagement in the labour market, on the one hand, and care, health, "well-being," or religion, on the other (Lister 2002). The idea is that, if workers have sufficient control over flexibility, then they can achieve equal distribution of unpaid and paid work between men and women. This is a very common view, especially within UK academic and policy literatures, and it effectively positions "balance" as the goal of so-called family-friendly policies. The Government Equalities Office, for example, stated in 2010 that "[d]ifferent individuals and families will have different ideas of the balance they would like to strike, but it is important that everyone has the opportunity to find an arrangement which suits them, their family and their employer" (United Kingdom 2010, 24). And the UK statutory equalities body, the Equality and Human Rights Commission, while more explicit about the gender issues involved, has also positioned balance as a core concern: "women, who now represent almost half of the workforce, face difficult and loaded choices over how they balance career and care, and all too often pay a penalty for the choices they make" (United Kingdom 2009, 6).

In particular, the UK regulatory paradigm of work-life balance, a result of many different influences, seems to be driven by a fundamental assumption that disequilibrium in labour markets and economic spheres can be resolved through liberal techniques of contract and contracting. As such, balance has been co-articulated with social and legal ideals of contractual negotiation, compromise, and resolution. Given critiques by feminist legal scholars of the foundational liberal principles of contract (Mulcahy and Wheeler 2005), it is worth maintaining some critical purchase on these close heuristic and conceptual connections. The aspirational language around balance fits easily into the contractual underpinnings of the employment relationship: workers and employers can achieve harmonious relations through bargaining over labour time, flexibility, and remuneration. Such language also evokes feminist critiques of social contract theories, in which men's social and political participation in work is enabled by women's unpaid labour (Adkins 2008). To some extent, therefore, both liberal approaches to contract, and feminist perspectives critical of these approaches, recreate an underlying concept of equilibrium, a state in which either workers and employers agree terms through contractual negotiation or, by contrast, the social contract dynamics through which women's unpaid labour subsidizes formal economic structures are made clear and challenged.

In recent UK parliamentary debates about new work-life balance measures in the Children and Families Bill, government ministers adopted the rhetoric of flexible work as economic strategy. Edward Timpson, Parliamentary Under Secretary of State for Children and Families, put it as follows: "We believe that supporting strong families and introducing flexible working practices is key to achieving business and economic growth. A new system of shared parental leave will support business by creating a more motivated, flexible and talented work force. Flexible working will also help widen the pool of talent in the labour market, helping to drive growth."[2] Government policy statements of this type position work-life balance and flexible working as contributing to two significant economic policy goals: economic growth and deficit reduction. Specifically, the coalition government's rationale appears to have been that flexibilizing working relations, allowing employees some leeway in determining their own working hours and working arrangements through contractual negotiations, brings "talented" people into workplaces, creates opportunities, promotes economic activity, and assists in the creation of growth in the new economy. The logic of such a move is neatly aligned with market-oriented approaches to labour regulation, in which rational actors negotiate their own optimum terms and conditions. Yet this idea of the market is also infused with an understanding of social reproduction that positions the resolution of the care

2 HC Deb 25 February 2013 c49.

dilemma as a key means of promoting economic growth. Within such a paradigm, women's participation in value-creating practices is facilitated so that they can accumulate and exchange labour and contribute to a growing economy (Adkins 2008). In this way, the motivating logic of the *Modern Workplaces* consultation and associated legal reforms in the Children and Families Act 2014 blends concepts of value production found in Fordist conceptions of labour with feminist critiques of the social contract, and with neoliberal market ideals to create a specific strand of socio-technical temporality: the idea of balance as a solution to a care dilemma.

"Doubting Properly"

If concepts in financial life, such as "real time," create and require instantaneous adjustments (de Goede 2005), then work-life balance requires flexibility, understood as adaptive negotiation. Flexibility is achieved as the subject and mechanism of labour policy through particular legal forms and technicalities. Specifically, in the United Kingdom, it is achieved through statutory provisions empowering employees to negotiate flexible working time with their employers through private law mechanisms in the employment contract. In this section, I trace one example of the temporalizing effects of these hybrid statutory/private law mechanisms, reflecting once again on the significance of legal form in co-producing time. The right to request flexible working in the United Kingdom's Employment Rights Act 1996 allows employees to make a request to alter their working schedule or other terms. Prior to the reforms to employment law brought about through the Children and Families Act, employers were under a legal obligation to follow a prescribed statutory *process* of considering such a request. My argument here is that the particularly temporalized dimensions of the legislated process were oriented towards building bureaucratic trust in a certain form of privatization, or regulatory unwinding, of care-related dilemmas back into the employer-employee relationship. The Children and Families Act altered the process, requiring only "reasonable" consideration of the request on the part of employers. These might appear to be merely technical changes and not worthy of further analysis, but the shifting legal-temporal mechanisms associated with considering flexibility requests have much to say about the enactment of regulatory approaches to unpaid care.

Sections 80F–I of the Employment Rights Act 1996, then, give employees a legislated, procedural right to request a change in their contracted terms and conditions to enable them to better accommodate child care. Such changes can include alterations to working hours (allowing an employee to begin later or leave earlier for the school run) or place of work. What was (and still is) interesting about the flexible working provisions in UK labour law is that they provide a statutory right to negotiate new contractual terms and conditions, something the employment contract purports to require or allow in any case. In others words, the right to request flexible work is a right to do what parties might usually be expected to do under the employment contract itself: negotiate and agree new terms as circumstances change.

Contracting is generally significant in labour regulation to the extent that the employment contract provides the paradigmatic legal means of understanding and regulating the individual relationship between employers and employees, as well as a home for enhanced legal rights provided by statute.[3] Employment contracts are usually understood as the source of both express (explicitly agreed) and implied obligations for both parties; in other words, they govern what employers and employees should, and should not, do. A further key principle and function of employment contracts is that terms are negotiated, and once they have been agreed to (or implied by the courts), a breach of any term will give rise to a legal remedy, such as a monetary award for damages.[4]

Many orders and valences of contract are at play in the articulation of balance as a social policy concern, measure, and socio-technical artefact. When we talk about "contracting," we can refer to the process of coming to a legal agreement governed by the formal principles of private law, or to a more informal agreement. In a different register, we might also refer to the dynamics by which people are taken by diseases or illnesses: contracting as "catching" refers to a process of incorporation or transmission – contagion even (Mitropoulos 2012, 18). As it is mobilized in labour market and economics discourses, work-life balance works in both registers: it resolves larger-scale disequilibrium through transmissive dynamics of private law bargaining. As a "proliferating" contractual genre (following Mitropoulos), balance helps place dilemmas of social reproduction within the constructed scale of macroeconomic

---

3 Many rights are available only to the privileged status of "employee," so the limits of employment status also function as the limits of employment protection.

4 Interacting with the employment contract are other sources of labour rights, such as statutory equality rights and collective agreements.

and labour market regulation. Indeed, the ubiquity of contractual techniques and logics within conversations about work-life balance provides a useful example of what Máiréad Enright and Illan rua Wall term the "public life of private law," or the proliferation of private law mechanisms into a wider range of hitherto "public" or "state" roles.[5]

More specifically for our purposes here, successive groups of ministers and bureaucrats in the Department for Business, Innovation and Skills (and equivalent departments over time), as well as legislative drafters, have relied on contractual mechanisms in creating, through the right to request, a responsibilizing system of negotiations between employers and employees. Through this system of negotiations, actions of autonomous and self-interested market participants are positioned as creating beneficial or self-correcting economic effects at the level of the labour market as a whole. The right to request flexible work does not amount to a direct right as between parties granted by legislation for an employee to *receive* a flexible working arrangement as such. It depends on a further step, the request, which mobilizes something akin to a private law process in which the role of the employer is central.

In the context of parental leave, an entitlement to unpaid time off to care (instead of flexible work, as such), the coalition government raised the goal of the "state getting out of the way" (United Kingdom 2011, 2), a clearing away of bureaucratic involvement so that privatized social actors could resolve workplace and care tensions on their own, and it is arguable that a similar logic has long structured the arm's-length nature of the right to request itself. The right to request flexible work itself evidences a wish to disentangle bureaucratic involvement, or to keep it apart from a market that is perceived to have self-regulating functions; but it does so in quite a distinct way. This is a context in which the legislated mode of action (the right to request flexible work) is, on the usual principles of contract law, not needed to achieve the outcome of negotiation that forms a key aspect of the socio-technical strategy. In other words, you do not need to legislate to give people rights to negotiate under their employment contracts: contract law provides those rights in any case, subject to certain limitations and conditions. On the usual principles of private law governing employment relationships in

5 See "The Political in the Contract Classroom"; available online at http://publicprivatelaw.wordpress.com/2013/09/17/the-political-in-the-contract-classroom/, accessed 5 September 2014.

the United Kingdom, an employee normally would be able at least to *commence* negotiations about flexible work. Contracts are always potentially negotiable and variable, with the other party's consent.[6] Anyone wishing to vary, say, their working hours would not necessarily have to resort to the legal route provided in the Employment Rights Act 1996 to do so; they could simply make a request for contractual variation.

As such, the right to request could evidence a weak bureaucratic trust in private law itself. If a route already exists in the form of the employment contract, why legislate at all, if not to shore this up? Sections 80F–I of the Employment Rights Act, on this approach, duplicate and enhance normal contractual principles, but within a framework of legislated rights. This could evidence some belief on the part of bureaucrats that the current legal paradigm needs patching up with a different type of legal mechanism. Either that, or creating a right over an already-existing legal relationship, which could achieve the same outcome, also has a performative and pragmatic function, instantiating a bureaucratic commitment to achieving "balance," worthy of interrogation on its own terms.

We are back to the question, however, of where any pragmatic function in such a measure might reside. Although it responsibilizes legal actors in the sphere of flexible work negotiations, this type of legal technicality is not deregulation in the usual sense. Instead, it is a more specific (statutory) right to do something that has been envisaged in another legal register (contract). The right leaves the usual contractual employment relations intact, but provides remedies if employers stray too far from the bounds of acceptable business reasoning, and a specific process for asserting this new hybrid through employment tribunals.

In other words, the private law of employment already perceives a certain degree of self-governing action. Prior to the changes brought about by the Children and Families Act 2014, what the right to request

6 And with consideration. In private law, consideration is something of value (including a promise to act or not to act) given by one party to another and is vital to the creation or lawful variation of a contract. This is significant because, without the employer's agreement and fresh consideration, any employee simply proceeding to vary their own working hours without agreement could, in theory, find themselves in breach of contract. The employer's remedies for this, depending on the seriousness of the breach and whether the employer suffered any loss, could include dismissal and/ or an action for damages (the latter claim is not often taken by employers against employees, except in situations where an employee is highly paid or key to a business).

added was the obligation on the part of the employer to consider a request in a *particular manner*, with specific stages of deliberation and a timeframe for the decision. These deliberative stages and their associated temporalities were not strictly required for negotiation under the private law of the employment contract. Responding to the relative differences in bargaining power held by employer and employee, the legal form chosen, then, was an inducement for employers not to *vary* the contract, as such, but to *engage in temporally structured negotiations* to vary. The legislated right to request mimicked the negotiation that in any case could be found in the employment contract, but imposed specific temporal requirements, something which contract law cannot easily provide. This was a legislated route to a particular, temporally delimited, sequence of actions.

What the flexible work request process added, in other words, was time. More specifically, the right to request temporalized the private law response to negotiations at the interface of social reproduction and work. As such, flexible working rights could have been defined as a type of regulatory "unwinding" (after Riles 2011) or the creation of responsible market actors as a way of managing risk. This is because bureaucratic preoccupations about balance and flexibility were achieved by imagining a new kind of self-regulating practice between employers and employees. But the point is that this practice was only "new" because of its temporal qualities. In fact, the rigid, legislated temporal requirements might suggest a failure to allow parties fully to privatize the deliberations. The process began with an employee's filling in a flexible working request form (or similar document) and submitting it to his or her employer. The employer then had to call a meeting within twenty-eight days to discuss the form, and had to make a decision about the request within fourteen days of the meeting. Employers could refuse requests only for business reasons outlined in the Employment Rights Act, for example, if the new working pattern would adversely affect quality and performance, impose extra costs that would damage the business, affect the business's ability to meet customer demand, if the employee would not have any work to do during the suggested working hours, and so on. If the employer refused a request on incorrect facts or for a reason not listed in section 80G of the Employment Rights Act, the employee could make a complaint to an employment tribunal for reconsideration of the original application or compensation.

The logic of the first part of this process encouraged something akin to the modulated suspension of certainty that Latour observed in his ethnography of the French Conseil d'État, characterized through periods, the exchange of documents, and the apparent open-minded deliberation of the decision-maker (here, the employer). Latour describes the process through the conseil as epitomizing what, in commonsense terms, would be defined as the "slowness of law." Yet, as he points out, these distancing procedures are required to ensure that the law "has doubted properly" (2004, 94). Having suspended certainty – and, indeed, actively fabricated doubt – a curious completeness takes over law: homeostasis, a type of all-encompassing, self-adjusting temporality (113), produced through a multitude of adjustments and changes in pace. From the present (postjudgment) vantage point, the legal principle confirmed through proceedings at the Conseil is as it has always been.

In our case, according to the previous version of the right to request, the employer had to make a decision about a flexible work request within fourteen days of the meeting. At this stage of the legal proceedings, the decision was final, and resulted in either new contractual provisions or the reassertion of the old contract. In fact, once the new form of the contract existed, the dilemmas that motivated the negotiations under the old contract became impossible to mobilize legally. The new-contract/right-to-request hybrid, here, operated only in sequence and not in synchrony: contractual provisions, once renegotiated, were only "new" or "old," never both.

This was definitely not flexibility in the normal sense of the word. The legislated right to request only provided flexibility to shift to a new permanent working regime and no guarantee, on the face of it, to shift back or shift again when required. This technical legal mechanism could be exercised only once every twelve months, as is still the case. As such, the employer's deliberation, the employee's submission to periods of time and form-filling, and the all-encompassing time of the new contract all contributed to an understanding of the flexible work request as inaugurating a type of regulatory unwinding, through which working arrangements could, at maximum, be renegotiated every twelve months, but with no guarantee that requested changes would be agreed to and with the proviso that newly negotiated arrangements might be with the employee for the remainder of his or her time with this employer.

What does it mean, then, that the process of considering requests for flexible working was later altered? Following the Children and Families Act, the temporalized statutory process was repealed and replaced with a duty on employers merely to consider requests in a "reasonable" manner, supplemented with a Code of Practice encouraging employers to respond to requests "promptly."[7] If anything, the assumption could be that, through the newly instantiated "reasonable" employer, flexible work requests were even further privatized and deregulated to a sphere even further away from bureaucratic control or concern. At least with the statutory mechanism of periods and deadlines, the right to request exerted some purchase over what, essentially, were contractual deliberations. But the introduction of "reasonableness" raises significant questions now as to what exactly the right to request adds to contract law that would not otherwise have been possible. By removing time-related requirements from the face of the legislation, the distinctive nature of this innovated and hybrid legal form, the right to request, might have been undermined. In this way, the shifting use of legal-temporal technicalities can mark shifting bureaucratic preoccupations with regulatory burdens and their management through distinct legal registers (contract, statute, for example).

If there is some bureaucratic doubt about the extent to which the previous version of the right to request effectively privatized the responsibility of achieving balance, then the detailed and highly temporalized requirements of the deliberation process provided reassurance. A modulated suspension of certainty ensured that the employer doubted properly, reconstituting human action within the universal, forward-marching ontological time of the moderns. Similarly, the epistemological horizon of doubt, which flexible work deliberations created, positioned the employer within the overarching world of linear time through which human actors could project forward and attempt to manage uncertainty. But the doubt was achieved through mundane, bureaucratic, temporalizing practices. Through these practices, bureaucratic trust in privatized negotiations was fortified and obligations apparently could shift regulatory scale from state to private actor. These legal mechanisms together recreated a sense of time passing irreversibly, which, as we saw in Chapter One, Latour terms a classificatory device of the moderns. Time, as a constructed technique of governing, mediated bureaucratic engagements with care, work, and the private law of the employment contract. Achieved through such legal techniques, flexibility thus appeared irreversible. Further than that, however, in aiming for "balance," legal flexibility appeared to recreate a thoroughly

7 See Employment Rights Act 1996, s80(G)(1)(a); and ACAS (2014).

modern ontology of forward-marching time. It is yet to be seen whether the new "reasonableness" obligation will have similar effects.

Flexible Things

The story so far, therefore, has legal technique acting in service of the time of the moderns. In this account, legal innovations such as the flexible work request play small but tangible roles in recreating specific strands of overarching time. Yet if flexibility is a legal technique that appears to recreate the idea of forward-marching time, then we might question who and what acts in relation to this technique. As Latour would have it, the Enlightenment story distinguishes between culture and "nature," and places human action within natural time. Greenhouse speaks of the bureaucrat with the hourglass starting and stopping time (1996, 22) as a means of referencing essential shifts in understanding time's significance to divine and human power, and the consequences this has for understanding liberal governance. By adopting alternative approaches to temporalization, we could think about the conative effects of flexible work negotiation practices, through which relationships between human and nonhuman actors sort or brew new ontologies, not merely new *experiences*, of time. Genres of modern time – for example, the forward-marching time of the flexible work request – can be counted as part of these newly brewed ontologies. They are created just as much by relationships between human and nonhuman actors as they are sustained by lived human experience and thought, or by "nature."

In this section, I analyse how things co-produce legal genres of flexibility through, among other practices, the operation of precedent. Taking moments when the apparently smooth negotiation of flexible work breaks down, in legal "cases," I focus on the human-nonhuman relationships involved. Furthermore, taking case reports themselves seriously, for their world-making effects, I analyse the patterning of legal things through precedent and its effects on legal-temporal orders of flexibility.

Flexibility populates labour regulation with an array of images, ideas, and effects. One of the most influential anthropological texts on the significance of flexibility in Western culture, Emily Martin's classic study in *Flexible Bodies* (1994), traces the emergence of a strong immune system as the epitome of embodied flexibility over the 1980s and 1990s. The immune system, according to Martin's interviewees, constantly changes to anticipate and respond to challenges; it is a perpetual-motion machine that produces specific antibodies to fit specific viruses (1994, 79–80) and whose flexible qualities have become more apparent in an age of just-in-time production. Martin finds that trends in the ways that management consultants and human resources specialists imagine good, functioning businesses coexist and overlap with the ways in which a wide range of scientists and activists imagine healthy, functioning bodies. In both cases, businesses and organic systems anticipate threat and adapt to change; they are constantly in flux, constantly at the ready for new problems and new opportunities. Flexibility within labour discourse is very similar: it requires organizations and labouring bodies to adapt, stretch, and contain. Employees are expected to cope with altered shifts and even with vastly new working patterns, such as "zero hours" contracts. Businesses are expected to retain staff by offering them working arrangements to accommodate child care and health appointments. All of these requirements are based on connected ideas of risk management and the entrepreneurial exploitation of opportunities.

These perspectives help us to think about how genres of flexibility have emerged in distinct areas of clinical and social life. In this sense, flexibility is not just a quality of human activity that can become the subject of law; it is co-produced as a legal artefact through relationships between legal technicalities, documents, and bureaucratic action. Working through case reports concerning flexible work disputes from the period from 2001 to 2010, it becomes apparent that things – "material forms" (Levi 2009) – have significant effects on the clusters of events and problems that become legal scenarios, as well as on the legal framing that leads to a decision.[8] The reports I found in this project cover a wide range of situations: the teacher who requested a daylight shift to

8 The decisions I analyse are those of employment tribunals, the Employment Appeal Tribunal, the Court of Appeal, and the House of Lords (now the Supreme Court) issued between 2001 and 2010 on issues of equality-related flexibility arguments. Employment-related cases are heard first in a local employment tribunal and can be appealed (on a point of law only) to the Employment Appeal Tribunal, the Court of Appeal, and finally the Supreme Court. The case reports all deal with UK-level decisions. I specifically have left out decisions of the European Court of Justice and the European Court of Human Rights so as to focus on UK-decided cases. I located the cases by searching on the widely used legal search engine Westlaw, using terms that have become prevalent in substantive equality law. For example, to yield cases on disability discrimination and scheduling, I searched, among other things, "'flexible working' AND 'reasonable adjustment'"; for sex discrimination cases, I searched, among others, "'flexible working' AND 'indirect discrimination.'"

help her cope with deteriorating vision;[9] the warehouse assistant who was refused flexible working to help her look after her grandchild, who lived with her;[10] the father who took one day off work to look after his son and was disciplined for absenteeism.[11] Tribunals considered a variety of requests for flexible or part-time work, including claims, respectively, by two police officers, a hairdressing tutor, a legal secretary, two lawyers, a recruitment manager, a pilot, an information technology specialist, an administrator, a sales executive, an airport check-in worker, a railway signalling operator, a sales assistant, and a Royal Navy employee.[12] It should be obvious to most readers familiar with critical approaches to law that relying on reports is usually a poor representation of legal problems and the way they are resolved "in context." Yet my focus on them has a specific aim: that of considering form as well as representation in law, and I will return to this point shortly.

Ron Levi's (2009) study proceeds through case searches oriented at tracing where gated communities emerged in legal decisions, in order to displace what he terms the "law first" approach to material objects, and I understand this strategy. In my study of case reports, by contrast, I aimed at picking out diverse instantiations of flexibility and their associated legal-material assemblages. Although the dilemmas in the reported cases ostensibly revolve around human disagreements and

---

9 *Meikle v Nottinghamshire County Council* (2005) ICR 1.

10 *Commotion Ltd v Rutty* (2006) ICR 290.

11 *New Southern Railway Ltd (formerly South Central Trains Ltd) v Rodway* (2005) ICR 1162.

12 See, respectively, *Chief Constable of Avon & Somerset Constabulary v Ms A Chew* (2001, unreported, case no: EAT/503/00) and *Mrs Suzanne Finnigan v Ministry of Defence Police* (2005, unreported, case no: EATS/0019/05); *Carshalton College v Mrs H Morris* (2002, unreported, case no: EAT/0673/01); *Sinclair Roche & Temperley & others v Sian Heard and Sian Fellows* (2004, unreported, case no: UKEAT/0738/03/MH); *Mrs D Fox v Betesh Fox & Co Solicitors* (2002, unreported, case no: EAT/0363/01); *Hardy & Hansons plc v Lax* (2005) ICR 1565; *British Airways plc v Mrs Jessica Starmer* (2005, unreported, case no: EAT/0306/05/SM); *Herbert Smith & others v Michelle Langton* (2005, unreported, case no: UKEAT/0242/05/DM and UKEAT/0437/05/DM); *Ms J Mitchell v David Evans Agricultural Ltd* (2006, unreported, case no: UKEAT/0083/06/SM); *Mrs H Shaw v CCL Ltd* (2007, unreported, case no: UKEAT/0512/06/DM); *Aviance UK Ltd v Mrs ML Garcia-Bello* (2007, unreported, case no: UKEAT/0044/07/DA); *Network Rail Infrastructures Ltd v Ms Patricia Gammie* (2009, unreported, case no: UKEATS/0044/08/BI); *Miss L A Rollinson v P & B Baldwin t/a United Colours of Benetton* (2005, unreported, case no: UKEAT/0873/04/CK); *Ministry of Defence (Royal Navy) v Mrs Adele MacMillan* (2004, unreported, case no: EATS/0003/04). For analogous cases in Australian equality law, see Owens (2006).

conflicts, disputes over flexibility and work-life balance are intimately attached to, and produced by, a range of nonhuman, material, actors. In *Network Rail Infrastructures v Gammie*, Patricia Gammie, a railway signaller, was refused an application to reduce her workweek from thirty-six hours to twenty-four upon her return from maternity leave on the basis that this arrangement would be too expensive, that it would lead to delays caused by the railway signalling box's not being occupied, and that Network Rail had failed to find someone to job share with her. She resigned shortly after that, because, as the employment tribunal put it, she was "beginning to run into difficulties with childcare and working full time."[13] In *Meikle* – a case concerning attempts to obtain accommodations for a visual impairment – daylight, classrooms, and small-print timetables appeared as actors in a conflict over a teacher's need for flexible working practices. In *Rutty*, a warehouse and its (apparently) fragile operating system in Tonbridge, Kent, was proffered as the business reason the claimant should not be allowed to work part time.[14] Finally, in *Finnegan*, driving distances, and hence a human-car relationship, motivated a Ministry of Defence police officer to request part-time work nearer to her home.

As legal actors, the status of the nonhumans in work-life balance disputes is not easy to discern. Unlike the regulated nicotine products that Rooke and colleagues analyse (Rooke, Cloatre, and Dingwall 2012) or Cloatre's patented drugs, their status as legally regulated things is not of immediate concern in the legal dilemmas at hand. Indeed, where they are mentioned in case reports, these nonhuman actors appear as bystanders or unspeaking witnesses – something reminiscent of, yet not wholly like, Cloatre's "silent regulatory tools" (2013, 100). Yet in many flexible-working cases, nonhuman actors variously blocked, invited, or thwarted human action, pulling labouring practices and time-related disputes in new directions. These movements are too diverse to summarize effectively here, but vehicles and their associated technical systems seem to have been particularly insistent legal agents (Grabham, in draft a). Cars and public transport are used to manage multiple child drops at school and preschool around parents' working days or other

13 *Network Rail Infrastructures Ltd v Ms Patricia Gammie*, para. 15. She won her claim for discrimination, but the case was referred by the Employment Appeal Tribunal on appeal to a fresh tribunal.

14 *Commotion Ltd v Rutty*, 293. The case report here is the decision of the Employment Appeal Tribunal, which upheld the employment tribunal's original decision.

care arrangements, and the failure of these vehicles and their associated systems to mitigate apparently conflicting demands, combined with their contribution to increased distances travelled and "fragmentation" of lives (Urry 2004), created a specific strand of vehicular distress in the cases covered.

We know from the work of sociologists such as John Urry (2000), Mimi Sheller (2004), and David Gartman (2004) that cars exert particular social and cultural logics and affective attachments. Our contemporary system of "automobility" not only has influenced social theory itself through the social science construct of Fordism, which itself relied on industrial complexes of car manufacturing and their associated innovations of management (Urry 2004, 26); it has also contributed infrastructural and planning practices that reconstitute the need for cars and that subordinate other forms of transport such as walking and biking, with their associated proximities and technologies. Urry (2000) terms this the "dominant culture of automobility," and hence it should be little surprise that automobility and its associated logics and things structure the meeting place of labour, care, and negotiated flexibility. The car that transported Ms Finnegan to work over huge commuting distances is only one example of this.

Yet it is not all about the car. A railway signalling box required a particular shift rota of Ms Gammie. Indeed, Ms Gammie's managers could not leave the Plean signalling box on its own:

> 9. … Plean had only one resident signaller working there instead of the required three. Three signallers in the area were on long term sick leave, one of whom was a relief signaller, and another relief signaller was about to go off on sick leave. He was having such difficulty in covering the requirements for manning the Plean box that managers were having to assist or other signallers were being asked to work overtime there on days when they would otherwise not have been working. Sometimes the box had to be left unmanned, a situation which limits train movements and can cause delays …
>
> 13. If a train is delayed such as by reason of a signal box being unmanned, the respondents have to pay penalties. In the case of Scotrail, they have to pay £8 per minute of delay. In the case of National Express, they have to pay £180 per minute of delay.[15]

---

15 *Network Rail Infrastructures Ltd v Ms Patricia Gammie*, 3.

Signalling boxes are quintessentially important to the functioning of rail systems; without them, trains cannot move. Leaving this particular box "unmanned" would lead to train delays, which then left train companies with a liability to pay penalties.

In the cases brought up through searches on flexibility, things co-produced timely dilemmas. Although it is possible to register the particularly insistent role of vehicles and their associated infrastructural demands, other "things" or material presences, such as daylight, also had effects. These things were sometimes of a type that we might normally associate with temporal ontologies, such as timetables and schedules, but many were not. Instead, an understanding of odd configurations of space and temporality is needed to account for their effects, something akin to Valverde's (2015) deployment of the chronotope. This is especially necessary for responding to vehicularized spaces and logics: automotive lives, and the dogged inability of the railway signalling box to operate without human intervention.[16]

Precedent: Form, Fact, and Patterning

Flexibility is, thus, many things. But in these cases, specifically through their case reports, flexibility also became a matter of form, fact, and patterning. If the "fact" is something that can be collected and patterned as much as it is treated as an epistemological object (Riles 2001, 139), then the instantiation of legal temporalities can similarly be analysed as a question of selection and collation, happening across legal decisions and in and between case reports. Furthermore, if things have shades of agency in relation to legal decision-making, then their effects can be felt through webs of norm-making established through case-law. At issue in this section, then, is the role of precedent in constituting flexibility, and the role of things in the brewing of precedent.

---

16 Furthermore, registering the sheer diversity of forms provides another angle on Levi's material-first approach. I accept that putting the legal concept of flexibility first in a case search limits a more receptive analysis of these things: it funnels them through law in specific ways, and it is productive to strategically avoid this. On the other hand, if it is possible to understand relationships between humans and material forms as particular kinds of assemblage, sometimes we need to see what happens when the assemblage coalesces around a temporal-legal mode.

The temporal orientation of precedent is a recurring object of study in legal theory (Postema 2004). As Richard Tur (2002) relates, the "declaratory" theory of the common law, which holds that judicial decision-making is inevitably retrospective, raises a number of problems about legal norms and time. Stating that the law is now what it has always been is a matter, as Tur puts it (quoting Kelsen) of articulating the "temporal sphere of the validity of the legal norm" (463). In other words, making an assertion about a legal decision's being future-oriented or rooted in already-existing principle recreates a particular stance towards the status and objectivity of law: law's capacity to describe and intervene in reality. It also requires particular understandings of the role of judges in relation to this objectivity; it requires asking whether they are acting in adjudicative or legislative fashion. The declaratory theory of precedent holds an understanding of law as eternal, timeless, and immutable (471), whereas prospective understandings of precedent articulate a noneternal, future-oriented temporal stance. These disagreements, then, are not only about the temporal orientations of the common law, but also about the effectiveness of judges, as actors, in creating legal time and the multiplicity of common law principles. Tur points out that declaratory theory postulates one overarching law, whereas the prospective approach can accommodate a legal split, between the law as it was then and the law as it is now (473).

Whereas theorists such as John Finnis hold that it is incumbent on judges not to apply a law unless it can be seen, all along, to have been developed as a legally appropriate standard, Tur (2002) argues that legal norms declared by judges through the operation of precedent can be prospective. Specifically, he charts specific cases in which what was held to be a previous legal norm was "not followed" – a hybrid position, which holds in place previous laws but claims they have been overtaken by new developments. Gerald Postema (2004), for his part, describes the temporalizing normative structure of common law as something akin to a melody. Melodies are heard, he argues, not merely in sequence but as a self-relating whole, which requires some element of projection in the moment of perceiving a melodic line. Understanding law's orientation as something akin to an unfolding melody can help us to understand the texture of legal normativity.

Drucilla Cornell has proposed an approach to legal interpretation and judging that confounds many of these perspectives by explicitly relating time to justice. Her Derridean interpretation of the role of the judge challenges legal positivist thinking by reinserting invention solidly back into interpretation. As Cornell puts it, the judge's responsibility towards memory has particular dimensions: "This responsibility is not to an accurate repetition through the recollection of legal norms, but to a refutation of the belief that what has been can ever be conflated with justice. Invention is inescapable if legal norms cannot be discovered purely through their mere recollection" (1990, 268). Cornell's theory of the temporal dimensions of judging and justice therefore proposes a split between law's memory, or processes of recollection, and its capacity to instantiate justice. It also requires a critical stance towards the (legal) privileging of the present. In this account, judging involves accounting for how and where, through what temporal means, one locates legal truth or normativity, whether in the past or through projections into the future, perhaps. As she states: "The unique Derridean contribution to legal interpretation is to show us why the act of memory in judging involves the seemingly contradictory notion that the judge, in his or her decision, remembers the future" (269).

Precedent, as legal technique and philosophical object, therefore articulates a range of concerns: justice, the status of recollection and memory, the temporal orientations of legal normativity, and the possibility of true legal invention. Yet accounting for the role of material forms in law also should prompt us to think about precedent's material dimensions: its connection to case reports and other things. In this account, things are textual as much as material – they are textually present, populating, and travelling through the legal practice of precedent just as easily as do legal principles.

To be more specific: through the case reports that formed the subject of my study on flexibility disputes, the thing-related principles associated with flexibility were patterned by virtue of legal citation practices required by precedent. Reports can be understood within legal assemblages as "living documents," inorganic actors that "feel" and produce social relations (Hunter 2008). All the case reports I looked at referred to principles established in previous cases, as is the usual practice in precedent. Yet precedent provided routes for legally significant things in earlier cases to become dislodged from their legal "homes" and travel into new scenarios through legal procedural and formal conventions. If the nonhuman actors were not always directly referenced, they nevertheless appeared in, and influenced, the outcomes of later cases. For example, in *MacMillan* – a request for part-time work to assuage a 120-mile roundtrip daily commute – a much earlier and very influential case, *London Underground v Edwards*, was discussed.[17] The legal issue at hand was the (now largely defunct) question of comparing pools of people with different characteristics to work out whether a claimant had been sufficiently disadvantaged by an employer's action. *Edwards* contained an infamous shift rota that disadvantaged women by requiring workers to start their shift at 4:45 a.m. and end at 1:30 p.m., sometimes working eleven consecutive days. This shift rota has considerable notoriety of its own in UK equality law and policy circles. Although legal precedent brought *Edwards* into *MacMillan*, nevertheless the legal treatment of flexibility in *MacMillan* assumed the nonhuman traces of the shift rota in *Edwards* through a process of reference and comparison: "The situation which arose in London Underground when the employers imposed a change to their rostering which resulted in one of 21 female train operators being unable to comply with the new rotas was referred to in detail by both parties. In that case the individual affected was a female single parent. The circumstances here are very different indeed."[18] In this case, the shift rota, as nonhuman actor, promoted the development of legal principle through a mechanism of comparison and divergence: the situation in *MacMillan* concerned a commute, but was decided with reference to the shift rota in *Edwards*, even though these "facts" were very different indeed. Through such a mechanism, a productive relationship emerged, within and across the case reports, between things such as the *Edwards* shift rota, the car and commuting distance in *MacMillan*, and the legal concept of flexibility.

Riles's conceptualization of documentary patterning is helpful here. In her study of the negotiations surrounding the *Pacific Platform for Action*, a gender and development policy document drafted in advance of the 1995 Beijing Conference on Women, Riles analyses the document both as independent object and as pattern (2001, 73). Treating the document as an anthropological object, she notes that its structure enabled a linear progression from "Preamble" to "Mission Statement" and eventually to "Institutional Arrangements" (78). However, each section consisted of self-contained paragraphs, which could be read in any order without losing understanding of the document. In turn, the form of this document was repeated in documents at other levels of negotiation, and this, coupled with rigid conventions, technical language, and a

17 *London Underground v Edwards* (1999) ICR 494.
18 *Ministry of Defence (Royal Navy) v Mrs Adele MacMillan*, 8.

preferred typeface, meant that innovative details were less important to drafters than the successful replication of language and patterns from one document to the next (79). Patterning itself was supported by the negotiators' seeming lack of interest in the meaning of keywords and phrases; instead they favoured the repetition of keywords, the rhythm and feel of particular words alongside each other (such as "structural adjustment") and word patterns ("universal" did not make sense unless it sat next to "human rights").

Case reports are less the subject of negotiation than are policy documents of this type, but they too are heavily stylized, formal, and, due to the mandates of legal provisions and clusters of policy knowledge, tend to contain patterned technical phrases and combinations of words ("flexible work," "unfair dismissal," "indirect discrimination"). Like policy documents of the type that Riles analyses, each of the case reports I looked at had been written with the expectation that it would be read and acted on at a different level. Reports are written with a consciousness of what exists outside the tribunal itself, cross-referencing paragraphs within case reports to paragraphs or pages within other case reports. All judgments begin with the names of the parties, proceed often to a summary of the main legal points and cases used in argument, and present the facts, the legal principle, and the decision in linear order, in consecutively numbered paragraphs. Furthermore, segments from lower court decisions are often quoted at length in higher court decisions, giving the impression of a world within a world: the analogousness of form reinforcing the impression of a tight legal network.

This is not just a matter of legal doctrine and interpretation, but of how legal assemblages orient themselves temporally. The sequential structuring of knowledge between case reports provides a key difference to Riles's policy documents, which could be read in any direction. In itself, finding that precedent operates prospectively is not new: as we have seen, many legal theorists have been contemplating this point for a while. The analysis in this chapter, however, has focused on the material means by which such forward motion has been achieved. Legal citation and referencing inaugurate prospective time by lifting particular constellations of artefacts, people, events, from one tribunal, and therefore one case report, to another. This suggests that precedent, at the very least, is more widely populated, and more strangely achieved, than hitherto imagined. In other words, the temporal effects of precedent can be conceived as material and materialized.

Conclusion

Bringing things, documents, and vibrant material concerns into the analysis of balance and flexibility might not obviously shift the political stakes of these powerful legal temporalities. In other words, focusing on the material and technical constitution of balance and flexibility might seem only to complicate the analysis and not necessarily to lead to any new feminist political insights or strategies. Yet, as we have seen, when mobilized through legal techniques and projects, even apparently progressive temporal constructs of balance and flexibility consistently recall the forward-marching, linear time of the moderns. Temporal techniques associated with flexibility, for example, instantiate new forms of contractual permanence while "unwinding" state responsibility for the gendered allocation of unpaid care. We might usefully question the otherwise apparently critical edge that balance and flexibility hold in feminist politics and legal strategies in favour of sustained attention to the means by which we practice and recreate time.

In the context of the insistent demands of generations of feminists – for example, through wages for housework and employer of last resort demands – some might argue that the stultifying effects of aiming for "balance" have ensnared utopian feminist visions of revaluing social reproduction into restrictive practices of negotiation and exclusion. Those who find their way through increasingly complex eligibility requirements to claim the right to request flexible work in UK law, for example, are met with onerous processes of form-filling and negotiation, raising concern over the transformative potential of work-life balance laws. Certainly, my own approach in recent years has become increasingly critical of what "balance" can achieve, politically, within feminist or other social policy initiatives.

Yet work-life balance laws and policies, embedded in mutating networks of gendered labour and value, also exert a range of contradictory logics and significant social effects. In other words, balance, in this context, might usefully be articulated as legal assemblage: a cluster of policy dilemmas, cases, humans, and artefacts, with an emergent collective agency. In Chapter One I suggested, following others, that we might try to avoid assuming in advance where the law arises within an assemblage, a stance easier to propose than to achieve. Yet doing so has implications for how we think about legal temporalities. Stepping aside from the temporal framework of the "moderns" (Latour 1993, 67), a paradigm characterized by the "arrow of time," definitive temporal breaks and, most important, the passing of time, work-life balance and flexibility appear much stranger, and more widely populated, than hitherto imagined. The picture that emerges is complex, involving a range of productive temporal mechanisms and horizons, many of which are apparently contradictory and all of which are linked to other policy concerns. The temporal dimensions of this kind of "balance" suggest a reckonable present, a form of measure, that acts through a logic of equivalence to renaturalize the separate domains of care and labour within the time of the moderns. Furthermore, the particular form of the right to request flexible work indicates that law's temporalizing qualities can have specific regulatory functions, shifting scale and reframing responsibilities. Finally, in tracing the lively actions of things in flexible work disputes, we can discern the materializing qualities of precedent. In such ways, we can take some small steps in analysing the diverse actors that constitute powerful legal-temporal ontologies and in understanding, through this process, the complexities of our own political positions.

Apple Crates and Hinges

In Whitstable, on the southeast coast of England, several antiques shops wait on the summertime tourist trade. From these shops, old and shabby objects – rickety benches, bed frames, novelty ten-foot statues of wart-hogs – can be purchased for eye-watering prices. My favourite horror is the pile of "Kentish apple crates" outside one place on the roundabout in town, each crate fetching the equivalent of around $40. Why does this bug me? Is it something about their price? The fact that they're being sold at all? Well, yes, but my first reaction to seeing this pile of entirely ordinary local receptacles has something to do with the style of their commodification. There is something not right about it all: these boxes, whose function was once to hold fruit, displayed alongside antique chairs and chests of drawers. Old apple crates in Kent, after all, are a bit like discarded coal sacks in Tyne and Wear: objects with which people have done their work in industries that have evolved (Kent) or been rendered defunct (the North East of England). Maybe this is why I feel there is something strange about reselling apple crates as ornaments.

There is more than a touch of indignant historical sentimentality to this. Nevertheless, Jean Baudrillard's theory of antiques might help us to understand objects such as these fancy crates, which, as he puts it, "appear to run counter to the requirements of functional calculation, and answer to other kinds of demands such as witness, memory, nostalgia or escapism" (2009, 41). Apple crates are certainly nostalgic. Yet Baudrillard is unsure about how antiques fit within his theories of the sign/symbolic values of objects. His provisional conclusion is that antiques signify time – more specifically, that the *function* of antiques is to signify time: "The antique object no longer has any practical application, its role being merely to signify. It is astructural, it refuses structure ... Yet it is not afunctional, nor purely 'decorative,' for it has a very specific function within the system, namely the signifying of time." Furthermore, as Baudrillard puts it, antiques embody not "real time" but the "signs of time": "Clearly it is not real time but the signs or indices of time that antiques embody ... Time ... is far less amenable than nature to abstraction and systematization. The living contradiction it enshrines resists integration into the logic of a system. This 'chronic' difficulty is what we see reflected in the spectacular connotation of the antique object" (Baudrillard 2009, 41).

It may be, then, that the apple crates are antiques because their nostalgic commodification signifies a constructed, orchard-laden time of fruitfulness and plenty that maps neatly onto a confabulated Whitstable era of local oyster fishermen, steam railways, and crinolines. In other words, the crates form one small but resonant part of Whitstable's persistent rehearsal of the late nineteenth century. In Baudrillard's account, antiques are spectacularized and set apart because they signify time, and because time is difficult to systematize it is especially tricky to integrate antiques into systems of knowledge and meaning. This might explain the uneasiness that apple-crates-as-antiques cause in me.

Yet objects also help to constitute new legal relationships. From a legal perspective, it is possible to think of apple crates in terms of their ownership. They are amenable in their own special way to a sale, and in particular to instantiating a new set of legal relations, above all perhaps, because they are (thought to be) old. If I were to put my irritation to one side and buy an apple crate from the antiques dealer, the crate as object would be more than merely a vehicle for the legal transaction; it would in many ways invite and constitute it. Recognizing the potential for the apple crate to act as a planter for a collection of hastily purchased seasonal flowers, for example, I might hand over the equivalent of $40, and in so doing, possession and ownership of the crate would shift to me. The sale would make no sense without the crate. In this way, even fleeting legal relationships such as the purchase of an apple crate have material effects as much as they establish human relationships.

In this book I have argued that objects co-produce legal temporalities in relationship with people, things, and matter. This account, and the scholarship on which it draws, contextualizes Baudrillard's assertion that "it is not real time but the signs or indices of time that antiques embody." Clearly, objects do signify time, but through the actions they invite objects also help to create new temporal ontologies, which are real as much as they are multiple. From signification, then, to what Bennett would term *conatus* "shades of material agency," the point of objects in this analysis is not merely that they carry or evoke temporal meanings, but that, through their actions, temporalities are brewed.

I have suggested in this book that the task of thinking seriously about law and time requires sustained attention to material objects and "vital matter." Offering a "praxiographic" approach to time, I have traced the percolation of legal temporalities in relationships between humans and nonhumans. Progression, likelihood, transition, and balance do not look like what we currently understand to be temporal concepts, but instead resemble something akin to temporal qualities or conditions for time: the expression of a moving-through-time (progression), a temporal orientation (likelihood), a reorientation (transition), or a settling of time (balance). Yet outside a modern temporal framework, where time is natural, linear, and distinct from humans and things, these temporal conditions and qualities percolate *as* time, and have their own effects. More specifically, these temporalities are achieved, in a manner similar to how science and technology scholars conceive of "uncertainty" (Moreira, May, and Bond 2009). They surface via distinct means and draw on a gaggle of temporal accomplices: in these accounts, reversals, prognosis, flexibility, and permanence. Inherently hybrid, as we have seen, these temporalities result from legal encounters with clinical knowledge, tests, and drugs, in the case of progression and likelihood, for example; from the meeting point of transgender rights with the bureaucratic imperative of categorization and documentation, in the case of transition.

Some legal temporalities, such as progression and likelihood, occupy, dissolve, or trouble the boundaries between law and scientific objectivity. The first two case studies in this book examined the role of legal-clinical temporalities in helping to ground the "reality" of HIV as a disability in law. In Canadian legal networks in the 1980s, for example, advisors and activists co-created a temporal ontology of urgency through innovated legal and quasi-legal strategies responding to the emergency of the new HIV epidemic. In both provincial human rights law and provincial welfare benefits law, the legal temporality of progression articulated legal dilemmas relating to HIV with the clinical "realities" of the virus. But AZT and antibody tests constituted "asymptomatic status" as a legal concern in diverging ways, such that symptoms were required to draw income assistance but not to make a human rights claim. Dilemmas over asymptomatic status and progression similarly marked UK legal concerns relating to HIV, characterized by early controversies over work-related antibody testing and HIV-related dismissals. With the introduction of the Disability Discrimination Act in 1996, however, asymptomatic status was linked to the newly required "likelihood" test, with its speculative practices and focus on "prognosis."

In turn, legal temporalities have arisen just as much through contestation and boundary work as through smooth collaboration. Boundaries of objectivity have timely effects both within law (for example, through the workings of jurisdiction in Chapter Two) and between law and other domains (for example, between lawyers and clinicians in Chapters Three and Four). These boundaries are also materially constituted: they result, for example, from object-concepts (such as drugs or symptoms) travelling between clinical and legal contexts. As Chapters Three and Four showed, clinicians and lawyers have often struggled to conceive of time in similar ways. Apparently shared "technical imaginaries" of time nevertheless have failed to align neatly with each other. At least one Canadian clinician found that his clinic's AIDS diagnosis of a patient for treatment reasons set in motion a set of practices within the Canadian military that led to the patient's losing his job. The "fact" of Simon Thwaites's new AIDS diagnosis, and its apparent significance in marking the "progression" of his condition, travelled much more effectively between diverging clinical and military classification systems than did the careful deliberations his clinicians made in getting him onto the new AZT treatment. In the United Kingdom, on the other hand, clinicians remained wary of enunciating prognosis with the clarity needed for the "likelihood" test, preferring instead to speak of the uncertainty of HIV progression.

As we saw in Chapter One, a range of scholarship on material cultures and in science and technology studies, for example, has begun to account for the co-constitution of objects and temporalities. Following Henare, Holbraad, and Wastell (2007), I have posed the question of where the (temporal) worlds are. Henare and colleagues would reply: here, in the things themselves. In a similar way, in each chapter I have attempted to trace the conative legal force of things – tests, medical reports, classification systems, statutory declarations, flexible work request forms, vehicles, telephones, drugs – as they help to enact specific temporal ontologies. Yet it is in this context that the strange and specific qualities of the "legal" should also be taken seriously. A recurring theme in this book, then, has been the materialization of law.

Dilemmas over the material qualities of legal form and the actions of form in legal-temporal assemblages recur across the case studies. Responding to Annelise Riles's invitation to reassess how ethnographers "know," I have attempted to register the world-making capacities of legal form, both through the material features of documentation and through the specificities of legal technique. Delegated negotiations over flexible work, which occupy a hybrid position between legislated right and the common law of the employment contract, are seen to adopt varying techniques of temporalization depending on bureaucratic approaches to the unpaid care burden. Furthermore, the common law principle and technique of precedent, for example, can be assessed for its material as well as its temporalizing features, suggesting that common law practices of legal invention or ratification (depending on one's outlook) are more widely populated than hitherto imagined (Chapter Five). Legal documents, such as statutory declarations, with their standardized form, in turn, can help achieve the temporalizing work of gender transition as a matter of law (Chapter Four).

We might say that, within these assemblages, or confederations (after Bennett), legal technicalities, like Latour's hinges, assist the "folding" of time, or the instantiation of distinct temporalities through relationships between human and nonhuman actors. We have seen that Latour himself would not agree with such an approach, yet in Chapter One I also proposed that the resources already exist within socio-legal theory to explore the folding or brewing of time through legal objects and relationships. The idea of brewing time is useful only if the split between the time of nature and the time of the social is set to one side. New types of time are not, on this account, new experiences of time within the paradigm of the moderns; instead, they constitute new worlds. This, furthermore, has what we perceive as legal effects. For example, the antibody test both registered and helped visualize the new phenomenon of the HIV retrovirus in Canada in the mid-1980s. When the technological artefact of the test came into contact with humans (as patients and clinicians), one result was a new temporal domain of asymptomaticity, vital to the emerging legal-temporal ontology of progression. Latour suggests that nonhumans register the past perfect, whereas human action registers the present. Asymptomatic status was co-articulated in Canadian and UK law with the innovation of the antibody test. To put it bluntly, the antibody test created a means of extending the temporality of HIV/AIDS backwards to the point of infection, understood as the point of "manifesting antibodies." Asymptomatic status registered the past perfect of the antibody test as a measurement that had already taken place within the current human time of the person living with HIV.

The reason this kind of temporal analysis might be worth the effort is that, as Louise Amoore and Marieke de Goede (2008) argue, regulatory ontologies of time do political things. Amoore and de Goede focus on the role of "pre-emption" tactics in the war on terror. In turn, the temporalizing tactics of intervention and law-making that occupy contemporary social justice concerns provide an urgent field of enquiry for law and society scholars. How we conceive of disability, gender transition, gendered working time, the question of when we call something a "crisis" and how we act in it, or how we bring about a longed-for and very real shift in legal status all produce "spaces of decision-making" (de Goede 2012, 194) in association with vehicles, clinical tests, and documents, for example, which give rise to legal, bureaucratic, and, essentially, political effects. The fact that nonhumans are participants in these spaces of decision-making serves only to politicize further our relationships with technical innovations, documentary practices, and legal technicalities. Arguing that HIV was enacted in Canadian law in the 1980s via the temporal legal artefact of progression, which itself was co-articulated with the development of the antibody test, does not have to flatten the social justice account of legal time or our assessment of who suffered in the early HIV epidemic, why, and how. Instead, permitting a role for nonhumans in the account of dominant legal temporalities has the potential to animate and politicize domains of action and social life within the analysis of legal time that, in any case, have long been understood as urgent and political through the work of treatment activism, for example (Epstein 2009). Likewise, intensifying our focus on legal technicalities in the achievement of flexibility should not, on its own account, depoliticize the urgent question of the gendered allocation of unpaid care and its effects on women workers. Instead, such an analysis asks about the desirability of apparently progressive socio-technical paradigms of "work-life balance" and flexible work by paying enhanced attention to their legal articulation through temporalized interventions into the common law of the employment contract.

To put this further into context, the conative, "not-quite-human," qualities of legal things have found willing collaborators in these case studies among lawyers, government ministers, legal claimants, bureaucrats, and legal activists improvising new temporalizing tactics. All these actions, whether or not they might be viewed as shaped by, resistant to, or expressive of, enduring normative paradigms, have helped to constitute legal time. Many have been intentionally political or have had political effects. Across different jurisdictions, these strategies include using "the tool we have now," "taking the money and running," and "spoon-feeding" clinicians to help constitute HIV as the proper concern of human rights and employment law. Bureaucrats in the United Kingdom's Department of Health, and Health and Safety Executive, presented as settled law a set of otherwise unsettled legal propositions about the viability of work-related antibody testing. In the domain of gender recognition, government ministers positioned "facts that are clear to lawyers" as the temporal long-stop of what otherwise would have been multiple potential gender "reversals." Legislative drafters and bureaucrats together found, in the "until death" provision, a technical legal expression for "permanence." In pursuing work-life balance as a policy goal, bureaucrats adopted temporally modulated contractual deliberations around flexible work as a means of trusting in the efficacy of regulatory unwinding. For their part, HIV and poverty law activists in Canada rerouted legal claims, closed files, and avoided funerals. Through these changes in strategy, frustrations, amendments, debates, and attempted manipulations, we can view the political human actions that contribute to legal temporalities.

Coming full circle, this book, then, engages the politics of vital materiality, alongside human subjectivity, in the analysis of legal time. Bennett's concluding manifesto in *Vibrant Matter* contains what she calls a "kind of Nicene Creed for would-be vital materialists," suggesting the following statement, or aspiration: "I believe that this pluriverse is traversed by heterogeneities that are continually *doing things* … I believe that encounters with lively matter can chasten my fantasies of human mastery, highlight the common materiality of all that is, expose a wider distribution of agency, and reshape the self and its interests" (2010, 122). In this book, I have attempted to trace the provisional, and thing-related, enactment of legal temporalities as they constitute new legal worlds as well as new legal knowledges. Through a variety of angles, case studies, and propositions, however, I have returned to the practices, and timely political implications of "doing things" (after Bennett) with law: a discipline, a set of activities, and a form of objectivity that have specific implications for how we understand time and temporality. As such, my timely legal analysis has become more and more enmeshed in dilemmas relating to materiality, politics, and ontology. If this complicates the analysis, then it also prompts new and alternative political theorizations of time's legal effects. What Frank O'Hara so eloquently termed "the eagerness of objects" brings me back, then, to the practice, and the potential, of brewing legal time.

Bibliography

ACAS (Advisory, Conciliation and Arbitration Service). 2014. "Handling Requests to Work Flexibly in a Reasonable Manner." London. Available online at http://www.acas.org.uk/media/pdf/p/6/Handling-requests-to-work-flexibly-in-a-reasonable-manner-an-Acas-guide.pdf.

Adkins, Lisa. 2008. "From Retroactivation to Futurity: The End of the Sexual Contract?" *NORA* 16 (3): 182–201. http://dx.doi.org/10.1080/08038740802300954.

– 2009a. "Feminism after Measure." *Feminist Theory* 10 (3): 323–39. http://dx.doi.org/10.1177/1464700109343255.

– 2009b. "Sociological Futures: From Clock Time to Event Time." *Sociological Research Online* 14 (4). http://dx.doi.org/10.5153/sro.1976.

– 2012. "Out of Work or Out of Time? Rethinking Labor after the Financial Crisis." *South Atlantic Quarterly* 111 (4): 621–41. http://dx.doi.org/10.1215/00382876-1724111.

Alessandrini, Donatella. 2014. "Research Note: Re-Thinking Feminist Engagements with the State and Wage Labour." *Feminists@law* 4 (1).

Amoore, Louise. 2004. "Risk, Reward and Discipline at Work." *Economy and Society* 33 (2): 174–96. http://dx.doi.org/10.1080/03085140410001677111.

– 2013. *The Politics of Possibility: Risk and Security Beyond Probability*. Durham, NC: Duke University Press. http://dx.doi.org/10.1215/9780822377269.

Amoore, Louise, and Marieke de Goede. 2008. "Transactions after 9/11: The Banal Face of the Preemptive Strike." *Transactions of the Institute of British Geographers* 33 (2): 173–85. http://dx.doi.org/10.1111/j.1475-5661.2008.00291.x.

Ashiagbor, Diamond. 2006. "Promoting Precariousness? The Response of EU Employment Policies to Precarious Work." In *Precarious Work, Women, and the New Economy: The Challenge to Legal Norms*, ed. Judy Fudge and

Rosemary Owens, 77–98. Oxford, UK: Haart Publishing. http://eprints.soas.ac.uk/10493/.

Bastian, Michelle. 2014. "Time and Community: A Scoping Study." *Time & Society* 23 (2): 137–66. http://dx.doi.org/10.1177/0961463X14527999.

Bastow, Karen. 1994. "Women, AIDS, and Family Benefits." *Canadian Journal of Women and the Law* 7:173–83.

Batty, David Batty. 2004. "Mistaken identity." *Guardian*, 31 July. Available online at http://www.guardian.co.uk/society/2004/jul/31/health.socialcare; accessed 12 June 2014.

Baudrillard, Jean. 2009. "Subjective Discourse or the Non-Functional System of Objects." In *The Object Reader*, ed. Fiona Candlin and Raiford Guins, 41–63. New York: Routledge.

Bedford, Kate. 2009. *Developing Partnerships: Gender, Sexuality, and the Reformed World Bank*. Minneapolis: University of Minnesota Press.

Bennett, Jane. 2010. *Vibrant Matter: A Political Ecology of Things*. Durham, NC: Duke University Press.

Beynon-Jones, Siân M. 2012. "Timing Is Everything: The Demarcation of 'later' Abortions in Scotland." *Social Studies of Science* 42 (1): 53–74. http://dx.doi.org/10.1177/0306312711426596.

Bhandar, Brenna. 2009. "Constituting Practices and Things: The Concept of the Network and Studies in Law, Gender and Sexuality." *Feminist Legal Studies* 17 (3): 325–32. http://dx.doi.org/10.1007/s10691-009-9128-3.

Birth, Kevin K. 2012. *Objects of Time: How Things Shape Temporality*. New York: Palgrave Macmillan. http://dx.doi.org/10.1057/9781137017895.

Blomley, Nick. 2011. *Rights of Passage: Sidewalks and the Regulation of Public Flow. Social Justice*. London: Routledge.

Bourdieu, Pierre. 2000. *Pascalian Meditations*. Trans. Richard Nice. Cambridge, UK: Polity Press.

Braverman, Irus, Nick Blomley, and David Delaney, eds. 2014. *The Expanding Spaces of Law: A Timely Legal Geography*. Stanford, CA: Stanford University Press. http://dx.doi.org/10.11126/stanford/9780804787185.001.0001.

Brenneis, Don. 2006. "Reforming Promise." In *Documents: Artifacts of Modern Knowledge*, ed. Annelise Riles, 41–70. Ann Arbor: University of Michigan Press.

Cabot, Heath. 2012. "The Governance of Things: Documenting Limbo in the Greek Asylum Procedure." *PoLAR: Political and Legal Anthropology Review* 35 (1): 11–29. http://dx.doi.org/10.1111/j.1555-2934.2012.01177.x.

Canada. 2013. Public Health Agency of Canada. "At a Glance – HIV and AIDS in Canada: Surveillance Report to December 31st, 2012." Ottawa. Available online at http://www.phac-aspc.gc.ca/aids-sida/publication/survreport/2012/dec/index-eng.php#footnote5; accessed 2 October 2014.

Canadian Human Rights Commission. 1996. "Policy on HIV/AIDS." Ottawa.

Candlin, Fiona, and Raiford Guins, eds. 2009. *The Object Reader*. New York: Routledge.

Casserley, Catherine, and Bela Gor. 2001. *Disability Discrimination Claims: An Advisor's Handbook*. Bristol, UK: Jordan Publishing.

Chávez, Karma R. 2012. "ACT UP, Haitian Migrants, and Alternative Memories of HIV/AIDS." *Quarterly Journal of Speech* 98 (1): 63–8.

Cloatre, Emilie. 2013. *Pills for the Poorest: An Exploration of TRIPS and Access to Medication in Sub-Saharan Africa*. New York: Palgrave Macmillan. http://dx.doi.org/10.1057/9781137313270.

Cohen, Cathy J. 1999. *The Boundaries of Blackness: AIDS and the Breakdown of Black Politics*. Chicago: University of Chicago Press.

Conaghan, Joanne. 2004. "Women, Work, and Family: A British Revolution?" In *Labour Law in an Era of Globalization: Transformative Practices and Possibilities*, ed. Joanne Conaghan, Richard M. Fischl, and Karl Klare, 53–74. Oxford: Oxford University Press.

Conaghan, Joanne, and Emily Grabham. 2007. "Sexuality and the Citizen Carer." *Northern Ireland Legal Quarterly* 58:325–42.

Conaghan, Joanne, and Kerry Rittich, eds. 2005. *Labour Law, Work, and Family: Critical and Comparative Perspectives*. Oxford: Oxford University Press.

Condren, Conal. 2006. *Argument and Authority in Early Modern England*. Cambridge: Cambridge University Press. http://dx.doi.org/10.1017/CBO9780511490477.

Conley, Robin. 2008. "'At the Time She Was a Man': The Temporal Dimension of Identity Construction." *PoLAR: Political and Legal Anthropology Review* 31 (1): 28–47. http://dx.doi.org/10.1111/j.1555-2934.2008.00003.x.

Cooper, Davina. 2013. "Time against Time: Normative Temporalities and the Failure of Community Labour in Local Exchange Trading Schemes." *Time & Society* 22 (1): 31–54. http://dx.doi.org/10.1177/0961463X11422279.

– 2014. *Everyday Utopias: The Conceptual Life of Promising Spaces*. Durham, NC: Duke University Press.

Cornell, Drucilla. 1990. "Time, Deconstruction, and the Challenge to Legal Positivism: The Call for Judicial Responsibility." *Yale Journal of Law & the Humanities* 2 (2): 267–97.

Costa, Mariarosa Dalla, and Selma James. 1973. *The Power of Women and the Subversion of the Community*. Bristol, UK: Falling Wall Press.

Cowan, Sharon. 2009. "Looking Back (To)wards the Body: Medicalization and the GRA." *Social & Legal Studies* 18 (2): 247–52. http://dx.doi.org/10.1177/0964663909103627.

Craven, Matthew, Malgosia Fitzmaurice, and Maria Vogiatzi, eds. 2006. *Time, History and International Law*. Leiden, Netherlands: Brill Publishers.

Crimp, Douglas, and Leo Bersani. 1988. *AIDS: Cultural Analysis, Cultural Activism*. Cambridge, MA: MIT Press.

Cunliffe, Emma. 2011. *Murder, Medicine and Motherhood*. Oxford, UK: Hart Publishing.

Currah, Paisley, and Lisa Jean Moore. 2009. "'We Won't Know Who You Are': Contesting Sex Designations in New York City Birth Certificates." *Hypatia* 24 (3): 113–35.

Currah, Paisley, and Tara Mulqueen. 2011. "Securitizing Gender: Identity, Biometrics, and Transgender Bodies at the Airport." *Social Research: An International Quarterly* 78 (2): 557–82.

Currah, Paisley, and Dean Spade. 2007. "Introduction to Special Issue: The State We're In: Locations of Coercion and Resistance in Trans Policy, Part 1." *Sexuality Research & Social Policy* 4 (4): 1–6. http://dx.doi.org/10.1525/srsp.2007.4.4.1.

Dada, Mehboob. 1990. "Race and the AIDS Agenda." In *Ecstatic Antbodies: Resisting the AIDS Mythology*, ed. Tessa Boffin and Sunil Gupta, 85–95. London: Rivers Oram.

Davis, Fred. 1960. "Uncertainty in Medical Prognosis Clinical and Functional." *American Journal of Sociology* 66 (1): 41–7. http://dx.doi.org/10.1086/222821.

Davy, Zowie. 2010. "Transsexual Agents: Negotiating Authenticity and Embodiment within the UK's Medicolegal System." In *Transgender Identities: Towards a Social Analysis of Gender Diversity*, ed. Sally Hines and Tam Sanger, 106–26. New York: Routledge.

Dean, Mitchell. 1999. *Governmentality: Power and Rule in Modern Society*. Thousand Oaks, CA: Sage.

de Goede, Marieke. 2005. *Virtue, Fortune, and Faith: A Genealogy of Finance*. Minneapolis: University of Minnesota Press.

– 2012. *Speculative Security: The Politics of Pursuing Terrorist Monies*. Minneapolis: University of Minnesota Press. http://dx.doi.org/10.5749/minnesota/9780816675890.001.0001.

De Landa, Manuel. 1997. *A Thousand Years of Nonlinear History*. New York: Zone Books.

Dinshaw, Carolyn, Lee Edelman, Roderick A. Ferguson, Carla Freccero, Elizabeth Freeman, Judith Halberstam, Annemarie Jagose, Christoper Nealon, and Nguyen Tan Hoang. 2007. "Theorizing Queer Temporalities: A Roundtable Discussion." *GLQ: A Journal of Lesbian and Gay Studies* 13 (2–3): 177–95. http://dx.doi.org/10.1215/10642684-2006-030.

Douglas, Stacy. 2011. "Between Constitutional Mo(nu)ments: Memorialising Past, Present and Future at the District Six Museum and Constitution Hill." *Law and Critique* 22 (2): 171–87. http://dx.doi.org/10.1007/s10978-011-9083-4.

Edelman, Lee. 2004. *No Future: Queer Theory and the Death Drive*. Durham, NC: Duke University Press. http://dx.doi.org/10.1215/9780822385981.

Engel, David M. 1987. "Law, Time, and Community." *Law & Society Review* 21 (4): 605–38. http://dx.doi.org/10.2307/3053598.

Epstein, Steven. 2009. *Impure Science: AIDS, Activism, and the Politics of Knowledge*. Berkeley: University of California Press.

Fassin, Didier, and Estelle d'Halluin. 2005. "The Truth from the Body: Medical Certificates as Ultimate Evidence for Asylum Seekers." *American Anthropologist* 107 (4): 597–608. http://dx.doi.org/10.1525/aa.2005.107.4.597.

Faulkner, Alex, Bettina Lange, and Christopher Lawless. 2012. "Introduction: Material Worlds: Intersections of Law, Science, Technology, and Society." *Journal of Law and Society* 39 (1): 1–19. http://dx.doi.org/10.1111/j.1467-6478.2012.00567.x.

Federici, Sylvia. 2012. *Revolution at Point Zero: Housework, Reproduction, and Feminist Struggle*. Oakland, CA: PM Press.

Fredman, Sandra. 2004. "Women at Work: The Broken Promise of Flexicurity." *Industrial Law Journal* 33 (4): 299–319. http://dx.doi.org/10.1093/ilj/33.4.299.

Freeman, Elizabeth. 2005. "Time Binds, or Erotohistoriography." *Social Text* 23 (3–4 84–85): 57–68. http://dx.doi.org/10.1215/01642472-23-3-4_84-85-57.

– 2011. *Time Binds: Queer Temporalities, Queer Histories*. Durham, NC: Duke University Press.

Fudge, Judy, and Rosemary J. Owens. 2006. *Precarious Work, Women And the New Economy: The Challenge to Legal Norms*. Oxford, UK: Hart Publishing.

Gartman, David. 2004. "Three Ages of the Automobile: The Cultural Logics of the Car." *Theory, Culture & Society* 21 (4–5): 169–95. http://dx.doi.org/10.1177/0263276404046066.

Gerrity, Martha S., Jo Anne L. Earp, Robert F. DeVellis, and Donald W. Light. 1992. "Uncertainty and Professional Work: Perceptions of Physicians in Clinical Practice." *American Journal of Sociology* 97 (4): 1022–51. http://dx.doi.org/10.1086/229860.

Gill-Peterson, Julian. 2013. "Haunting the Queer Spaces of AIDS: Remembering ACT Up/New York and an Ethics for an Endemic." *GLQ: A Journal of Lesbian and Gay Studies* 19 (3): 279–300. http://dx.doi.org/10.1215/10642684-2074512.

Goss, David, and Derek Adam-Smith. 1995. *Organizing AIDS: Workplace and Organizational Responses to the HIV/AIDS Epidemic*. Abingdon, UK: Taylor & Francis.

Grabham, Emily. 2010a. "Dilemmas of Value in Post-Industrial Economies: Retrieving Clock Time through the Four-Day Work Week?" *Connecticut Law Review* 42 (4): 1285–97.

– 2010b. "Governing Permanence: Trans Subjects, Time, and the Gender Recognition Act." *Social & Legal Studies* 19 (1): 107–26. http://dx.doi.org/10.1177/0964663909346200.

– 2011. "Doing Things with Time: Flexibility, Adaptability, and Elasticity in UK Equality Cases." *Canadian Journal of Law and Society / La Revue Canadienne Droit et Société* 26 (3): 485–508. http://dx.doi.org/10.3138/cjls.26.3.485.

– 2014. "Legal Form and Temporal Rationalities in UK Work–Life Balance Law." *Australian Feminist Studies* 29 (79): 67–84. http://dx.doi.org/10.1080/08164649.2014.901280.

– In draft a. "Taking Bloods on a Destroyer: Vehicles and the Enactment of Risk in UK and Canadian Equality Law."

– In draft b. "Time and Technique: The Legal Lives of the 26 Week Qualifying Period."

Grabham, Emily, and Jenny Smith. 2010. "From Social Security to Individual Responsibility (Part Two): Writing Off Poor Women's Work in the Welfare Reform Act 2009." *Journal of Social Welfare and Family Law* 32 (1): 81–93. http://dx.doi.org/10.1080/09649069.2010.484226.

Grant, Isabel, Martha Shaffer, and Alison Symington. 2013. "Introduction." *University of Toronto Law Journal* 63 (3): 462–5. http://dx.doi.org/10.3138/utlj.0302.

Greenhouse, Carol J. 1996. *A Moment's Notice: Time Politics across Cultures*. Ithaca, NY: Cornell University Press.

Grosz, E.A. 1999. *Becomings: Explorations in Time, Memory, and Futures*. Ithaca, NY: Cornell University Press.

Haigh, Richard, and Dai Harris, eds. 1990. *AIDS: A Guide to the Law*. London: Routledge.

Halberstam, Judith. 2005. *In a Queer Time and Place: Transgender Bodies, Subcultural Lives / Sexual Cultures*. New York: New York University Press.

Harper, Richard. 1998. *Inside the IMF: An Ethnography of Documents, Technology, and Organizational Action*. San Diego, CA: Academic Press.

Henare, Amiria J.M., Martin Holbraad, and Sari Wastell, eds. 2007. *Thinking through Things: Theorising Artefacts Ethnographically*. London: Routledge.

Hines, Sally. 2013. *Gender Diversity, Recognition and Citizenship: Towards a Politics of Difference*. New York: Palgrave Macmillan. http://dx.doi.org/10.1057/9781137318879.

Holbraad, Martin. 2011. *Can the Thing Speak?* London: Open Anthropology Cooperative Press.

Hunter, Shona. 2008. "Living Documents: A Feminist Psychosocial Approach to the Relational Politics of Policy Documentation." *Critical Social Policy* 28 (4): 506–28. http://dx.doi.org/10.1177/0261018308095300.

Incomes Data Services. 1993. *HIV, AIDS and Employment*. London: Incomes Data Services.

Irving, Dan. 2008. "Normalized Transgressions: Legitimizing the Transsexual Body as Productive." *Radical History Review* (100): 38–59. http://dx.doi.org/10.1215/01636545-2007-021.

Jacob, Marie-Andrée. 2007. "Form-Made Persons: Consent Forms as Consent's Blind Spot." *PoLAR: Political and Legal Anthropology Review* 30 (2): 249–68. http://dx.doi.org/10.1525/pol.2007.30.2.249.

Jacob, Marie-Andrée, and Annelise Riles. 2007. "The New Bureaucracies of Virtue: Introduction." *PoLAR: Political and Legal Anthropology Review* 30 (2): 181–91. http://dx.doi.org/10.1525/pol.2007.30.2.181.

Jain, Sarah Lochlann. 2007. "Living in Prognosis: Toward an Elegiac Politics." *Representations* 98 (1): 77–92. http://dx.doi.org/10.1525/rep.2007.98.1.77.

Lamble, Sarah. 2008. "Re-telling Racialized Violence, Re-making White Innocence: The Politics of Interlocking Oppressions in Transgender Day of Remembrance." *Sexuality Research and Social Policy* 5 (1): 24–42.

Latour, Bruno. 1992. "Where Are the Missing Masses? The Sociology of a Few Mundane Artifacts." In *Shaping Technology/Building Society: Studies in Sociotechnical Change*, ed. Wiebe E. Bijker and John Law, 225–58. Cambridge, MA: MIT Press.

– 1993. *We Have Never Been Modern*. Trans. Catherine Porter. Cambridge, MA: Harvard University Press.

– 2004. "Scientific Objects and Legal Objectivity." In *Law, Anthropology, and the Constitution of the Social*, 73–114. Cambridge: Cambridge University Press. http://dx.doi.org/10.1017/CBO9780511493751.003.

– 2005. *Reassembling the Social: An Introduction to Actor-Network-Theory*. Oxford: Oxford University Press.

– 2010. *The Making of Law: An Ethnography of the Conseil d'État*. Translated by Marina Brilman and Alain Pottage. Cambridge, UK: Polity Press.

Levi, Ron. 2009. "Gated Communities in Law's Gaze: Material Forms and the Production of a Social Body in Legal Adjudication." *Law & Social Inquiry* 34 (3): 635–69. http://dx.doi.org/10.1111/j.1747-4469.2009.01160.x.

Lezaun, Javier. 2012. "The Pragmatic Sanction of Materials: Notes for an Ethnography of Legal Substances." *Journal of Law and Society* 39 (1): 20–38. http://dx.doi.org/10.1111/j.1467-6478.2012.00568.x.

Lister, Ruth. 2002. "The Dilemmas of Pendulum Politics: Balancing Paid Work, Care, and Citizenship." *Economy and Society* 31 (4): 520–32. http://dx.doi.org/10.1080/03085140220000020661.

Lung, Shirley. 2010. "The Four-Day Work Week: But What about Ms. Coke, Ms. Upton, and Ms. Blankenship?" SSRN Scholarly Paper 1652180. Rochester, NY: Social Science Research Network. http://papers.ssrn.com/abstract=1652180.

Lynch, John. 2000. "AIDSTimes Representing AIDS in an Age of Anxiety." *Time & Society* 9 (2–3): 247–67. http://dx.doi.org/10.1177/0961463X00009002006.

Lynch, M., and R. McNally. 2003. "'Science,' 'Common Sense,' and DNA Evidence: A Legal Controversy about the Public Understanding of Science." *Public Understanding of Science* 12 (1): 83–103. http://dx.doi.org/10.1177/0963662503012001246.

Macfarlane, Karen. 2013. "'Does He Know the Danger of an Oath?': Oaths, Religion, Ethnicity, and the Advent of the Adversarial Criminal Trial in the Eighteenth Century." *Immigrants & Minorities: Historical Studies in Ethnicity, Migration and Diaspora* 31 (3): 317–45. http://dx.doi.org/10.1080/02619288.2013.802866.

Martin, Emily. 1994. *Flexible Bodies: The Role of Immunity in American Culture from the Days of Polio to the Age of AIDS*. Boston: Beacon Press.

Mawani, Renisa. 2014. "Law as Temporality: Colonial Politics and Indian Settlers." *Irvine Law Review* 4:65–96.

Melissaris, Emmanuel. 2005. "The Chronology of the Legal." *McGill Law Journal* 50:839–61.

Mitropoulos, Angela. 2012. *Contract and Contagion: From Biopolitics to Oikonomia*. [n.p.]: Minor Compositions.

Mol, Annemarie. 1999. "Ontological Politics: A Word and Some Questions." *Sociological Review* 47 (S1): 74–89. http://dx.doi.org/10.1111/j.1467-954X.1999.tb03483.x.

– 2003. *The Body Multiple: Ontology in Medical Practice*. Durham, NC: Duke University Press.

Monk, Daniel. 2009. "Reckless Trials? The Criminalization of the Sexual Transmission of HIV." *Radical Philosophy* 156 (July–August): 2–6.

Moreira, Tiago, Carl May, and John Bond. 2009. "Regulatory Objectivity in Action Mild Cognitive Impairment and the Collective Production of Uncertainty." *Social Studies of Science* 39 (5): 665–90. http://dx.doi.org/10.1177/0306312709103481.

Mulcahy, Linda, and Sally Wheeler. 2005. *Feminist Perspectives on Contract Law*. Abingdon, UK: Routledge Cavendish.

Muñoz, José. 2009. *Cruising Utopia: The Then and There of Queer Utopia*. New York: New York University Press.

Namaste, Viviane. 2000. *Invisible Lives: The Erasure of Transsexual and Transgendered People*. Chicago: University of Chicago Press.

Napier, B. 1989. "AIDS, Discrimination, and Employment Law." *Industrial Law Journal* 18 (2): 84–96. http://dx.doi.org/10.1093/ilj/18.2.84.

National AIDS Trust. 2004. *Memorandum on the Draft Disability Bill 2004*.

O'Hara, Frank. 1991. *Frank O'Hara: Selected Poems*. Ed. Donald Allen. Manchester, UK: Carcanet Press.

O'Malley, Michael. 1996. *Keeping Watch – A History of American Time*. Washington, DC: Smithsonian Institution.

Owens, Rosemary. 2006. "Engendering Flexibility in a World of Precarious Work." In *Precarious Work, Women, and the New Economy: The Challenge to Legal Norms*, ed. Judy Fudge and Rosemary Owens, 329–52. Oxford: Hart Publishing.

Patton, Cindy. 1990. *Inventing AIDS*. New York: Routledge.

Persson, Asha. 2004. "Incorporating Pharmakon: HIV, Medicine, and Body Shape Change." *Body & Society* 10 (4): 45–67. http://dx.doi.org/10.1177/1357034X04047855.

Pickersgill, Martyn. 2011. "Connecting Neuroscience and Law: Anticipatory Discourse and the Role of Sociotechnical Imaginaries." *New Genetics & Society* 30 (1): 27–40. http://dx.doi.org/10.1080/14636778.2011.552298.

Platero, Raquel. 2011. "The Narratives of Transgender Rights Mobilization in Spain." *Sexualities* 14 (5): 597–614. http://dx.doi.org/10.1177/1363460711415336.

Postema, Gerald J. 2004. "Melody and Law's Mindfulness of Time." *Ratio Juris* 17 (2): 203–26. http://dx.doi.org/10.1111/j.1467-9337.2004.00264.x.

Pottage, Alain. 2004. "Our Original Inheritance." In *Law, Anthropology, and the Constitution of the Social: Making Persons and Things*, ed. Alain Pottage and Martha Mundy, 249–85. Cambridge: Cambridge University Press. http://dx.doi.org/10.1017/CBO9780511493751.009.

– 2014. "Law after Anthropology: Object and Technique in Roman Law." *Theory, Culture & Society* 31 (2–3): 147–66.

– 2012. "The Materiality of What?" *Journal of Law and Society* 39 (1): 167–83. http://dx.doi.org/10.1111/j.1467-6478.2012.00576.x.

Pottage, Alain, and Martha Mundy, eds. 2004. *Law, Anthropology, and the Constitution of the Social: Making Persons and Things*. Cambridge: Cambridge University Press. http://dx.doi.org/10.1017/CBO9780511493751.

Prior, Lindsay. 2008. "Repositioning Documents in Social Research." *Sociology* 42 (5): 821–36. http://dx.doi.org/10.1177/0038038508094564.

Rayside, David M., and Evert A. Linquist. 1992. "AIDS Activism and the State in Canada." *Studies in Political Economy* 39:37–76.

Renz, Flora. In progress. "The Gender Recognition Act 2004 and Transgender People's Legal Consciousness." PhD diss., University of Kent.

Richland, Justin. 2013. "Perpetuities against Rules: Law, Ethnography and the Irresolution of Inheritance." *Law, Culture and the Humanities* 8 (3): 433–47. http://dx.doi.org/10.1177/1743872110380872.

Richmond, Bernard. 1990. "HIV and Employment." In *AIDS: A Guide to the Law*, ed. Dai Harris and Richard Haigh, 36–52. London: Routledge.

Riles, Annelise. 2001. *The Network Inside Out*. Ann Arbor: University of Michigan Press.

– 2006a. "(Deadlines): Removing the Brackets on Politics in Bureaucratic and Anthropological Analysis." In *Documents: Artifacts of Modern Knowledge*, ed. Annelise Riles, 71–94. Ann Arbor: University of Michigan Press.

– 2006b. *Documents: Artifacts of Modern Knowledge*. Ann Arbor: University of Michigan Press.

– 2008. "The Anti-Network: Private Global Governance, Legal Knowledge, and the Legitimacy of the State." *American Journal of Comparative Law* 56 (3): 605–30. http://dx.doi.org/10.5131/ajcl.2007.0018.

– 2011. *Collateral Knowledge: Legal Reasoning in the Global Financial Markets*. Chicago: University of Chicago Press. http://dx.doi.org/10.7208/chicago/9780226719344.001.0001.

Robertson, Mark. 2005. "An Annotated Chronology of the History of AIDS in Toronto: The First Five Years, 1981–1986." *Canadian Bulletin of Medical History* 22 (2): 313–51.

Rooke, Catriona, Emilie Cloatre, and Robert Dingwall. 2012. "The Regulation of Nicotine in the United Kingdom: How Nicotine Gum Came to Be a Medicine, but Not a Drug." *Journal of Law and Society* 39 (1): 39–57. http://dx.doi.org/10.1111/j.1467-6478.2012.00569.x.

Salamon, Gayle. 2010. *Assuming a Body: Transgender and Rhetorics of Materiality*. New York: Columbia University Press.

Sanger, Tam. 2008. "Trans Governmentality: The Production and Regulation of Gendered Subjectivities." *Journal of Gender Studies* 17 (1): 41–53. http://dx.doi.org/10.1080/09589230701838396.

Schultz, Vicki. 2010. "Feminism and Workplace Flexibility." *Connecticut Law Review* 42 (2): 1203–21.

Scott, Dayna. 2005. "When Precaution Points Two Ways: Confronting 'West Nile Fever.'" *Canadian Journal of Law and Society* 20 (2): 27–65. http://dx.doi.org/10.1353/jls.2006.0026.

Scott, David. 2014. *Omens of Adversity: Tragedy, Time, Memory, Justice*. Durham, NC: Duke University Press.

Serres, Michel, and Bruno Latour. 1995. *Conversations on Science, Culture, and Time*. Ann Arbor: University of Michigan Press.

Shannon, Jennifer. 2007. "Informed Consent: Documenting the Intersection of Bureaucratic Regulation and Ethnographic Practice." *PoLAR: Political and Legal Anthropology Review* 30 (2): 229–48. http://dx.doi.org/10.1525/pol.2007.30.2.229.

Shapiro, Barbara. 1983. *Probability and Certainty in Seventeenth Century England: A Study of the Relationships between Science, Religion, History, Law and Literature*. Princeton, NJ: Princeton University Press.

Sheller, Mimi. 2004. "Automotive Emotions: Feeling the Car." *Theory, Culture & Society* 21 (4–5): 221–42. http://dx.doi.org/10.1177/0263276404046068.

Shippen, Nichole. 2014. *Decolonizing Time: Work, Leisure and Freedom*. New York: Palgrave Macmillan. http://dx.doi.org/10.1057/9781137354020.

Silversides, Ann. 2003. *AIDS Activist: Michael Lynch and the Politics of Community*. Toronto: Between the Lines.

Society of Occupational Medicine. 1992. *What Employers Should Know about HIV and AIDS*. London: Society of Occupational Medicine.

Sontag, Susan. 2001. *Illness as Metaphor and AIDS and Its Metaphors*. New York: Picador.

Southam, Christopher, and Gillian Howard. 1988. *AIDS and Employment Law*. London: Financial Training.

Spade, Dean. 2007. "Documenting Gender." *Hastings Law Journal* 59 (1): 731–832.

– 2011. *Normal Life: Administrative Violence, Critical Trans Politics, and the Limits of Law*. Brooklyn, NY: South End Press.

Standing, Guy. 2011. *The Precariat: The New Dangerous Class*. London: Bloomsbury Academic.

Treichler, Paula A. 1999. *How to Have Theory in an Epidemic: Cultural Chronicles of AIDS*. Durham, NC: Duke University Press.

Trent, Bil. 1988. "Armed Forces Unveils AIDS Policy." *Canadian Medical Association Journal* 138:1129–32.

Tur, Richard H.S. 2002. "Time and Law." *Oxford Journal of Legal Studies* 22 (3): 463–88. http://dx.doi.org/10.1093/ojls/22.3.463.

United Kingdom. 1986. "AIDS and Employment." London: Department of Employment, and Health and Safety Executive.

– 2000. "Report of the Interdepartmental Working Group on Transsexual People." London: Home Office.

– 2003a. Joint Committee on Human Rights. "Draft Gender Recognition Bill: Nineteenth Report of Session 2002-2003. Vol I: Report. (HL Paper 188-1; HC 1276-1)." London.

– 2003b. Joint Committee on Human Rights. "Draft Gender Recognition Bill: Written Evidence." London.

– 2009. Equality and Human Rights Commission. Working Better: Meeting the Changing Needs of Families, Workers and Employers in the 21st Century. London. Available online at http://www.equalityhumanrights.com/sites/default/files/publication_pdf/working_better_final_pdf_250309.pdf; accessed 20 April 2010.

– 2010. Government Equalities Office. *Working Towards Equality: A Framework for Action*. London.

– 2011. Department for Business, Innovation and Skills. *Consultation on Modern Workplaces*. London.

Urry, John. 2000. *Sociology beyond Societies: Mobilities for the Twenty-First Century*. London: Routledge.

– 2004. "The 'System' of Automobility." *Theory, Culture & Society* 21 (4–5): 25–39. http://dx.doi.org/10.1177/0263276404046059.

Valverde, Mariana. 2015. *Chronotopes of Law: Jurisdiction, Scale and Governance. Social Justice*. London: Routledge.

van Loon, Joost. 2002. "A Contagious Living Fluid Objectification and Assemblage in the History of Virology." *Theory, Culture & Society* 19 (5–6): 107–24. http://dx.doi.org/10.1177/026327602761899174.

Waldby, Catherine. 2004. *AIDS and the Body Politic: Biomedicine and Sexual Difference*. London: Routledge.

Waldby, Catherine, and Melinda Cooper. 2010. "From Reproductive Work to Regenerative Labour: The Female Body and the Stem Cell Industries." *Feminist Theory* 11 (1): 3–22. http://dx.doi.org/10.1177/1464700109355210.

Watt, R.A. 1992. "HIV, Discrimination, Unfair Dismissal, and Pressure to Dismiss." *Industrial Law Journal* 21 (4): 280–92. http://dx.doi.org/10.1093/indlaw/21.4.280.

Weait, Matthew. 2007. *Intimacy and Responsibility: The Criminalisation of HIV Transmission*. Abingdon, UK: Routledge Cavendish.

Weeks, Kathi. 2011. *The Problem with Work: Feminism, Marxism, Antiwork Politics, and Postwork Imaginaries*. Durham, NC: Duke University Press. http://dx.doi.org/10.1215/9780822394723.

Williams, Lucy. 2005. "Poor Women's Work Experiences: Gaps in the 'Work/Family' Discussion." In *Labour Law, Work, and Family*, ed. Joanne Conaghan and Kerry Rittich, 195–216. Oxford: Oxford University Press.

Wilson, Petra. 1992. *HIV and AIDS in the Workplace: An Examination of Cases of Discrimination*. London: National AIDS Trust.

– 1994. "Colleague or Viral Vector: The Legal Construction of the HIV-Positive Worker." *Law & Policy* 16 (3): 299–322. http://dx.doi.org/10.1111/j.1467-9930.1994.tb00127.x.

Winterton, Rosie. 2002. "Government Announcement on Transsexual People, 13 December 2002." Department for Constitutional Affairs. London.

Zerubavel, Eviatar. 1985. *Hidden Rhythms: Schedules and Calendars in Social Life*. Berkeley: University of California Press.

Index

www.ingramcontent.com/pod-product-compliance
Lightning Source LLC
LaVergne TN
LVHW090159080826
844660LV00013B/871/J

* 9 7 8 1 4 4 2 6 4 6 0 5 6 *